EDITED BY ANDRÉ W. M. GERRITS
AND DIRK JAN WOLFFRAM

Political Democracy and Ethnic Diversity in Modern European History

STANFORD UNIVERSITY PRESS

STANFORD, CALIFORNIA

2005

Stanford University Press
Stanford, California

© 2005 by the Board of Trustees of the
Leland Stanford Junior University.
All rights reserved.

Printed in the United States of America
on acid-free, archival-quality paper

Library of Congress Cataloging-in-Publication Data

Political democracy and ethnic diversity in modern European history / edited by
André W. M. Gerrits and Dirk Jan Wolffram.
    p. cm.
 Papers originally presented at the conference on Ethnic diversity and political
democracy in modern European history, organized at the University of
Amsterdam, March 2002.
 Includes bibliographical references and index.
  ISBN 0-8047-4975-2 (cloth : alk. paper)—ISBN 0-8047-4976-0 (pbk. : alk. paper)
  1. Europe—Politics and government—Congresses. 2. Democracy—Europe—
History—Congresses. 3. Pluralism (Social sciences)—Europe—History—
Congresses. 4. Ethnicity—Europe—History—Congresses. I. Gerrits, André.
II. Wolffram, Dirk Jan.
JN8.P65 2005
323.14—dc22

2005002180

Original Printing 2005

Last figure below indicates year of this printing:
14 13 12 11 10 09 08 07 06 05

Typeset by Classic Typography in 10/14 Janson

Contents

Acknowledgments

The editors are grateful to all the participants of the conference on *Ethnic Diversity and Political Democracy in Modern European History*, organized at the University of Amsterdam in March 2002, for sharing their academic insights into the complicated and topical relationship between democracy and ethnic or cultural diversity. The contributions to this book were initially presented and discussed at this conference. We thank Simona Piattoni, Paul Scheffer, George Schöpflin, Siep Stuurman, Bart Tromp, and Peter van der Veer in particular for their stimulating role during the conference. We also thank Christina Bechter and Ayfer Sen, who found the time, despite the heavy burden of their MA work in European studies at the University of Amsterdam, to assist us in all kinds of practical issues. They did a great job. We are grateful to all the people who were involved in the production of this volume, in particular for the support and assistance we have received from Kim Lewis Brown of Stanford University Press during the production of the book, and Victor van Bentem of the history department of the University of Groningen for his excellent text processing.

The conference was made possible by grants from the Netherlands Organization for Scientific Research (NWO) and the Institute for Culture and History of the Faculty of Humanities of the University of Amsterdam.

ANDRÉ W. M. GERRITS
DIRK JAN WOLFFRAM
DECEMBER 2004

Contributors

FRANK ANKERSMIT is professor of philosophy of history and historiography at the University of Groningen, the Netherlands. He is the author of *Narrative Logic: A Semantic Analysis of the Historian's Language* (The Hague: Nijhof, 1983); *History and Tropology: The Rise and Fall of Metaphor* (Berkeley: University of California Press, 1994); *Aesthetic Politics: Political Philosophy Beyond Fact and Value* (Stanford: Stanford University Press, 1997); *Historical Representation* (Stanford: Stanford University Press, 2001); and *Political Representation* (Stanford: Stanford University Press, 2002).

IVAN T. BEREND is professor of history at the University of California, Los Angeles. He is the author of, among other works, *Central and Eastern Europe 1944–1993: Detour from the Periphery to the Periphery* (Cambridge: Cambridge University Press, 1996); *Decades of Crisis: Central and Eastern Europe Before World War II* (Berkeley: University of California Press, 1998); and *History Derailed: Central and Eastern Europe in the Long Nineteenth Century* (Berkeley: University of California Press, 2003).

ANDRÉ W. M. GERRITS is associate professor in European studies at the University of Amsterdam. Among his works are *The Failure of Authoritarian Change: Reform, Opposition and Geo-Politics in Poland in the 1980s* (Aldershot: Dartmouth, 1992); *Troubled Transition: Social Democracy in East Central Europe* (Berlin: Friedrich Ebert Stiftung, 1999); and *Social Democracy in Central and Eastern Europe* (Berlin: Friedrich Ebert Stiftung, 2002).

IDO DE HAAN is professor of history at the University of Utrecht. He has published volumes in Dutch on the political debate on citizenship and the state, on the memory of the Holocaust in the Netherlands, and on the Dutch constitution. He also has written articles in English on the persecution of the Jews, and on child health and citizenship.

ANDREW C. JANOS is professor of political science at the University of California, Berkeley, in the fields of comparative politics and East European studies. His writings include *The Politics of Backwardness in Hungary* (Princeton: Princeton University Press, 1982); *Politics and Paradigms: Changing Theories of Change in Social Science* (Stanford: Stanford University Press, 1986; *Czechoslovakia and Yugoslavia: Ethnic Conflict and the Dissolution of Multinational States* (Berkeley: University of California Press, 1997); and *Eastern Europe in the Modern World: The Politics of the Borderlands from Pre- to Postcommunism* (Stanford: Stanford University Press, 2002).

BRUNO NAARDEN is professor of Russian history at the University of Amsterdam. His main publication in English is *Socialist Europe and Revolutionary Russia: Perception and Prejudice 1848–1923* (Cambridge: Cambridge University Press, 1992). His contribution to this volume on ethnic diversity and political democracy is an offshoot of his research for the *Srebrenica Report*, which was commissioned by the Dutch government and published in 2002.

AVIEL ROSHWALD is professor of history at Georgetown University in Washington, DC. His publications include *Ethnic Nationalism and the Fall of Empires: Central Europe, Russia and the Middle East, 1914–1923* (London: Routledge, 2001); and *Estranged Bedfellows: Britain and France in the Middle East During the Second World War* (Oxford: Oxford University Press, 1990). He is coeditor with Richard Stites of *European Culture in the Great War: The Arts, Entertainment, and Propaganda, 1914–1918* (Cambridge: Cambridge University Press, 1999).

PHILIPP THER teaches history at the European University in Frankfurt/Oder. In 1998 he published *Deutsche und polnische Vertriebene: Gesellschaft und Vertriebenenpolitik in der SBZ/DDR und in Polen 1945–1956* (Dissertation, Freie Universität Berlin). In 1997–1998 he was a John F. Kennedy Fellow at the Center for European Studies at Harvard University. Between 1998 and 2002 he worked as a researcher at the Center for Comparative History of Europe in Berlin. In 2001 he edited with Ana Siljak *Redrawing Nations: Ethnic Cleansing in East-Central Europe, 1944–1948* (Harvard Cold War Studies Book Series. Lanham: Rowman & Littlefield Publishers, 2001).

EUGEN WEBER was educated at Cambridge and the Paris Institute des Sciences Politiques. Until his retirement he held the Joan Palevsky Chair of Modern History at UCLA. Among his many works are *Peasants into Frenchmen: The Modernization of Rural France, 1870–1914* (Stanford: Stanford University Press, 1976); *France, Fin de Siècle* (Cambridge, MA: Harvard University Press, 1986); and *Apocalypses: Prophecies, Cults, and Millennial Beliefs Through the Ages* (Cambridge, MA: Harvard University Press, 1999).

DIRK JAN WOLFFRAM is assistant professor in the history department of the University of Groningen. He has published volumes in Dutch on local variants of consociationalism, on Dutch land reclamation, and on social politics. He has also published articles in English and Italian on Dutch history and on administrative history.

POLITICAL DEMOCRACY AND ETHNIC
DIVERSITY IN MODERN EUROPEAN HISTORY

CHAPTER ONE

Introducing the Problem

The Historical Relation Between Ethnicity and Democracy

ANDRÉ W. M. GERRITS AND DIRK JAN WOLFFRAM

This book on the historical relation between democracy and ethnicity is based on the contributions to the conference "Political Democracy and Ethnic Diversity in Modern European History," which we organised at the University of Amsterdam in the spring of 2002. The conference addressed three basic questions: First, can ethnic homogeneity be perceived as a condition of democracy, or is it a historical coincidence that modern democracies developed in relatively ethnically homogeneous societies? Second, how relevant is ethnic diversity or homogeneity in explaining the success (continuity) or failure (discontinuity) of democracy in Europe during the nineteenth and twentieth centuries? And third, how did democracies, in comparison with other political systems—empires and dictatorships in particular—cope with ethnic diversity?

The emergence and development of democracy is one of the central concerns of political science. This volume is limited to one "variable," one "condition" of democracy: the (causal) link between ethnicity and democratization in Europe, West and East. The classical contradictory statements of the two British political thinkers John Stuart Mill (1861) and Lord Acton (1862) represent a challenging starting point for discussion. "Free institutions are next to impossible in a country made up of different nationalities," Mill wrote in 1861. "Among a people without fellow-feeling, especially, if they read and speak different languages, the united public opinion, necessary to the working of representative government, cannot exist" (1958, 230). Lord Acton was considerably less pessimistic. Steeped in benign imperialist thinking, he rejected Mill's gloomy interpretation and questioned the congruence of political and national boundaries as a positive value per se. Precisely the multinational state "provides against the servility which flourishes under the shadow of a single authority," he opined. "Diversity preserves liberty" (1862, 169).

At the end of the twentieth century, by far the bloodiest and most horrifying in history, in which human nature appeared capable of unprecedented evil executed in a scientific, systematic way, European democracy showed many faces. Democracy in the traditional democratic countries, victorious in both world wars, has not been seriously challenged (with the occasional exception of France), but on the other hand, democracy has proved not to be a particularly successful export commodity to Central and Eastern Europe.

The Nature of Ethnicity

In this volume, the issue of democracy and ethnicity is approached from an essentially historical perspective. This implies that we are primarily concerned with neither the present wave of democratization in the former communist world, nor with the current challenges to the traditional democracies of Western Europe—in particular the process of European integration (and the subsequent erosion of "national" democracies), and the unprecedented challenge of "multiculturalism," the very specific problems related to the integration of relatively large numbers of non-European immigrants. Additionally, we do not intend to add novel theoretical approaches to the plethora of explanations and interpretations available.

Our point of departure is the definition of democracy of Larry Diamond, Juan Linz, and Seymour Lipset, which contains the crucial notions of competition, inclusion, and freedom, thereby stressing the dimension of change, or democratization (1995, 6–7). Additionally, we define ethnicity as an essentially politico-cultural category, which embraces a potentially large number of characteristics, such as religion, language, and, although much more vague, a sense of historic solidarity, or, as the German language so aptly expresses it, *Schicksalsgemeinschaft* (roughly, "a community sharing a common destiny").

In research on the "causes" of democracy in Europe the variable of ethnic diversity or homogeneity is rarely analyzed as a separate, a specific condition; and if it is, it is mostly linked with class and/or (other) socioeconomic factors. Metahistorical or structural explanations focus primarily on the social and economic underpinnings of democracy and dictatorship, on modernisation, and first and foremost on the growth and development of capitalism.[1] "That capitalism and democracy go hand in hand is a widely held belief. Indeed it is a commonplace of Western political discourse," as Dietrich Rueschemeyer puts it. He adds, however, that "racial and ethnic divisions may also affect the chances of democracy directly," and admits that his framework "has to give more room to a direct impact of ethnic fragmentation on the chances of democracy" (1992, 1, 48, 287).

As yet, though, politico-cultural issues do not figure prominently in most analyses, and when they are taken into account, they are generally considered as variables of modernisation: from nationalism[2] and the formation of national states[3] to the role of warfare and the military (Dawning 1992) and the growth of the international state system (Preece 1998). The impetus to an alternative approach, as made by Stein Rokkan and Derek W. Urwin, who combined territorial and cultural factors in their explanation of peripheral political action, remains limited to Western Europe and does not call into question the relation between ethnicity and democracy.[4] The same goes for the analysis by Alvin Rabushka and Kenneth A. Shepsle of democratic instability in plural societies. They simply define plural societies as unstable, because of the salience of ethnicity. No attempt, however, is made to connect the development of the political system with the gradual overcoming of ethnic cleavages, and with the integration of minorities into the nation-state (Rabushka and Shepsle 1972, 20 and passim).

On the other hand, ethnic diversity is often perceived as particularly difficult to reconcile with democracy, as one of the most complicated issues for democracies to handle (Diamond and Platter 1994, xix; Horowitz 1985, 570). "Democracy is exceptional in severely divided societies," as Donald Horowitz writes, and "unless precautions are taken, democratic arrangements tend to unravel fairly predictably in ethnically divided societies"(1985, 681).

Ethnic cleavages seem to be more fundamental than divisions of class, profession, or, for that matter, political preference. They are generally perceived as "permanent and all-compassing," as a matter of exclusion and inclusion, "predetermining who will be granted [or] denied access to power and resources" (Diamond and Platter 1994, xviii). Ethnic identity particularly relates to the "supportive culture," to the sense of identification in terms of geographical extension and its legitimate quality, on which every durable form of political system essentially rests (Berg-Schlosser and Mitchell 2000, 9). This identification reflects the major values of each society, shaped by historical experiences, by specific symbols and rituals, and transmitted through socializing agencies as families, media, churches, and political parties. Ethnic cleavages, and the division into subcultures (including their network of intermediate structures), more so than social and economic divisions, have the potential to undermine these common cultural values. In this sense, cultural homogeneity, or, in specific cases, cultural heterogeneity "pacified" by pluralist, consociational arrangements at the elite level, may not be a prerequisite or a condition of democracy, as the case studies in this book testify, but it certainly helps. This seems particularly so because ethnic or cultural cleavages are rarely isolated phenomena. They often concern socioeconomic and political divides too.

In his chapter "The Eternal Stranger," Eugen Weber focuses on the paradox between the *inclusive* and the *exclusive* dimensions of modern democracies. Democratic nation-states developed strong inclusive mechanisms, but they equally had to adjust to and cope with the inevitability of (growing) diversity. Weber discusses, partly based on his personal experience as a German-Jewish emigrant from interwar Romania, how democracies continuously have been challenged by this paradox; how they have, from the beginning of the modern nation-state to the current postindustrial societies, balanced the need to incorporate and to exclude the stranger.

Western European Democracies

The antagonism between democracy and ethnic diversity is not irreconcilable, as the history of the established western European democracies demonstrates: the basic features of modern western democracy, pluralism and a high level of welfare, actually are the outcome of a process of overcoming social and ethnoreligious cleavages. Ido de Haan analyzes the development of a national political space in the Netherlands and France in the nineteenth century. He shows that the centralized monocultural French republic and the pluralist decentralized Dutch constitutional monarchy were both products of a process in which nation building contained the articulation of national and cultural (religious) diversity on a political level.

In the traditional, nineteenth–century democracies (Great Britain, Scandinavia, the Netherlands, Belgium, France) a stable political system, based on constitutional rights and political representation, was firmly established. Sharp socioeconomic—(frequently with a cultural, sometimes an ethnic component), linguistic, and religious cleavages characterised several of the democracies at the western fringe of Europe at the end of the nineteenth century. Church and political party formed the core of these societal pillars. Depending on specific circumstances, differences of class, religion, language, or ethnicity dominated politics (Lijphart 1968), or, in the word of Lipset and Rokkan, there was a "hierarchy" of cleaving issues in each political system (1967).

The introduction of universal suffrage (often combined with proportional representation) aggravated these cleavages. Nevertheless, stable democracies developed, based on civic virtue (Almond and Verba 1963) and trust in government (Warren 1999). Subnational or intermediary arrangements, such as corporatism and consociationalism, contributed to this stability (Steiner and Ertman 2002). Consociationalism is based on segregation, on separation of different cultures, ethnicities, or religions, and functioned from the end of the nineteenth century as an informal political system. This enabled the national integration of religious and political (socialist) groups into the liberal democracy, through the even distribution of state subsidies and commodities among the different ethnic and religious groups. Its most pure form was visible in the Netherlands (with its complex antagonisms among Protestants, Catholics, socialists, and liberals) and in Belgium (where Catholics, liberals, and socialists competed with each other, and cleavages were exacerbated by the question of language), but traits of it can be seen in every western European political system.

After the Second World War the political and social stability of the Continental European democracies was further enhanced by the introduction of active government policies of industrialisation and the creation of the welfare state. Neocorporatist arrangements were of crucial importance. Under the guidance of the state, employers and trade unions negotiated many of the most important socioeconomic issues. These contacts evolved into the creation of a series of organisations dealing with various crucial socioeconomic questions and arrangements. With Mussolini's fascism in mind, corporatism is generally considered as authoritarian, nondemocratic, and hierarchical. However, neocorporatist arrangements in Europe after 1945 did not collide with democratic principles. They comprised economic planning, a combination of social-democratic and Christian-democratic ambitions for an elaborate welfare state, resulting in a combination of state control and private enterprise.

Consociationalism and corporatism proved effective in mitigating religious and social cleavages. consociationalism offered a way out of ethnoreligious instability, whereas neocorporatism successfully overcame socioeconomic cleavages and paved the way for the introduction of the welfare state. The ensuing political stability was based on the maintenance of a high level of welfare (De Swaan 1988). Due to the extent of the subjects negotiated within neocorporatist structures, the margins for socioeconomic government policies were reduced considerably indeed.

Political stability appears to rest on the ability of the political system to find a balance, an equilibrium among conflicting interests. This balance is found within representative political bodies, political parties included. Moreover, political stability is greatly enhanced if categorical interests can be articulated freely. Only if relevant interests and conflicts are politicized, within and between political parties, can these conflicts ultimately be solved by compromise in the political arena. Basically, the integration of minority groups within a political party and, subsequently, within the nation-state, is a feature of all modern democracies, as has been demonstrated in one of the classical studies on political participation: Lipset and Rokkan's volume on *Party Systems and Voter Alignments* (1967).

The importance of political parties in the integration of conflicting interests is underlined by the analysis of the other successful example of political integration: the British two-party system. In the Lipset and Rokkan volume, the British Conservative Party is presented as the first modern catch-all party, comprising lower, middle, and upper classes. Its electoral success (as compared with the Labour Party) from the end of the nineteenth century until the 1960s lay in its ability to secure working class votes with a specific, albeit nonrevolutionary, social program (McKenzie and Silver 1967). This resembles both consociationalism, in its sociopolitical consequences, and neocorporatism, in its socioeconomic effects. Mazower has characterized Margaret Thatcher's "authoritarian form of neoliberalism," the conservative effort to decrease state involvement to the benefit of individual liberty, as a disruption of this carefully built-up social equilibrium (Mazower 1998, 336–38).

Generally, both the British two-party system based on district representation, and the continental political system, primarily based on proportional representation, have proven to be resistant to authoritarian challenges and serious economic strains. Consociationalism and neocorporatism stabilised politics for the most part of the twentieth century. They are more than imperfect political arrangements. Consociationalism still is an expression of democratic values, whereas neocorporatism can be seen as offering the socioeconomic basis for political stability by managing the welfare state, a fair distribution of social public benefits, and a balanced economic development (Scholten 1987).

Especially in the last decades of the twentieth century, Western Europe was confronted with tensions within society as a result of the influx of non-European immigrants and the revival of xenophobia and racism. Until the 1980s, the basic feature of political democracy was undisputed: in democratic societies, democracy was upheld by strong political parties, with a firm footing in society and with a program in which all political issues were weighed and placed into an ideological perspective. The fall of the Berlin Wall and the demise of the Soviet Union had a profound impact on western politics. Traditional bonds fell apart; consociationalism started to crumble. Nowadays, political participation (voting, membership of political parties and pressure-groups) is seen as a nexus between the individual and society. Active political participation though, is incongruent with the classical theory of consociationalism, as formulated by Arend Lijphart in 1968 in *The Politics of Accommodation*. He considered passive acquiescence of the electorate as a necessary precondition for stability in societies dominated by ethnic or religious cleavages. In our view, Lijphart underestimates the importance of the expression of interests within pillarized organisations, which necessitated active participation. Democracy only works if it is supported by active political

participation of some sort, and a lack of democratic dedication (and participation) not only explains the waning of democracy (in the interwar decades
for example), but it may also threaten the future of democracy. As Frank
Ankersmit argues in Chapter 9, political participation has to precede cultural
integration.

Ankersmit tackles the tricky relationship between democracy and mass
immigration. Based partly on historical analysis, he considers the need to integrate large numbers of immigrants in the west European nation-states a
challenge comparable to earlier processes of social and political integration,
particularly of the late nineteenth-century labor force. Taking as a point of
departure the universal constitutional and political rights of immigrants in
western democracies, Ankersmit criticises current approaches of (cultural)
integration and advocates a process of emancipation and acculturation by
means of social and political organization and confrontation (comparable to
the earlier politicisation of the labor-capital dichotomy and the political integration of the socialist movement). Historical evidence shows that immigrants develop into full-grown citizens, into generally accepted members of
the nation, only by means of struggle and political organization. Cultural
differences should be politicized, he argues, as this is the only way to reach
acculturation in a democratic multicultural society.

East Central Europe

Whereas Western Europe showed a relative political stability, and, as a result, the capacity to set up the welfare state, Central and Eastern Europe
faced instability, political violence, authoritarian and totalitarian rule, and
economic backwardness. However, as we have underlined before, there is no
simple one-to-one relationship between ethnicity and democratic instability.
In fact, the perception of ethnoreligious cleavages as a sociopolitical problem was often the *result* of democratization.

In East Central Europe the historical link between ethnic homogeneity
and democratization seems even more complex, more multidimensional
than in the western part of the continent (see Sugar 1980). In general, the
role of the state in homogenizing populations has been far more drastic and
violent than in Western Europe. Ivan Berend evaluates the relevance of eth-

nic heterogeneity in the twisted and frustratingly long road to democratic governance in East Central Europe, and comes to the conclusion that the success or failure of democracy is rooted in a complex context of social, cultural, economic, and political development. His central argument is that lack of ethnic homogeneity was a basic impediment of democratization in Eastern Europe, but only within the specific environment of backwardness and a flawed nation-building process. As he argues, economic and social backwardness and failed modernisation in the nineteenth century and, consequently, the growing gap between the advanced core countries of Europe and the eastern part of the continent were far more decisive barriers to democratization than ethnic diversity. "In the environment of peripheral socioeconomic backwardness, and only in this environment, lack of ethnic homogeneity, indeed, became a basic impediment of democracy," he writes in Chapter 3. In this respect, the history of East Central Europe clearly illustrates the deformation of democracy at birth. Whether its modern history of despotism, closely related to ethnic conflict, will frustrate further democratization in the postcommunist era remains to be seen. Berend is not overly optimistic.

Aviel Roshwald discusses one of the most vexing questions surrounding the historical relationship among imperial authority, democratization, and ethnic nationalism. He focuses on the late nineteenth-century European empires (Habsburg, Romanov, and Ottoman) and asks to what extent the introduction of constitutional forms and (democratic) electoral politics contributed to their fall. Could imperial authority coincide with democratization, or were they essentially mutually exclusive? Roshwald questions the rosy picture (still rather attractive in conflict-ridden Europe today) of the lost world of the European empire-states (the Habsburg Empire in particular) as benign, patriarchal political regimes graciously presiding over the peaceful development of multicultural societies. He claims that the imperial regimes' relative tolerance of diversity was not a product of fundamental ideological commitment to ethnocultural pluralism, but a function of their dynastic legitimacy, including the attempt to promote official nationalisms. The historicist perspective Roshwald proposes suggests that these imperial orders were rather incubation vessels for morally and politically irresponsible forms of nationalism than a sincere attempt to introduce a type of modern multiethnic democracy. From a contemporary perspective we can learn from their experiences, he concludes, but more by studying their mistakes than their accomplishments.

In the multinational empires of Central Europe, assimilation of "national minorities" was commonly believed to be a matter of only a few generations. An optimism, as Philipp Ther has argued, that was "deeply rooted in liberal idealism and sometimes in supremacist and racist nationalist ideas" (2001a, 47). This optimism proved to be misplaced. Attitudes began to harden, as the ethnic identities proved to be more persistent than expected. The *façade* democracies of the interwar years, products of foreign intervention mainly, degenerated into dictatorships within a decade (Czechoslovakia, as is well-known, being the only exception). Ethnic diversity, interethnic tensions, jealousies, and conflicts certainly had an adverse effect on political stability (and on democracy-building) in the region, as did the intolerant, "majoritarian" type of nationalist discourse and policy, which the elites in most of the newly established countries felt prompted to follow. The actual demise of the façade democracies, however, has been mostly conditioned by other factors. The economic crisis and its social consequences were of particular importance, as were the political pressures from outside, especially from frustrated neighboring states and expansionist regional great powers (Italy, Germany, and Russia). In other words, ethnic diversity as such may not have been the major condition of democratic breakdown, but the ethnocentric approach and intolerance of many of the more powerful political actors in the region, facilitated by societies' ethnic heterogeneity, certainly contributed to the emergence of autocratic regimes, based on quasi-national identities and strongly homogenizing political strategies. Even in Czechoslovakia, ethnic cleavages, or nonidentification with the current political order on the basis of an ethnically defined identity, burdened the country from the very beginning. The establishment of the Czechoslovak Republic was accomplished peacefully, with the exception of the German-inhabited territories and Ruthenia, the least developed part of the new country. Both regions had to be occupied by military force before they were formally integrated into the state. As John Bradley concludes: "German districts remained under an occupation regime for a long time; Slovakia appeared as an annexed province with Hungarian masters replaced by Czechs; and Ruthenia never obtained its much-advertised autonomy. In fact it became a unique example of colonial occupation in Central Europe" (2000, 90). Germans remained the most recalcitrant citizens of the republic, while their legal status remained uncertain for a good while. Their frustration would eventually enable National-Socialist Germany to fatally weaken East Central Europe's only democracy.

Homogeneous states, however, appeared to be as unstable as heterogeneous states. Interwar Austria was a remarkably uniform society, both ethnically and religiously. It was also a highly unstable and volatile country, though, whose democracy collapsed soon after its tenth anniversary. The demise of democratic rule in Austria could not have been related to ethnic divisions. The most crucial factors involved were a lack of internal political cohesion, a devastating economic crisis, and, particularly, subversive interference by outside powers. Hungary was almost equally ethnically homogenous, but its democratic experiment lasted even less time. In this case, ethnic issues may have played a role, but only indirectly. The antidemocratic and "hegemonic" consensus of the major part of its political elite could be seen within the context of its overall goal, namely to regain the lost "historical territories." In short, domestic ethnic or religious diversity proved largely irrelevant factors in the breakdown of democracy in either Austria or Hungary. Czechoslovakia on the other hand was an outspokenly divided country, whose democracy happened to survive most of the interwar period. The solidity of the administration and the large measure of consensus among (most of the) political elite guided Czechoslovakia through the first two decades of its existence. Despite the fact that ethnic cleavages weakened the internal cohesion of the young republic, and that cross-border ethnic problems, more than other factors, contributed to its precarious international position, only the subversion and machinations of eager dictatorial enemies and dubious democratic friends would finally seal the fate of the region's only democracy. Up to 1926 Poland was a parliamentary democracy, but after Józef Piłsudski's coup d'état it became a flawed dictatorship at best. As divided as the Second Republic was, the breakdown of its democratic system was more the result of the frustrations and ambitions of powerful individuals, in combination with the divisiveness and impotence of its legislature, than of ethnic cleavages per se, as real as they were. With respect to the subversive effect of ethnic divisions on the democratic polity, the case of Romania seems to be more relevant. "The root cause of all Romania's crisis is the failure of its ruling class to resolve the essential problem of integration and assimilation of the various provinces acquired at the end of the First World War ... into the body politic, social, and cultural of the 'Greater' Romania that had been created," Stephen Fischer-Galati claims (2000, 381). The question is of course: was this "body politic" ever democratic? Whatever the answer to the question is, one thing seems to be sure: in Romania ethnic diversity can only have functioned as a strong argument against democratization. The need for national integration, combined with an overriding concern to keep their monopoly of power, made the political elite inherently intolerant of diversity, any kind of diversity, whether ethnic or political.

Andrew Janos analyzes the three waves of democratization in Europe. He explores the special problems related to the "export" of the western nation-state model in Central and Eastern Europe, in particular within the nexus between multiethnicity and democracy before the Second World War and under contemporary conditions. He seriously questions the notion of the universality of the west European nation-state under the specific conditions of East Central Europe, which applies both to the early phase of (flawed) democratization (final decades of the nineteenth century and the interwar years) and to contemporary postcommunist democratization. Janos remains cautiously optimistic about the prospects for democracy in Central and Eastern Europe.

In Chapter 6, Philipp Ther elaborates on the tragic fate of democracy in the German-speaking states. He asserts that democratization was seriously hampered in the German Empire from 1871 by "national engineering," by the policies of ethnic homogenisation, especially in the Polish part of Prussia. This in turn would negatively influence the development of democracy in Central Europe during the interwar years. The post-1945 communist regimes elaborated on the unprecedented example of ethnic homogenization (or genocide) during the German occupation from 1939 to 1945. Forced population transfers were a prominent feature of early communist rule. Twelve million ethnic Germans were expelled from Central Europe, Poland, and the Czech lands in particular (an expulsion authorized by the Great Powers), as were large numbers of Poles from the Soviet Union, Ukrainians from Poland, and Hungarians from Slovakia. The expulsions supported the communist rulers' claim on "new" territories and provided them with much-needed capital for social and economic reconstruction, as Ther shows. Ethnic engineering by the communist parties further homogenized (a political asset per se) and "revolutionised" their societies, and strengthened their national credentials. In other words, ethnic cleansing sustained communism's (feeble) legitimacy considerably, particularly in Poland and Czechoslovakia.

German genocide and communist ethnic cleansing implied far-reaching demographic change in East Central Europe. They made the region more homogeneous than it had ever been in modern history. The attempts at cultural homogenization, from the empires in the nineteenth century, through the flawed nation-states of the interwar decades, to the widespread political engineering of the first few years of communist rule, were not particularly supportive of the growth of democracy in the region—to put it moderately.

The renaissance of national and ethnic conflicts in postcommunist East Central Europe has often been explained by the "freezer" metaphor: Traditional nationalist controversies, resentments, and conflicts were supposedly covered for more than forty years by a layer of ice (the *Pax Sovietica*), and only revived when the ice began to melt, when (international) political conformity and harmony enforced by the Soviet Union collapsed. This metaphor is only partly true. Nationalism and the minority issue were never put in a freezer. Indeed, they were frequently used and manipulated by the communist regimes. They were a constituent part of the communist experiment from the very beginning, and they served as one of the most powerful, albeit ultimately ineffective, instruments for acquiring legitimacy (Gerrits 1992, 9). All "communisms" were to some extent "national," at least that is what the communist rulers aspired to. With the exception of the major multinational communist states (the Soviet Union, Yugoslavia, and to a lesser extent, Czechoslovakia) communist state nationalism, however, was the nationalism of the dominant ethnic group. Ethnic minorities could hardly be expected to recognize themselves in the collective mythology of the nation and in the supreme value of the national state.

In practice, the communist regimes have treated the issue of ethnic minorities in widely divergent ways. With few exceptions (Bulgaria during the 1980s and Romania under Nicolae Ceaușescu), forced migration remained limited to the first postwar years. After the communist parties had consolidated their power, ethnic minorities generally acquired equal rights, and, often for the first time in history, individuals from minority groups reached positions of political power. On the whole, as the historian Robert King asserts, in post-1948 East Central Europe minorities probably enjoyed a better position in society than they did before the Second World War (1973, 73). A mixture of ideological assumptions and practical considerations guided the ethnic policies of the communist regimes. Given Marx's well-known underestimation of the power of ethnic identification, it should not come as a surprise that communist ideologues stuck to the idea that class would be superior to nation as the main source of identification, or, in more practical terms, that a "union-wide" identity (Soviet patriotism or "Yugoslavism") would ultimately replace particularistic forms of national identity. The communist regimes may have been generally aware of the potential explosiveness of lasting ethnic identities and antagonisms, but their policies remained rather ambiguous, if not contradictory—and this was part of the reason national awareness continued to stay alive. National and ethnic differences were recognised, but rather half-heartedly. Federal arrangements were created, though with important exceptions. One of the more enigmatic and, with the benefit of hindsight, more fateful decisions taken concerned the redrawing of internal borders in the Soviet Union and postwar Yugoslavia. This gave the major ethnic groups, differently from precommunist times, their own, quasi-autonomous administrative entities, thereby sustaining their cultural identities and facilitating the subsequent break-up of the multinational communist states along traditional ethnic lines.

This is not the place to discuss extensively postcommunist political reform and democratization in general. We are interested though in the intricate relationship between ethnic diversity or homogeneity and political democratization. To put it more precisely: should the ethnic "issue" be considered as an important explanatory variable, as a necessary or sufficient condition of postcommunist democratic change? Historically, based on west European experience, democracy and nationalism are closely, if not causally, linked. "Nationalism was the form in which democracy appeared," as Liah Greenfeld asserts, "contained in the idea of the nation as a butterfly in a cocoon" (1992, 10).

Democracy can only rest on a strong cohesive identity, which the nation (nationalism) seems particularly suitable to facilitate. Be that as it may, the political interpretation of the nationalism-democracy matrix changed radically under the influence of interwar crisis, fascism (national socialism), and war. Democracy and nationalism became increasingly considered as mutually hostile, as exclusive. The relationship between democratization and nationalist conflict in postcommunist East Central Europe has been far more ambivalent, however, than many people in the West initially wanted to believe. Bruno Naarden shows how western images of East Central Europe, including ideas on ethnic diversity and the region's suitability for democracy, have evolved over the last two centuries, closely connected as they were to our perception of cultural fault lines in Europe. Naarden focuses primarily on stereotypical notions of Central Europe and the Balkans. He comes to the conclusion that in the case of the demise and violent disintegration of communist Yugoslavia, many western observers (and participants in the conflict) were caught within a web of flawed analyses, myths, and stereotypes concerning the role and relevance of the ethnic factor in the Yugoslav civil war. They were either ignoring ethnicity altogether, or isolating it as the predominant cause of the country's collapse. Both interpretations, Naarden suggests, are untenable.

When communism collapsed and a range of new states appeared on the map of Europe, the dominant political idea was that democratization was actually the best antidote available to nationalist conflict. This notion may have been comforting, but it was essentially ahistorical and politically misleading. Under the conditions of postcommunism, democratization rather stimulated than discouraged nationalist sentiments and conflicts. It gave powerful groups and individuals more room to politicize and mobilize frustrated (national) sentiments than the limited parameters of the communist order had done (Snyder 2000). Defective democracies are more numerous among the new nation-states of East Central Europe than among the old ones. Within the states emerging from the disintegration of the Soviet Union, Yugoslavia, and Czechoslovakia, the issue of nation building was high on the political agenda and it often complicated and delayed democratization. The conflicts it generated ranged from mild protests and controversies to repression and civil war (major exceptions: the Czech Republic and Slovenia, but they are among the economically most advanced countries in the region, bordering as they do the European Community).

The ethnic or minority issue, however, was neither the only nor the most important factor in the collapse of communism. Generally, one may seriously qualify the relevance of ethnic diversity as a major historical condition of democratization, and of democratic or communist breakdown in East Central Europe. Nevertheless, ethnic diversity seems to make a difference. Of the ten postcommunist countries in East Central Europe to which the Freedom House in 1997 gave the highest "democratic reform score," and among the ten countries that the United Nations Development Program placed most prominently on the Human Development Index Value (also 1997), seven are among the ten ethnically most homogeneous in the region.[5] Scepticism seems justified, though (Fish 2001, 62). Is the level of ethnic homogeneity an important variable of democratization in postcommunist Europe; or is it a mere empirical coincidence that among the more successful reformers, the more stable democracies, we also find the more ethnically homogeneous countries? Is the statistical relationship really convincing, and if so, has it any predictive value? Is it worthwhile at all to search for commonly present, independent variables, which explain democratization or the lack thereof in a region as diverse as former communist Europe? We tend to believe that if ethnic homogeneity is an explanatory variable of democratization in post-communist Europe at all, it is definitely only one of the conditions of democracy, and most probably not the crucial one. Other factors seem decisively more important: historical experience with democracy; geographical proximity to the West—and everything, including extensive financial and political assistance, that comes with it; the level of socioeconomic development, particularly the distribution of wealth; the nature and duration of communist rule and the record of the noncommunist opposition; and the measure of pluralism within the state or the extent to which power is divided, including specific constitutional arrangements. Obviously, as some major exceptions (ethnically heterogeneous countries with a credible democratic record, such as Estonia and Latvia) show, ethnic homogeneity cannot be considered a *condition* of democracy in the postcommunist world. We do believe, however, that it may be considered a positive factor, and we therefore question the idea that "progress or regress on the road to democracy" in East Central Europe is fully "independent" of ethnic or cultural diversity (Anderson 2001, 154). This interpretation, as we see it, underestimates the democracy-sustaining effect of ethnic homogeneity. The essential issue again is not so much the measure of ethnic heterogeneity as such, but the extent to which this issue can be politicized and manipulated (for reasons that may have very little to do with the actual size of the minorities). It is this kind of calculating politicization of ethnic diversity that creates the ethnic type of nationalism that is at odds with a democratic political culture and polity.

CHAPTER TWO

The Eternal Stranger

Democracy and Diversity

EUGEN WEBER

In 1952, Claude Lévi-Strauss wrote a pamphlet for UNESCO entitled *Race and History*, where he explained that all societies have words to designate good guys, who are members of the group, and bad guys, who are not—who are outsiders. In the 1940s, when I grew up in the Lake District, in the northwest of England, countrymen still repeated "Here's a stranger, heave a rock at him"; although by then they did it with a smile. "Diversity," writes Lévi-Strauss, "results in great part from the desire of each culture to oppose itself to those that surround it, to distinguish itself from them, in one word to be itself."[1] But the diversity of others can be troubling, as it would be to find in a mirror an unfamiliar figure—perhaps an apparition or a ghost—staring back.

Strangers are strange. Hence the derisive dismissals of outlanders that survive in our speech. Barbarians were people who did not speak like the Greeks, but in some incomprehensible babble. For the Slavs, German-speakers were *Niemec*, again incomprehensible, hence dumb. Civilizations come in many shapes and sizes. But all are about common standards, reverences and dis-criminations—in language, remembrance, and literature, where identity (or imagined identity) looms once it has been forged, and shaped, and reshaped.

Society represents itself to itself as it imagines itself to be. If you don't fit the representation or are thought not to fit it, then you don't belong. More: you don't share the humanity that society attributes to itself and, in earlier ages or stages, denies to those outside its bounds, characterized as defective, botched, flawed, and potentially mischievous. That is what ethnologists rec-ognize in what we call primitive or archaic tribes that they study today. We hear echoes of the view in a pamphlet that Dean Swift published in 1737, where he denounced the perpetual swarms of foreign beggars (meaning for-eign to the city of Dublin, whether they were English, or Irish from outside the city), "fitter to be rooted out of the face of the earth, than suffered to levy a charge upon the city they infest" (Swift 1737).

Then came the nation: the abstract notion of a collective entity presented as an extended family allegedly united by its assertion of communal particu-larism, by continuity, by a common past and a common future. Since inclu-sion implies exclusion, the attitudes and practices of small-scale communities were transferred to the larger—which also claimed or assumed unanimity and tried to keep cuckoos out of the national nest so that, during the French Rev-olution, *étranger* was used to designate political foes, traitors to the revolu-tionary cause, nobles, Britons, and all who conspired against the nation.

The rather novel entities called nations asserted their personality by way of an inclusive national language: French, not some dialect or *patois*; English, not Welsh or Gaelic; Hungarian, not Latin; Norwegian, not Danish; Finnish, not Swedish. They supported their personality by national fictions called folklore: not just by tales and ballads, but costumes like the kilt. And, of course, they used instruction and indoctrination. Léon Bourgeois, a great political figure of the early Third Republic, described the principle behind these efforts in a *fin-de-siècle* book about the education of French democracy:

> A society cannot live in security and peace if the men who compose it are
> not united and voluntarily disciplined by a common conception of life, of its
> aims and of its duties. The ultimate aim of national education is to create
> this unity of minds and consciences (Bourgeois 1897, preface).

In due course the concept of nationality was going to generate legislation to regulate strangers, outsiders, and foreigners—their immigration, residence, registration, taxation, access to employment, and eventually to social benefits. But for a long time, rules and controls administered by skimpy bureaucracies counted for little. Until the second half of the nineteenth century, barriers and borders remained porous; and oversight was slack or nonexistent. More important, into the 1880s, conception and perception of the foreign other was hazy and dubious. In England it is not much of a political issue, rather a socio-economic one. In France, assimilation and integration are important goals, but Ernest Renan refuses any ethnic identification of a nation that melds Celtic, Iberic, Germanic, and Latin contributions. "There is no pure French race," he proclaims at the Sorbonne in 1882, "but one French people, product of process, of fusion, of building, of choice, and of a plebiscite of every day" (1947, 896, 903–4).

Anyway, national identifications of *us* versus *them* continued rare well into the 1880s—probably because national references were exceptional in much of the national territory, and their carriers (press and politicians) were little heard among the masses. The étranger continued to be the outsider to the local community: Belgian or Flemish in the north, Piedmontese in the southeast, Auvergnat in Paris, and so on. Perceptions of difference and ensuing suspicion or rejection are to be found rather in relations between town and country, with country folk disliking townsmen as *forains*, outsiders, intruders, and townsfolk dismissing yokels at best as exotic, at worst as primitive savages. Under the July monarchy and still at mid-century, migrant masons of the Creuse, 200 or 250 miles from Paris, encounter the same scorn there and the same biases as their Algerian successors a century later.

Then, in the 1880s, as the press is freed from censorship, journalism, which used to be mainly political or literary, shifts toward sensationalism. Newspapers begin to look for news stories that will sell their shoddy tattle to newly literate readers and, as international friction grows, brawls that used to pass unnoticed between French and Italian or Flemish workers are exaggerated and used to fit and feed prevailing fashion. Sporadic clashes, disorders, pilfering, and ignorable tensions turn into problems: *le problème Juif, le problème Gitan*—and rejection of the other becomes an incandescent rage. "The condensation of political passions in a small number of hatreds that are very simple and related to the deepest roots of the human heart," wrote Julien Benda, "is a conquest of the modern age" (1927, chapter 1).

Modern democracy rests on parliament and on the press. Both address and court universal suffrage which really comes into its own in the last third or the last quarter of the nineteenth century; and, with it, demagogy, of which, at the *fin-de-siècle*, xenophobia is the raw material and the topic of choice. How shall we mobilize the masses, get them into the streets, into the voting booth, into buying the papers now selling at prices that they can afford? Whether you are a socialist or a nationalist, it will be us against them. National abstractions become concrete and passionate as Germans threaten the French, the French threaten the Germans, and foreigners come to be seen as a threat to security and economy both. The nation must be protected; the labor market must be protected; outsiders must be identified, neutralized, expelled, kept out.

In the mid-1880s, Franco-German mistrust leads to a serious crisis, exploited on the French side by a bellicose show-off, General Georges Boulanger. The sensationalism of Boulangist politics and the marketing of Boulanger himself mobilize sections of the electorate that had paid no heed to politics and elections; in Paris, they raise electoral participation by 10 percent by the end of the decade—you might say that they press democracy forward. And concerns for national security coincide with economic crisis and rising unemployment to produce the Decree of 1888, requiring all resident foreigners to carry identity cards. Then, in 1895, comes a census of migrants, designed to improve the surveillance of "nomads of an ethnic character," meaning Gypsies. By 1912, Gypsies in France were required to carry an anthropometrical identity card.

Meanwhile the trickle of Jews leaving Russia and Eastern Europe for the West was becoming a stream. Michael Marrus has described them speaking Yiddish, dressed in traditional garb, poverty-stricken and distressed, crowding the wharves in Hamburg, Bremen, and Amsterdam, but also other urban centers of the West. "It did not take long," adds Marrus, "before such uninvited guests became unpopular. By the end of the century, European opposition to Jewish migrants was widespread, nourished by popular anti-Semitism and xenophobia . . . " (1985, 35)It was the Jewish inflow that persuaded the otherwise easygoing British to pass an Alien Act in 1905.

Jews, of course, are the stereotypical resident or refugee alien; and those Jews who assimilated were continually being tarred with the brush of what Bernard Lazare called the unregenerate hordes who had not, or would not, or could not be like us (Weber 1986, 131). But in some societies xenophobia zeroes in on other groups—notably the Irish, pet aversions of nineteenth-century British miners and textile workers, as of late-nineteenth-century Americans. Arthur Schlesinger Jr. refers to the abhorrence with which old Yankees viewed the Irish "as intense as against Blacks." And the distinguished Black champion, W. E. B. du Bois recalls that when he grew up in western Massachusetts in the 1870s, "the racial angle was more clearly defined against the Irish than against us" (Schlesinger 2000, 55, 56). Which is only to say that every place and time has its preferred others, treated as targets of exclusion and derision.

Every society, too, has its marginalized, marginalizing, and criminogenic urban pathologies: insalubrious, overcrowded, deprived, and precarious ghettos, slums, and *bidonvilles* that run from the Flemish quarters of Roubaix in the 1860s to Italian mining settlements in early twentieth century Lorraine, to Jewish sections of Belleville and the Marais in the *Belle Époque*, to the Armenian shanties of Issy-les-Moulineaux in the 1920s, to the Portuguese and North African bidonvilles of the 1960s and 1970s, and the problem tenements of the 1990s.

But in the age of nations and nationalism, one of Europe's major problems was the diversity and the number of populations ruled by masters of a different stock, different culture, and different language. Before the First World War some sixty million Europeans lived under an alien jurisdiction. Now, it is a modern axiom that rule by strangers is worse than rule by one's own: better for people to rule themselves—even messily, even badly, than to be ruled by foreigners, even if the foreigners do a decent job. This persuasion, broadly speaking, helped to set off the Great War, after which only about 25 million Europeans had foreign masters to resent.

Self-determination means widespread acceptance of the determinations of a dominant group, or resignation to them. When resignation flags trouble follows, as it did in eastern and southeastern Europe. Greece, Yugoslavia, Romania, Poland, Czechoslovakia had been forced to sign treaties providing minorities with basic human rights, and chauvinists and irredentists with battle cries. The machinery of these and other national states, most of them functioning under allegedly representative democratic and parliamentary rules, unloosed millions of *Heimatlosen* and refugees for whom new and old nations would not or could not assume responsibility: nearly 10 million of them, including 1 or 1.5 million forcibly exchanged between Greece and Turkey, 2 million Poles, over 2 million Russians and Hungarians (thousands of the latter camping for years in railway stations), 1 million Germans, and hundreds of thousands of Armenians (who would have been more numerous if their fellow nationals had not been murdered by the million). Nansen passports, internationally recognized identity cards issued by the League of Nations to stateless refugees, were invented for these groups in 1922.

Passports themselves were generalized as a result of the war. Before 1914, travel documents were few or nonexistent except in backward realms like Russia and the Ottoman Empire, which required them for internal travel. The passports we are used to came in with the war and the post-war, complete with photographs and all sorts of vulgar personal details, once reserved for vagrants, that shocked and scandalized my parents and grandparents.

I am too young to have been shocked by passports. But I can testify to ethnic diversity in Romania between the two World Wars: it was rife, and it worked badly. Romania was not really a democracy but, along with corruption, ethnic friction was the most representative thing about it. Romanians had over the centuries assimilated or accepted Greeks, Ruthenians, even Poles; but they disliked and despised Gypsies, Jews, Hungarians, Bulgarians, and Turks. The Jews, eager to assimilate into cultures they admired (like the French, English, German, and Hungarian) found little in Romania to respect and remained largely undigested, while the Romanian authorities, along with those of Hungary and Poland, repeatedly tried to solve what they called the Jewish problem by massive evacuation to other lands. Anti-Semitism was particularly acute because peasants' sons moving upward found Jews installed in the professions and in commerce. The more vigorous the competition, the more vigorous the xenophobia. Fanned by the press, the fear kept exploding; especially, as one might expect, at moments of political and economic crisis. And, while the Romanian situation may have been exceptionally fraught, you could find it reproduced in more stable and more democratic societies, like France, the biggest immigrant haven beside the United States.

France was never densely populated for its size, which means that immigration was encouraged whenever employers needed labor, and resented only in hard times, when outsiders were denounced for taking work from natives and bread from their mouths. In those times the discourse darkens and veers to us versus them themes, to zoological similes, to illegality and delinquency and costs that went unnoticed when the benefits of the foreigners' presence outweighed their oddity and the menace of contamination. So, normally in France as in the United States, immigrants were first marginalized and denigrated, then assimilated and integrated. There were bloody hiccups in the late 1840s and at the turn of the century, but the system worked until the Depression and specifically until 1932.

That was when French industrial production plunged to one-third of what it had been in 1929, just on the eve of a new and more numerous flow of refugees. And that was when, in France and elsewhere, an era of real animosity opened. When Dutch, Belgian, Swiss, and British set to screening out refugees; and when, in 1933, French, Dutch, and Belgian representatives to an international labor conference in Geneva complained of the calamitous effects that refugees were having on their collapsing labor market.

The United States had closed its gates in the 1920s. Now France declared itself saturated. No one was willing to become a dumping ground for refugees. The radical Right discourse of today was a commonplace of the 1930s too, and that reflected wide popular (and also literate) assent. The rights of man are only what some men concede to others. Legislation that excludes aliens from access or shelter or jobs is the work of citizens defending their fellow-citizens and widely perceived to be doing so. Nor is legislation always needed to designate an out group or keep an out group out. Designated others come in many shapes and sizes—they can be Catholics or Protestants, Jesuits or Masons, communists or capitalists. But the model of choice is one that is ethnically identifiable and visually recognizable. In Finland, for example, xenophobia and racism are preferably directed against people who don't look like the Finns. Gypsies illustrate this picture par excellence.

Typically Gypsies refer to themselves as Roma, meaning man or human, and to non-Gypsies as Gadje, a pejorative term that means something like barbarian or bumpkin. A community affirms its identity by identifying what it is not, or not like. Gypsies do so too when they distinguish between Roma and others in matters of hygiene, diet, relations with animals, speech, and by avoiding contact whenever possible.

In some ways, Roma were (and some still are) like Jews—that is, visibly, sometimes assertively, different—but their blackness, equated with inferiority and evil, and their vagrant ways that meant they did not really belong anywhere, made them even more suspect and persecuted than the Jews. Since their arrival in Europe in the fourteenth century, Roma have been accused of poisoning wells, spreading plagues and epidemics, stealing children, and eating other people—the most recent charge of cannibalism dates to 1927. And if one hardly hears about the hundreds of thousands deported from Germany, Austria, Czechoslovakia, Holland, Belgium, France, Yugoslavia, Romania, Russia, and Bulgaria during the last war to perish in Polish camps, that is presumably because no one cared then and no one cares now, except those who thought "Good riddance."[2] If you ask how democracies react to ethnic diversity, to a stubborn assertion of the right to be different, policies and treatment of Gypsies offer a very clear answer that the politically correct would rather not heed.

Democracy is no guarantee of anything, not even of democracy itself, or of so-called human rights. The people, after all—as Horace, who had fought in Rome's civil wars, wrote under the reign of Augustus—the people is a many-headed beast. But, to the extent it functions, democracy is likely, sometimes at least, to express the prejudices of its members as well as their aspirations. A democratic state is a free association; and freedom to associate includes the right to exclude.

In this connection, although our focus is European history (which is why I refrain from mentioning multiple ethnic conflicts the world over), I want to cite the example of a Eropoid country, Australia. Some years ago, a fish-and-chip shop owner called Pauline Hanson ran for parliament in a Queensland constituency near Brisbane, on a call to end Asian immigration. In her first speech in parliament, Hanson declared the country in danger of being swamped by Asians. "They have their own culture and religion, form ghettos, and don't assimilate. A truly multicultural country can never be strong or united."[3] The elite and articulate public was outraged. But the Australian elections of 2001 were fought on the anti-immigration issue. And while, or because, the Australian election commission advertised the vote in twenty-six different languages, the opponents of immigration won. Gerard Henderson, head of the Sydney Institute writes that "Historically in Australia there has been opposition to newcomers, as there has been in most democratic immigrant societies," but he insists that the country is not racist, and a pretty tolerant and accepting society, with a high level of intermarriage and a low level of ethnic crime (*New York Times*, November 9, 2001).

Indeed, prejudice expressed at one level does not exclude acceptance at another. Henderson mentions intermarriage. In France, where xenophobia sometimes flares, marriages between French and foreigners have practically doubled in the past twenty years, and marriages between French and North Africans have multiplied by a factor of nine. Gérard Noiriel, in his masterful study of the French melting pot, concludes that the very intensity of xenophobic derision accelerates the process of assimilation.[4] This view may be debatable; but to the extent that it holds water, there is plenty of accelerant around.

The Australian experience repeats and confirms what happened in Austria; it confirms what happens in France, where Arabic is now the second language (as Spanish is in the United States), and where three-fourths of respondents feel that there are too many Arabs. It also confirms what is happening in Germany, where Turkish is the second language, where two-thirds of the population oppose further immigration, where the children of Turks who have lived there for decades are still called foreigners, and where attacks on refugee hostels evoke sympathy for "our protesting children." The heterophobia of Le Penists in France, of skinheads in Germany, of Haiderists in Austria, is only an exaggeration or caricature of widespread attitudes.

"Exorcise racist intolerance?" asks Fernand Braudel in his last important work, *The Identity of France*. "But don't such ideologies reflect real oppositions, power struggles sparked by the demographic explosion that makes living together more fraught?" Individual or tribal, "true creativity implies a certain deafness to the appeal of other values that can go as far as their rejection, even to their negation." Abiding identity goes with a degree of impermeability. So Braudel recognizes "the problem of *otherness*, that is the feeling that a foreign presence is other, a challenge to one's own self and identity, to such a degree that this real or imagined difference provokes in both parties unease, scorn, fear or hate" and generates "reciprocal forms of rejection that cannot be denied" (1988, I, 43, 47, 208, and *passim*). Immigrants, he declares, must make a choice; and so must host societies that seem reluctant to do so.

The siren calls of well-intentioned intellectuals (like Alain Touraine, who wrote a fine book to argue that democracy cannot exist without diversity of beliefs, origins and opinions (Touraine 1994, 26) are heeded mostly by other well-intentioned intellectuals. Amplified by the media, they sound like public opinion; but one wonders how deep that goes, and how far. Politics, after all, are less about liberties for others than about advantages for oneself. Political discourse originates and largely takes place at non-popular levels. It may percolate to wider audiences, but ordinary people, most people, usually have other fish to fry, other agendas; and ideas fascinating to their betters do not necessarily engage those whose main concern is to earn a living, find shelter and preserve it, put food on the table and, if possible, enjoy some degree of security and comfort.

But security, nowadays, seems in as short supply as in the first half of the nineteenth century that Louis Chevalier described in his classic *Classes laborieuses et classes dangereuses* (1958). On the fringes of law and order orphan territories loom, criminogenic "projects" and their spill-off. One might call the predators they generate desocialized, but they have scarcely been socialized in the society that their hosts consider their own. In fact, like other gangsters, these dysfunctional others function quite well in their own world. Where general social rules lose hold or fail to take hold, unruly living is a form of adaptation. Territorial delinquencies reflect the exclusion and the self-exclusion of clans closing themselves off from a society that they believe has closed them off. In cultures of resentment and defiance transgression socializes, delinquency establishes peer status. And the rest of the people no longer face criminal lost sheep, but herds.

This generates acrimony and contention. For those who regard immigrants as invaders, native culture and identity have to be defended. For progressives, meanwhile, immigrants have replaced the working class as the new social heroes, ethnic consciousness has taken over from class consciousness. As identitarian claims forge ahead of redistributive claims, social justice translates into ethnic justice. But ethnicities are multiple, fragmented, and given to reciprocal rejections. Tolerance thrives in inverse proportion to physical proximity. Even a sympathetic observer like Touraine cannot help noting the running conflict in suburban Paris projects between Blacks and *beurs* (North Africans) on the one hand, and South Asians, whom the Blacks call *hindous* or, more often, *others*. Despite their more recent arrival in the country, these others have integrated better than the Blacks in French society, which is one reason for resentment. But they are also blamed for being more interested in economic success than in mixing with their non-white neighbors.[5]

Braudel remarked that Islam, which he saw engaged in a process of reverse colonialism in Europe, is more than a religion: "a whole civilization full of vigor, an entire way of life" (1988, 214). Traditional Muslim teaching discouraged Muslims from living in infidel states, except for temporary visits to trade or negotiate. More recent interpretations, though, notably those of Islamists, claim that Europe too is a land of Islam (*Dar al-Islam*) and that *sharia*, the Islamic law, extends to Europe—a theory with unsettling implications for countries where immigrants seethe and terrorists breed. A reflection of this occurred in Strasbourg in April 2002 during the presidential campaign, where *Le Monde* reported young beurs yelling, among other obscenities, "We don't want to live in a country that has Jews in it"(April 9, 2002). To which the obvious rejoinder would be: then why not leave? Many wish they would: two thirds of the French polled in 1988, three quarters in 1995.[6] But this is easier said than done when the sovereign people is fragmented and confused.

So nothing is quite as it used to be. New ideologies replace traditional solidarities. Habitual cleavages—Right/Left, capital/labor—give way to novel ones—sexual, generational, religious, or ethnic. Ideologies turn to fads and fads to ashes. Familiar perspectives fade, clash, and collide; the new ones fail to fuse in a coherent (let alone common) system. Established institutions prove slow to recognize competing claims, let alone act on them. Notions of representativity, legitimacy, trust, all crack. Alliances are made and unmade according not to long-standing principle or tradition but to the moment's juncture. Surveys compete with elections; initiatives, referenda contend with parliamentary laws. The bombardment of news and images thickens, and bumps up levels of expectation that institutions in low gear don't fit. Rhythms accelerate, experience gets more crowded, immediacy rules, impatience intensifies and turns democracy into dromocracy (as in the Greek for a race). Media and media-made opinions reflect and expect short-term reactions, maximize trends and trendy notions, leave little time for reflection, now replaced by emotion, sentiment, flash panics, and stampedes. Capricious, impressionable, tyrannical, what passes for public opinion turns from a political factor into an urgent force.

The issue, in this context, is less xenophobia or racism or prejudice, than the immediate everyday experience that has been intimidated and bottled up by pressure of political correctness, yet smolders waiting for an opportunity to flare. What about? Take your pick: costs associated with the increasing number of immigrants, criminality, indifference to local standards and expectations, irritation at interdicts that feel stifling, bitterness when the political and administrative elite turn a blind eye to discomforting transgressions. Elected representatives and governments no longer *represent* a sovereign people with whom they don't sit down to dinner but rather the values and the mindsets far from those of the vulgar crowd. This has always been so, but expectations have changed and so have opportunities to express them. Among the ideologically homeless who feel unrepresented, populist protest clamors: a plague on all your houses.

Folk may well feel bedeviled. Léon Bourgeois's unity of minds and consciences unravels; Renan's plebiscite of every day turns up conflicting answers. Westerners feel torn between the claims of national narrative that sounds increasingly anachronistic;[7] of an encroaching Europe that displays more geography than history; of a shadowy humanity too often evoked for manipulative ends.

It brings to mind the question Chateaubriand raised in his memoirs: "What would a universal society look like that included no particular country, that would not be French or English or German or Spanish or Portuguese or Italian or Russian or Tartar or Turkish or Persian or Indian or Chinese or American, or rather that would be all these societies at once?" (*Mémoires*, book 44, chapter 5). The screech of values crashing, the rasp of standards scraping, the thump of pedigrees jostling for prevalence in societies where manners and mindsets change so rapidly, rattle and perplex. If opinions, ideas, practices, and creeds are free and equal in their diversity, so are identities free to roam among national, ethnic, linguistic, gender, or generational affiliations. Shelley's *Prometheus Unbound* ends in apocalypse that leaves us "free, uncircumscribed . . . Equal, unclassed, tribeless and nationless . . . Pinnacled dim in the intense inane." We're not quite there yet, but it's not far off.

Perhaps *le droit à la différence* is one of those comforts (rather like Sports Utility Vehicles) that is fine as long as things go well. But things can go less well, and that will send ominous signals in times when unanimity has been replaced by multanimity, and when assertion of human rights encourages ethnic and religious groups to demand the right to self-determination—to particularisms and intolerances and exclusions of their own. Also to privileges not available to other citizens, like Muslim prayer halls in the work place. "The cult of ethnicity," Arthur Schlesinger declares, "exaggerates differences, intensifies resentments and antagonisms, drives ever deeper the awful wedges between races and nationalities. The endgame is self-pity and ghettoization" (1998, 106). The right to be different has become part of human rights. Why not the right to be the same?

Democracy may be a scam: what we call the populace when we need it. But, at its best, it is a process—the continuous creation of endless exchanges, communications, gossip, parleys, debates, and negotiations. A democracy is, in the first place, a way of life where people dare tell each other things they think important, and where they rely on the right to speak like grownups, not like dissembling children. But democratic societies and democratic institutions can be hoist with their own liberality or inattention. Open to democratic-sounding arguments about rights and freedom, they find it hard to withstand claims that are actually designed to obstruct individual escape from the customs and constraints of ethnic or religious groups and individuals' integration as free agents in the secular democracy around them.

Muslim or Hassidic groups, for example, that negotiate particular redefinitions of public space and special facilities for special practices maintain the cohesion threatened by assimilation or integration; reaffirm communal distinctiveness in schooling and diet, behavior and dress; and avoid or at least delay absorption in the surrounding society. But, as they do so, they place the cohesion of that society at risk. Loyalties diverge, national and personal dignity no longer coincide, moral commitments grow murky.

Tired, poor, huddled masses, the wretched refuse of all teeming shores drawn to democratic welfare states like flies to honey, help to dismantle them. A heavy influx of strangers may cause disruption and friction at the best of times. More so when the mien, conduct, and religious beliefs of the newcomers differ obtrusively from those of the society that is expected to absorb them; and their numbers make absorption, let alone assimilation, difficult.

Until mid-twentieth century, industrial and agricultural labor, mostly unskilled, eased integration. In postindustrial economies, illegality, marginality, criminality, educational deficiencies, and precarious service jobs, turned large-scale proletarian immigration into an ongoing problem.

Like some of their neighbors, the French had considered immigration quotas in 1938 and again in 1945. The issue came up again in 1991, after President Mitterand declared that "the threshold of tolerance" had been reached. Quotas were meant to favor "useful and assimilable incomers originating from countries ethnically, religiously, culturally closest to France, not African or Asian."[8] But the tide of dark, proliferating others could not be stemmed, and small wars of race were compounded by religious conflict. One man's piety is another man's bigotry; claims for religious rights were denounced as intrusive privilege. In that realm as in others, multicultural policies and ethnic heterogeneity began to deconstruct what took a long time to put together. Modern democracy proclaimed the rights of the individual. Multiethnicism asserts the rights of cultural collectivities; and multiculturals tend to act like advocates of ethnocentric apartheid. When group rights trump individual rights, democratic societies lose their bearings and fragment.

But being different is not in itself a value; and the particularism of embitterment, of self-assertion, or of self-indulgence does not promise well for those societies where it has been whipped up.[9] Should then diversity be deferred to or disparaged? Is particularism permissible, dismissable, or simply in the eye of the beholder? Once upon a time most peoples were chosen peoples, triumphalist, exclusivist and peculiar unto themselves. Nowadays few in the western democracies would claim that solipsistic role. The limits of humanity and of the tribal group no longer coincide. Strangers are no longer rejected out of hand as scruffy, defiled, subhuman. Yet emblematic others continue to delineate identities and affirm them. Eloquent claims that the world is one and humankind kin the world over (even when the kin camps in your back yard) discountenance and do not quite convince. But they are a step in the right direction, as long as you don't miss your footing.

In the beginning there was multiplicity. In the beginning there was conflict. They lie in ambush until chapter III of Genesis, but scarcely relent thereafter. Within a few chapters, men discover differences of speech (chapter XI), migration and demographic problems (chapter XIII), warfare between neighboring communities (XVI), ethnic differences (XXVI), and the narcissism of minor differences justifying slaughter (XXXIV). This pretty much continues until you get to Deuteronomy (which is also rather bloody-minded), where Moses shines one ray of light into the gory darkness: "Love ye therefore the stranger; for ye were strangers in the land of Egypt."

And that, as we know, ended badly too. More seem to prefer Aristotle's advice to Alexander, to treat only the Greeks as human beings, and look upon all other peoples as animals or plants.[10]

We who read the papers and watch the TV news know that the love Moses prescribes does not go far. Foresight and keeping an eye out for trouble are more effective. And if you are looking for trouble, diversity offers promising possibilities.

We have overcome the primeval chaos of multiplicity, of multiple babbles and mutual incomprehensibility, by transferring a sense of pretence of community to large-scale entities, artificial but equipped with a semblance of law and order, where inevitable diversities have been relegated to the private sphere, where tolerance is activated by indifference, and many potential conflicts are sublimated in consumerism. Why should democracies—if given an opportunity to express their will—abandon their imperfect achievements, prosy though they may be, for new sources of friction and breakdown?

CHAPTER THREE

Democracy and Ethnic Diversity

The Case of Central and Eastern Europe

IVAN T. BEREND

Can ethnic homogeneity be perceived as a condition of democracy or is it a historical coincidence that modern democracies developed in relatively ethnically homogenous societies? Can we explain the success or failure of democracy in Europe on the basis of ethnic homogeneity or diversity? My point of departure in answering these questions is to comment on the complex origins of the various types of authoritarian regimes, based on the nineteenth-century historical experiences of Central and Eastern Europe. In other words, I will analyze the lack of democracy in the area *in statu nascendi*, at the stage of birth (see Berend 2002).

One certainly cannot state that lack of ethnic homogeneity is an insurmountable barrier on the road to democracy. The success or failure of building democracy is rooted in social, cultural, economic, and political development. Most important, economic and social backwardness, failed modernization, and consequently lagging behind the advanced core countries of the world system, Eastern Europe became a cradle of revolt against the core's domination and values, including democracy. In the environment of peripheral socioeconomic backwardness, and only in this environment, lack of ethnic homogeneity, indeed, became a basic impediment to democracy. The historic road toward democracy has been paved only in those countries of Europe that in the early modern period emerged as rich core countries of the nineteenth-century world system. As Barrington Moore stated in his often-quoted work on the *Social Origins of Dictatorship and Democracy*, a "contract as a mutual engagement freely undertaken by free persons, derived from the feudal relations of vassalage . . . constitutes a crucial legacy to modern Western . . . free society.." In these countries "a rough balance [emerged] between the crown and the nobility, in which the royal power . . . left a substantial degree of independence to the nobility . . . [as] a decisive precondition for modern democracy." However, the most important development, Moore maintains, is the commercial revolution in agriculture and "the ways in which the landed upper classes and the peasants reacted to the challenge of commercial agriculture . . . " A successful bourgeois transformation paves the way for political democracy. The lack of these historical factors: the weakness of towns and town dwellers, the reintroduction of serfdom and the "manorial reaction" to the advance of commerce did not allow the prerequisites of modern democracy to develop in Central and Eastern Europe. The socioeconomic and political development of these countries thus created the "social origins of dictatorship" (Moore 1967, xvii, 415, 417).

Along with these far-reaching medieval and early modern roots, in the nineteenth century failed industrialization and social modernization were sources of further serious negative political consequences. The persistence of the landed nobility, the emergence of an *Ersatzklasse* (substitute class), a pervasive bureaucratic-military elite, a substitute for an advanced middle class, and the weakness of modern urban burgher and well-to-do peasant elements in these predominantly rural, uneducated peasant societies created formidable hurdles on the road to parliamentary democracy. Instead, during the nineteenth century, authoritarian regimes emerged, and in the twentieth century, various types of "modernization dictatorships" followed—Mussolini's Italy and Stalin's Soviet Union being the best examples.

Peripheral backwardness, however, is far from just an economic, social, and cultural phenomenon. It is closely connected with the nation-building process. Central and Eastern Europe, which became a part of the world system in the sixteenth century on the periphery of a rising capitalist west European core, not only remained agricultural, largely preserving its traditional societal structure, but it also lacked a western absolute state, the cradle of the nation and the homogenizing force of centralized power. Instead, all of the countries of the region lost their independence between the fifteenth and eighteenth centuries, the Balkans first, the Czech and Hungarian kingdoms later, and Poland last. The entire area became part of three huge multiethnic states, the Ottoman, Habsburg, and Russian empires. The peripheral socioeconomic situation, combined with the lack of independent statehood or nation building, were the main factors leading to the rise of authoritarian political regimes.

The Nineteenth Century

The Central and Eastern European political and intellectual elite, at the turn of the eighteenth and nineteenth centuries, under the influence of a mixture of western Enlightenment and romantic nationalist notions, shared a zeitgeist of faith in progress and nation. They believed in the possibility of learning from the admired West, adopting western institutions, and changing their own destiny and history. The main goal of the peoples of the area was to create a nation and an independent nation-state, and to join "civilized Europe." Legislation and institution building, the introduction of modern constitutions, parties, and parliamentary systems were strongly influenced by western examples.

Cultural traditions, socioeconomic environment, and incomplete nation building, however, had special political consequences. Despite attempts to follow the West, a rather different outcome was reached. The nonindustrialized countries, struggling for independent nationhood, were unable to follow the western road. Nations, unable to realize their national dreams, became frustrated and militantly hostile toward the "enemies of the nation," whether oppressor great powers or rival oppressed nationalities living in the same area.

The most devastating blow to democratic development in the nineteenth century thus was launched by this developmental problem—the lack of a nation-state—as well as the seemingly insurmountable obstacles to creating one in an age of exalted nationalism. An existential fear for the national community penetrated the societies of Central and Eastern Europe. The elites and, under their influence, gradually the peasant masses as well, felt increasingly oppressed by dominant foreign powers. The middle-class Czechs suffered national humiliation because they could not use their mother tongue in offices. Poles could not tolerate the fact that the official language in public schools was Russian. Slovaks and Romanians felt like second-class citizens in Hungary. Moreover, in the age of nationalism all the socioeconomic pains were interpreted as consequences of foreign oppression. In this political framework, oppressed nationalities began to fight for independence against the oppressor Ottoman, Russian, and Habsburg empires.

Unlike in the West, where nations emerged within the boundaries of existing states, state and nation were not the same units in this area. In addition, emerging but oppressed and subordinated nationalities, jumbled together in the "belt of mixed population," became rivals in competition for the same goal: national independence. As a consequence, they confronted each other and often collided head on. Central and Eastern Europe became a hotbed of hostile, fundamentalist nationalism, which penetrated politics and became the leitmotiv of authoritarianism.

The struggle for autonomy and independence against Germanizing Austria, and Russifying Russia in the Czech lands and Poland, the attempt to assimilate non-Magyar nationalities and create an "indivisible Magyar nation" in multiethnic Hungary, the concept of creating a Great Serbia, Great Croatia, Great Romania, and Great Bulgaria by incorporating neighboring fellow-nationals and the territories in which they lived, led to permanent confrontation and warfare among neighboring nations with mixed populations.

This environment nurtured the desire for stronger power. It revitalized and legitimized the unquestioned leading role of an autocratic monarch, the noble elite, the state bureaucracy, and the army as "saviors of the nation." Longing for a strong nation-state that might be able to cure burning national, social, and economic ills generated heated nationalism throughout the nineteenth century. Romantic idealization of people and prophet-intellectuals, and longing for charismatic, almighty leaders capable of leading the people to the Promised Land created an atmosphere conducive to strong, authoritarian national policies. The romantic notion of a self-sacrificing struggle for the nation was translated into hostility toward "enemies of the nation": oppressors, aliens, minorities, and rival neighbors (Bibó 1986, vol. 1, 330–43). "What emerged in eastern Europe between the end of the eighteenth century and roughly the middle of the next," summarized Peter Sugar, "was the autocratic, centralized state run by a more-or-less despotic ruler with the help of a steadily growing bureaucracy... The next fifty years, roughly the second half of the nineteenth century, saw the gradual weakening of the power of the autocrat, but not the diminishing of authoritarian rule in Eastern Europe" (Sugar 1999, chapter VI, 9, 10). Western emerging democratic great powers had a strong influence on the entire continent, and in Central and Eastern Europe they often played a direct role in influencing political arrangements. Newly autonomous countries of the region introduced western constitutions and legal codes. To quote Sugar again: "That the inhabitants were considered citizens, that parties were permitted, that parliaments functioned, that rulers became 'constitutional monarchs' are also clear indications of the influence of the western model. Yet, all these changes" were only a pseudo-transformation, "at best skin deep; under this thin layer of western veneer the reality remained unchanged" (1999, chapter VI, 11, 12).

The difference between adopted western law and eastern reality was also marked. In the eastern half of Europe, as László Péter attested, "an autocratic principle of the law" remained during the nineteenth century. "This difference in the presumption of the law between the two parts of Europe had momentous consequences. While in Western Europe where the law was silent, the citizen was said to be free, in the legal systems beyond the Rhine, the opposite prevailed: where the law was silent (the individual and the social group were not expressly protected by laws), it was the state authorities who were, so to say 'free' . . . The state authorities in Central and Eastern Europe could lawfully issue decrees and act at their own discretion in matters which interfered with the individual and the group" (1997–98, 12–13, 18–20). The government extended its authority to the sphere of civil rights, maintaining close supervision over associations, banning those considered to be dangerous for the security of the state. Individual rights, in these systems, were concessions from the government.

The history of Central and Eastern Europe clearly illustrates the deformation of democracy at birth. In Romania, the road toward independence was opened in 1866, with the election of a constituent assembly. The constitution of 1884 was modeled on the Belgian Constitution of 1831 and reflected modern western democratic values. The architects of transformation believed in a spectacular change: Romania will be, proclaimed the Bucharest newspaper *Steaua Dunării*, a true "Belgium of the East" (Hitchins 1994, 19). Civil liberties, freedom of association and the press were legally protected. Form and substance, however, were fundamentally different. The regime remained highly authoritarian. First of all, though universal male suffrage was granted, only a fragment of the citizenry gained political rights. The electors were divided into three uneven categories. People with large landed property, 1.5 percent of the eligible voters, elected 41 percent of the representatives. A second group of higher taxpayers, professionals, and primary school graduates, another 3.5 percent of the voters, elected 38 percent of the representatives. On the other hand, 95 percent of the voters, the entire poor and uneducated masses, had only indirect votes: fifty people elected a single representative. The king, not the parliament, formed the government. Elections were controlled by the government through the minister of interior's appointments of the prefects of the *judeţe* (counties); they guaranteed government victory. Small wonder, the government always had an absolute majority in parliament: in the 1883 elections, for example, the governing Liberal Party gained more than 91 percent of the votes. Both chambers were obedient, rubber-stamping bodies. In real terms, the government responsibility to the parliament was a mere formality. The judiciary, in practice, was subordinated to the executive and legislative branches of power. State and church were not separated. The two leading political parties sought unrestricted political power, and were authoritarian once in government, enriching their clientele. The German prince Carol, who was invited to the Romanian throne, tried to convince the great powers in November 1870 that the western institutional system was inappropriate in unindustrialized Romania without a strong middle class. He proposed a revision to the Paris Treaty (1856) in favor of a "powerful regime" with the autocratic power of a prince. Although he failed to revise the treaty, in practice, he used the "spoils system" of political corruption and became an autocratic ruler (Scurtu 1988).

The legitimacy of the authoritarian regime in Romania was guaranteed by a continual struggle to create an independent "Romania for the Romanians." This was directed against not only foreign tutelage, but also "aliens" within the country—mostly Jews, who, partly because of an intensive eastern immigration during the nineteenth century, made up 5 percent of the country's population. Anti-Semitism became an integral part of the national creed (Fischer-Galati 1969, 385–86). Romania remained virtually the only country of Europe that refused to give citizenship to Jews up until the First World War. An unparalleled early-twentieth-century *jacquerie*, a spontaneous peasant uprising, also turned out to be the deadliest anti-Jewish pogrom, in 1907. Thousands of shops and houses were destroyed, Jews were beaten and killed, and thousands escaped only by leaving everything behind (Ilincioiu 1991). *Moldava de Sus*, a populist newspaper, which declared in its editorial that the "Yids" are the enemies of the Romanian people, urged a mass uprising. "Perhaps out of impoverished ancient Moldavia, today overwhelmed and stifled by Yids, once more a man . . . will rise up and start a new *hetairia* against the Yids . . . All true Romanians will give it assistance and will struggle until they have achieved such a crucial victory, so as to save our ancestral land and our race from the plague and the infernal plans of the Yids" (*Moldova de Sus*, March 1, 1907, in Eidelberg 1974). Political anti-Semitism, by channeling social dissatisfaction into the reservoir of xenophobia, gained a tremendous impetus.

An equally strong influence on Romanian nationalism, similar to the general trend in the Balkans, was the goal of creating a Greater Romania, uniting all Romanians. In the "belt of mixed population" various ethnic groups were hopelessly intermingled, and many Romanians lived together with Ukrainians, Hungarians, and Bulgarians in Bessarabia, Bukovina, Transylvania, and Dobrudja. Both the loss of southern Bessarabia to Russia in 1878 and the acquisition of southern Dobrudja from Bulgaria in 1913 fueled Great Romanianism and the unification of all Romanians living in neighboring Transylvania, Bukovina, Banat, Crişana, Maramureş, and Bessarabia. The main enemy in this drive to unity (as in the case of Serbia) was Austria-Hungary.

Bulgaria, also under the tutelage of the great powers according to the Berlin Treaty, enacted a western-style, liberal constitution in Tirnovo in 1879. Universal male suffrage, parliamentary power in a one-chamber system, and civil liberties were guaranteed. The next day, a German prince, Alexander von Battenberg, was elected Prince of Bulgaria. The young soldier-prince was dissatisfied with the democratic constitution. The scenario was strikingly similar to the Romanian one. Prince Alexander complained: "The present constitution is not suited to the country. It places the person of the Ruler in continual opposition to the National Assembly . . . the people lack the most elementary requisites for constitutional life . . . I wish . . . the necessary authoritative powers . . . [to defend] the interest of the State" (Koch 1887, 70–72). He did not hesitate: on May 9, 1881, a coup was carried out. Alexander dismissed the government and demanded extraordinary power for seven years. The parliament, "elected" under overt and strict military control, unanimously accepted Alexander's demands in July: the prince became a dictator. The "national mission" of the governments legitimized authoritarian rule. In post-Treaty-of-Berlin (1878) Bulgaria, the main nationalist goal was the liberation of "all Bulgarian territories," i.e. Eastern Rumelia, Thrace, and Macedonia, and the reestablishment of Great Bulgaria. Macedonia, however, was claimed by Greece and Serbia as well. This nationalist program became the basis of the alliance between the king and the army, and autocratic rule. An Internal Macedonian Revolutionary Organization (IMRO) was founded. Armed bands launched ongoing attacks, and prepared a general uprising in 1903.

In 1912, the Balkan League of Bulgaria, Serbia, and Greece against Turkey practically liberated the entire peninsula, a situation sanctioned by the Treaty of London in May 1913. While the Bulgarian forces occupied eastern Thrace, Greek and Serbian troops liberated Macedonia. In June, Bulgaria decided to reverse the outcome of the allied victory over Turkey and attacked Serbian and Greek troops to recapture Macedonia. This led to the Second Balkan War, when Romania and Turkey attacked Bulgaria from the north and east, and the Greeks and Serbs attacked from the south and west. After the humiliating defeat, the Treaty of Bucharest (August 1913) gave the largest portion of Macedonia to Serbia and Greece, while Romania took southern Dobrudja, and Turkey regained most of Thrace and Edirne. The dream of Great Bulgaria, which had permeated the history of independent Bulgaria for more than a generation before the First World War and generated permanent warfare, faded away.

Serbian politics was defined by wars, coups, and assassinations. Fighting for autonomy, independence, and then for a Great Serbia, which would unite all the Serbs who lived in neighboring countries, deformed national politics: "From 1882 on," concluded Ivo Lederer, "Serbian political parties . . . gradually ceased to distinguish between issues of . . . democratization and modernization on the one hand and the national 'mission' of all-Serbian

unity . . . on the other (1969, 407). The 1869 constitution, which was enacted after Prince Michael Obrenović had been assassinated, established autocratic rule in Serbia. Unlike most of the other countries of the region, it
granted a liberal franchise, but strongly limited the role of the *Skupshtina*
(parliament), which did not have the right to initiate laws or modify government bills. The government was not responsible to the parliament. The
prince, who had the right to appoint and dismiss governments, had the upper hand. This was illustrated when the Radical Party won the 1883 elections. King Milan refused to appoint a Radical government and formed the
conservative Hristić government instead. The rivalry between the political
elite and the king was often decided by brute force and murderous actions.
The question was not one of democratic or autocratic rule, but rather who
would exercise authoritarian power. During the July 1901 elections, agitated
demonstrators filled the streets of Belgrade. The police callously arrested
and killed demonstrators. New elections were held in at atmosphere of un-
fettered police terror in May 1903. The Radical Party withdrew from the
ballot. In June, twenty-eight officers invaded the royal palace, killed the
royal couple, and threw their bodies from the palace windows. The conspir-
ators also killed the prime minister, the minister of interior, loyal officers,
and two brothers of the queen. Real parliamentary democracy remained absent in the Balkans, along with a serious deficit in civil liberties.

Serbia was more successful in realizing the Great Serbian dream. Under
the banner of *Srpstvo*, the entire Serbian political elite believed in the national mission of establishing all-Serbian unity. After having gained independence, the central goal of Serbian politics was the territorial acquisition
of Macedonia and Bosnia-Herzegovina. This led to permanent warfare—a
military campaign in Bosnia in 1876, a war against Bulgaria in 1885, and
participation in two Balkan wars in 1912–13.

Oppressive Russian rule generated a series of bloody revolts in parti-
tioned and occupied Poland: armed revolts were launched against Russia by
three consecutive generations between 1794 and the 1860s. The national
cause in the somewhat modernized country was renewed in the latter part of
the nineteenth century. An integral nationalism included an awakened peas-
antry into the national camp. In 1893, the National League, and then in
1897, the National Democratic Movement (*Endecja*) of Roman Dmowski
launched successful propaganda campaigns to strengthen national spirit and

advocate an independent Polish state. Dmowski maintained that without struggle, the nation "degenerates morally and disintegrates." Poland, maintained Dmowski, first must defeat its internal enemies and guard against racial contamination. He opened the front against Jews, calling for strengthening the national spirit by boycotting Jewish business, and "spiritually isolating Polish life from Jewish influence." The mass emigration of Jews as a "final solution" became a tenet of the exclusive nationalist Endecja program. Polish nationalism from this time on, like Romanian nationalism, became inherently anti-Semitic. The most extreme expression of Polish anti-Semitism was the crusade launched by the magazine *Rola* after 1881. Its editor, Jan Jeleński published protofascist brochures, *Our World of Finance* (1874), and then *The Jews, the Germans, and Us* (1876). Jeleński and *Rola* made fashionable the concept of struggle for national survival and advocated a ruthless tribal struggle against the Jews. One of Jeleński's close collaborators, Konstanty Wzdulski, demanded the immediate expulsion of Jews. At the end of 1881, a bloody anti-Jewish pogrom engulfed Warsaw. Dmowski spoke about a well-organized Jewish conspiracy, which, "according to a plan" and based on a "very well-developed internal organization," was designed to conquer Poland and create a "settlement for the Jewish nation" (Porter 2000, 164–66, 176–79, 229). Besides the Jews, other ethnicities were also hated. The oppressor Russians were considered to be an Asiatic horde. "Who can deny," stated Zygmunt Miłkowski in his *Wolne Polskie Słowo* "that Moscow is the heir . . . of the Golden Horde?" Lithuanians and Ukrainians were considered to be part of the Polish nation. Poland had a "civilization mission" in Lithuania and Ukraine, territories that have "been our property for five centuries . . . Nearly everything that has any lasting value [there] at all . . . is the result of Polish thought and Polish will." Dmowski argued that Ruthenians (Ukrainians) do not exist; they are only a "pitiful type of Pole." "Ukraine never did exist, does not exist, and will not exist." Ukrainian nationalism in Galicia was declared to be a "purely artificial creation." Instead, the Polish nationalists offered Polonization, or assimilation as an alternative (Porter 2000, 184, 223–25).

Compared to the Ottoman and Russian empires, the Habsburg Empire embodied the most enlightened absolute power in Central and Eastern Europe. The first two-thirds of the nineteenth century, however, was characterized by unquestionable autocratic rule, with strong censorship, an army of police spies who closely controlled the subjects, and a politically influential Catholic Church. The liberal constitution of 1848, a result of the revolution, was revoked, and the "entire administrative system had thus become purely authoritarian" (Macartney 1968, 440). However, the Habsburg monarchy introduced western legal institutions at the end of the 1860s: censorship was abandoned, freedoms of speech, press, property, belief, and association were granted. Citizens became equal before the law, and the judiciary was separated from executive power. The empire, nevertheless, preserved its autocratic character. The monarch's supremacy was based on the bureaucracy and the army, the "cement" of the monarchy. The huge, self-serving bureaucracy of three million people (in 1914), preoccupied with its own advancement and preservation of privileges, grades, and ranks, became a major player of authoritative power (Hayes 1992, 69). "The *Reichsrat* had become in fact little more than . . . an advisory body to the Crown." Although the parliament, which was elected by 5.9 percent of the population, had some control, "where . . . fundamentals were at issue, the Monarch's will was enforced, if necessary, over Parliament's head" (Macartney 1968, 561–67).

The 1867 *Ausgleich* (Compromise), however, reestablished a great portion of Hungarian independence. An independent Hungarian government was formed, responsible to the Hungarian parliament. The monarchy was transformed into a dualist state, renamed Austria-Hungary. The Austrian emperor was crowned King of Hungary and the most important portfolios of the government of the Dual Monarchy—defense, foreign affairs, and finance—became "common affairs." The joint army used German as the language of command. A so-called economic compromise kept a customs union, and divided common expenditures, and payments of state debts, according to a quota system.

The Hungarian elite regained domination over all ethnic minorities in the country, which were half of the population. Transylvania, Voivodina, and the so-called Military Frontier, mostly populated by ethnic minorities, became integral parts of Hungary.

Autonomous Hungary introduced a modern European parliamentary system. The franchise was limited to about 6 percent of the population, which was not unusual at that time in Europe. This percentage, however, did not change with time. Besides, the open ballot made elections controllable by the administration. The legislative, executive, and judicial branches were each given separate powers. Liberal European institutions and legislation were introduced. Basic human rights, equality before the court, and equal rights for all citizens, including minorities, were guaranteed. A liberal law regulated the rights of the nationalities (Law XLIV/1868). Nationalities were allowed to use their native language at various local levels and schools; they were equally eligible to hold any position. Jews were emancipated. Personal freedom for minorities, thus, was guaranteed.

Collective national rights and representations, however, were rejected. As Ferenc Deák, the father of the compromise stated: "In Hungary there is only one, indivisible political nation, the Hungarian." Consequently, the official language of legislation and government as well as of higher courts was Hungarian. Compulsory and free basic education was introduced (Law XXXVIII/1868) and accompanied by intensive school construction and teacher training.

Political practice and the autocratic principle of law, however, differed from institutionalized freedoms. The authoritarian reality of power, the most important characteristic of the politics of backwardness, was independent from constitutional and legal formalities. Hungarian governments issued decrees to regulate society. The judges, according to Law XIX/1869, besides statute law and lawful custom, were required to proceed by applying government decrees as well. The authority of the government was strengthened because statutory law secured only fragments of personal and civil rights. In 1878, a confidential circular of the prime minister ordered local authorities to permit assemblies "only if six to ten 'distinguished citizens' stood surety for the meeting" (Péter 1997–98, 17, 22, 25–27). The governing force, the *Szabadelvü Párt* (Liberal Party) founded in 1875, was virtually unchallengeable. It maintained a comfortable absolute majority for thirty years. In 1881, 225, in 1887, 261, in 1910, 258 representatives of 413 belonged to the government party. The only "accident" during the nearly fifty years in power, when the government party failed to secure a parliamentary majority, occurred in 1905. When the united opposition won the elections, the emperor rejected the result and appointed the captain of his *Darabont* bodyguard unit as prime minister of Hungary. Elections like those held in 1910 became the scene of brutal violence: 194 infantry battalions and 114 cavalry squadrons terrorized voters in 380 constituencies. Military force, of course, was only the *ultima ratio* to save the situation. In most cases corrupt county administrations, subordinated to the government, closely controlled and successfully manipulated the open ballot elections. "Electoral corruption—the purchase of votes, the use of forgery, and intimidation— . . . became routine," stated Andrew C. Janos on the liberal Hungarian era of the 1870s–1880s. If needed, they provoked unrest and arrested voters of the opposition. "The administrative bureaucracy were welded into a single, powerful machine . . . "making" the elections and perpetuating the . . . majority . . . The political machine emerged as the single most important actor on the Hungarian political stage. The autocratic tendencies . . . were further mitigated . . . by a number of habits, conventions, and quasi-institutions that operated as correctives in the absence of free competition and represented built-in restraints on the arbitrary exercise of power . . . they were most effective in protecting the personal and political rights of the members of the establishment . . . they were also instrumental in blunting the harshness of the bureaucratic regime towards the lower classes and the national minorities" (1982, 97–101) Democratic institutions, such as freedom of the press and parliamentary opportunities for the opposition also served to restrain the arbitrary exercise of power. Corrupt practices were made public, and use of the filibuster placed some limits on the majority's law-making machinery.

The foundation of the far-right *Országos Antiszemita Párt* (National Anti-Semite Party) in 1883 signaled emerging political anti-Semitism, but remained unimportant. The party was unable to gain more than seventeen seats in 1884, and disappeared in the early 1890s. The party, however, launched a vitriolic campaign against Jewish immigration and introduced the theory of "Jewish conspiracy against the Christian nation" and other elements of German-Austrian political anti-Semitism in Hungary. It also played a central role in creating a vicious anti-Semitic campaign by reinventing the medieval blood-libel, the accusation of ritual murder of a Christian girl in Tiszaeszlár in 1882.

Although political anti-Semitism could not gain a foothold, antiminority, assimilationist nationalism dominated Hungarian politics. Under the banner of the "indivisible unitary Magyar nation," a forced assimilation policy characterized the half-century existence of autonomous Hungary in the Dual Monarchy. Against the letter and spirit of the nationality law, minority representatives were effectively excluded from high official positions. Although in 18 of 62 counties (excepting Croatia) between 66 and 96 percent of the population belonged to the Romanian and Slovak majority, the *Főispán* (high sheriff) and his deputy in these counties were always Hungarians. In 1891, 60 percent of the population in Transylvania was Romanian and 6 percent of the officials were ethnic Romanians. A total of 3 to 4 percent of the appointed persons to positions in district courts, government ministries, university chairs, and education supervision were Romanians. Although the use of native languages was allowed in district courts by the Nationality Law of 1868, the reorganization of the judicial system in 1869 practically eliminated this right and Magyarized the entire justice system. Almost the same thing happened to primary and secondary education, where the use of mother tongues was guaranteed in the Nationality Law, but in practice, the school system became the main tool of assimilation. At the secondary level all state schools became entirely Magyar; German, Slovak, Romanian, and Ukrainian languages were not used at all. In 1903 only 14 secondary schools were non-Magyar out of the existing 190. As Béla Grünwald stated at the time: "The secondary school is like a huge machine, at one end of which the Slovak youth are thrown in by hundreds, and at the other end of which they come out as Magyars" (Seton-Watson 1963, 400). Primary schools were partly run by minority churches. Even in these schools, however, 18 to 24 hours (of 26-hour units) were reserved for Magyar education, according to the 1902 ministerial decree.

Successive Hungarian governments suppressed any kind of national movement that threatened the indivisible Magyar national state and the dualistic structure of the monarchy. The most ardent advocates of Romanian, Slovak, Croat, and Serb national self-determination were persecuted, and, if required, ethnic unrest was suppressed. Between 1886 and 1908, 362 Romanians were sentenced to imprisonment and fined about 100,000 crowns for political offenses (Seton-Watson 1963, 405). Three Slovak representatives in the Hungarian parliament, among them Milan Hodža, future prime minister of Czechoslovakia, were arrested and imprisoned in 1906. A show trial was arranged against Vavro Šrobár and Andrej Hlinka in the same year. Another show trial was held in Hajdúdorog in March 1914, when Father Mureşan and fourteen Romanians were sentenced for resisting the transfer of seventy-five parishes from the Romanian Uniate Church to Magyar control and the introduction of the Magyar language into the liturgy.

The number of representatives of minorities—half of the population—declined from 26 to 8 in the Hungarian Parliament in the early twentieth century. Less than 2 percent of the representatives represented half of the population, namely the ethnic minorities.

Forced assimilation, however, became counterproductive. The homogenous and closed Romanian and Slovak peasant communities preserved their language and identity. Between 1880 and 1910, the number of Hungarian-speaking minorities doubled, but only 22 percent of the minorities spoke Hungarian (Hanák 1988, 414–18).

Authoritarian power and overwhelming nationalism was thus everywhere dominant in Central and Eastern European politics. Nationalism was the triumphant political mainstream, which legitimized authoritarian regimes. These trends characterized politics in the region of incomplete nation building. Nationalism motivated oppression, assimilation, political and armed conflicts among nationalities, and among newly created nation-states.

The Twentieth Century

The twentieth century history of the area is a well-known story of despotism, which was closely related to ethnic conflicts. The Versailles Treaty system, though its leading slogan was the right for self-determination, did not solve the ethnic-national conflicts of the area, but created new ones. True, just and identifiable ethnic borders do not exist in Central and Eastern Europe, the "belt of mixed population." But the peacemakers, most of all France, did not even try to create just borders but followed their own political interests. In place of Austria-Hungary, three independent states were created, and huge chunks of the monarchy were given to transforming neighboring countries. Rump Austria became ethnically rather homogenous. Independent Hungary, which lost two-thirds of its former, mostly minorities-inhabited territory, also became ethnically homogenous, but three million Hungarians remained outside the new borders in minority status. A great part of them, in southern Slovakia, northern Transylvania, and in the Voivodina region of Yugoslavia, lived next to the Hungarian border. Newly independent Albania was also ethnically homogenous, but nearly half of the Albanians remained outside the country, next to the Albanian border in newly created Yugoslavia. The demand for border revision and to regain the old territories and/or to unite all Hungarians and Albanians became the leitmotiv of interwar Hungarian and late twentieth-century Albanian politics.

The victors of the First World War sought to create relatively strong allies in the central and eastern European area behind Germany and were ready to realize the dream of Great Romania: the country with nearly 138,000 square kilometers territory and 7.5 million inhabitants gained huge new territories, Transylvania and the so-called Partium, a part of Bukovina, Bessarabia, and Dobrudja. Great Romania became a country of more than 304,000 square kilometers with nearly 18 million inhabitants. Nearly one-third of the population belonged to ethnic minorities.

The same idea inspired the peacemakers to accept another national dream, the unification of the Czechs and Slovaks, by creating a relatively small multinational states with huge German and Hungarian minorities, who lived next to the border of their "home" countries. The founding fathers of the new Czechoslovak state believed in the existence of a Czechoslovak nation and rejected Slovak autonomy demands. The new country became a hotbed of ethnic and national conflict. The same was true for newly created Yugoslavia, which, besides Serbs, Croats, Slovenes, Macedonians, Bosnians, and Montenegrins, also had huge Hungarian and Muslim Albanian minorities. The Serbian-led Yugoslav state, similarly to Czechoslovakia, sought creating a Yugoslav nation and rejected autonomy for the Croats. New, explosive ethnic conflicts emerged, which almost destroyed the Yugoslav state within a decade after its foundation and generated two deadly civil wars and ethnic cleansings during the years of the Second World War, and then again during the 1990s.

Mutilated countries, which lost large territories and population, focused on revenge and irredentism. Minority ethnic groups in small multinational states, such as the Croats in Yugoslavia and Slovaks in Czechoslovakia, also wanted to change the status quo, first demanding autonomy, but, from the 1930s, independence. These countries and minority nations became natural allies of revisionist fascist-nazi regimes. They turned to Hitler and Mussolini and, in alliance with them, attacked their neighbors. To gain nazi assistance, they tried to adjust their regimes to Nazi Germany.

There were only two types of countries in the region: either multiethnic, such as Poland, Romania, Yugoslavia, and Czechoslovakia; or truncated with huge ethnic communities outside the national borders, such as in Hungary, Albania, and Bulgaria, and, after the dissolution of Yugoslavia, Serbia. National struggle, border revision, forced assimilation of minorities, and attempts to unite the entire nation played an ongoing and important role in the creation of the authoritarian regimes of József Piłsudski in Poland and Miklós Horthy in Hungary, the alliance with Hitler and Mussolini, the emergence of so-called royal dictatorships in the Balkans, and the fascist, "independent" Croat and Slovak states, established by Hitler. During and after the Second World War history's most dramatic ethnic cleansing engulfed the region: the Jewish holocaust killed 4 million Jews in the area (another 1 to 2 million were killed elsewhere), and more than 5 million ethnic Germans were expelled.

After the war, the nearly half-century dominance of state socialism forcibly suppressed the national question within these countries, but Soviet domination and occupation revived it. Meanwhile, in some of the countries, ruthless attempts were made to homogenize the nation-states. Assimilationist policy in Romania and Bulgaria and a dramatic new, delayed nation-building attempt in the small multinational countries generated ethnic conflicts in the entire region. After the collapse of state socialism, all of the multinational states broke down: Czechoslovakia peacefully, Yugoslavia in bloody wars and ethnic cleansing. Ethnic conflicts penetrated the entire twentieth century in Central and Eastern Europe and became a major obstacle to undisturbed democratic transformation.

CHAPTER FOUR

Democracy, Ethnicity, and the Nation

Nineteenth-Century France and the Netherlands

IDO DE HAAN

"Our performance is not altogether innocent." With this warning Abraham Kuyper, the leader of the Dutch protestant movement, started his famous lecture at the opening of the protestant Free University in Amsterdam on October 20, 1880. The dangerous message he presented was that the Dutch nation did not need to be unified. He argued that his fellow antirevolutionary protestants were entitled to an independent place within the Dutch nation, to be sovereign within their own sphere of life. Kuyper stipulated that his group should not be regarded as a faction, "i.e. an artificial group"; and neither as a fraction, "i.e. a separate piece," but as a *volkspartij*, a popular party, or *volksdeel*, a part of the nation. Moreover, Kuyper argued, this *pars Christiana* was "despite itself a national party" which, through its temporary partiality, was able to inspire the nation with a higher ideal (1880, 6).

In a few lines, Kuyper had described the model—this model of what came to be called *verzuiling*, or pillarization—in which the Dutch political landscape would be molded for most of the twentieth century. When Kuyper formulated his vision of nonartificial groups with a separate standing within a larger national unity, pillarization was not yet a reality, as he was fully aware. All century long, he said, the nation had been wrestling through a crisis. Some people mistakenly assumed that this was a struggle between rich and poor, or between clericalism and liberalism. These issues were not at stake, according to Kuyper. The essential tension was between those who argued in favor of the sovereign state and those, like himself, who pleaded for the sovereignty of the separate parts within the nation. Modestly Kuyper concluded there was in his endeavor a certain protest against the political culture of his times.

Kuyper's dangerous idea gradually turned into conventional political wisdom, according to which the Netherlands formed a pillarized nation. Every pillar within the nation long remembered its own struggle for recognition within this pillarized framework. An emancipatory historiography was an essential part of each pillar's collective identity. Yet at the same time all parties completely forgot about how difficult it had been to get used to the idea that the nation should be divided in parts and parties. During most of the nineteenth century, political debates were not about which rights every part of the nation should be granted, but about how the nation should be divided in parts—or even more fundamental, whether it was possible and desirable to distinguish parties within the nation. Only in the final quarter of the nineteenth century, did people begin to argue in favor of partitioning the nation in different popular parts. And only after universal suffrage was introduced, in 1917, did a truly pluralistic model of the nation develop (see De Haan 2003).

Now there is a well-known argument that democracy requires a strong measure of cultural homogeneity. When ethnic identities, religious confessions, or other cultural orientation vary widely, civilized politics quickly turns into civil war. As one of the founding fathers of contemporary political science, Sidney Verba, once argued, the importance of a national identity "cannot be overstressed": "It is the sense of identity with the nation that legitimizes the activities of national elites and makes it possible for them to mobilize the commitment and support of their followers." Democracy requires nation building, for "the absence of a well-defined sense of identity creates a host of tensions and frustrations" (1965, 512–60, 529–30).

The most radical version of this idea can be found in the work of Carl Schmitt. In his preface to the second edition of *Der geistesgeschichtliche Lage des heutigen Parliamentarismus* (1926), Schmitt argues for a distinction between parliamentarism and democracy. The former is based on the idea "that laws arise out of conflict of opinions" between independent and reasonable individuals. Democracy, on the other hand, requires "first homogeneity and second—if the need arises—eradication of heterogeneity." The reason is that democracy, according to Schmitt, should be defined as "the identity of governed and governing," which manifests itself by a substantial and unitary general will. From a democratic point of view, all obstacles to the unity of the general will—such as widely divergent cultural orientations—have to be obliterated. And since it is only the will of the people that counts, there is no protection for minorities or individuals beyond the reach of the democratic will (1985, 1–17 and *passim*).

As unpleasant as Schmitt's arguments may be, they nevertheless seem to be corroborated both by the liberal tendency to limit democracy by constitutional safeguards, and by the tendency of newly developing democracies to eradicate cultural difference. Tocqueville among others voiced the characteristic liberal worry that "it is in the nature of democratic governments that the rule of the majority will be absolute, because outside the majority nothing will resist" (1981, 1: 343). For the actual eradication of cultural difference as the corollary of democratization, a case in point seems to be the French Third Republic, which under the guidance of Jules Ferry pursued a secularization of social life as an essential precondition for the development of a democratic republic. We have to defend, Ferry argued in *La Revue Pedagogique* of 1882, "the spirit of new generations, of those young and innumerable resources of the republican democracy, shaped in the school of science and reason" (quoted in Mayeur 1973, 113). The *loi Ferry* establishing the *école laïque* (state school system) was the high point of what Pierre Rosanvallon has called the *démopédique* of the Third Republic: the idea that the state should educate its citizens in order to become rational and reliable participants in the political process (1992, 356). It inaugurated a period of fierce anticlericalism and of a cultural politics aimed at the construction of a secularized political culture.

When we compare the French Third Republic to the Dutch political culture in the last quarter of the nineteenth century, it seems we have two very different models of the relation between democracy and cultural homogeneity. While the French case seems to confirm the conventional political wisdom that democracy requires an eradication of cultural difference, the

Dutch case appears to offer a radical alternative. In the Netherlands, de-mocratization seemed to be accompanied by the emergence of a new and vigorous pluralism. So, how should we conceptualize the relation between democracy and cultural homogeneity?

One way to solve this puzzle is by rejecting all generalizations in histori-cal judgments. France is France, and the Netherlands are something com-pletely different. However, though "it depends" may be a prudent historio-graphical starting point, as an end to academic debate it is too shallow. Not only would it be interesting to know which differences actually accounted for the success of the French or Dutch model; we should also be aware of the possibility that the countries still share some crucial characteristics. The dif-ferences between the French and Dutch political culture may be more a matter of degree, timing and pace than of fundamentally divergent histori-cal trajectories.

Democratization

To compare the Dutch and French ways to link democracy and cultural dif-ference, we should start by asking along which lines democracy developed in France and the Netherlands. According to the classical statement of modern democratic theory of Robert Dahl in *Democracy and Its Critics* (1989), mod-ern democracy involves at least free and fair elections for representative bodies, an accountable government, civil and political rights, independent associations, and free media for enlightened understanding. In Dahl's study, as in many other works on democracy, the questions of who is member of the demos and what is the composition of the nation are only cursorily addressed (Dahl 1989; Goldblatt 1997, 46–70; exceptions are Mann 1993; Balibar 1992).

With respect to the introduction of political rights, France had an early start, but a slow finish. After the limited suffrage of the 1793 constitution, the empire, the Bourbon regime, and the July monarchy, universal suffrage was introduced in 1848, and, after a short interlude in which the vote was re-stricted, reconfirmed after the coup d'état of December 2,1851. Since then, all men over the age of twenty-one have had the right to vote, and over the age of twenty-five the right to run for office—for women the right to vote was introduced only in 1946.

The constitutional revision of 1848 in the Netherlands also introduced a change in the electoral laws; in this case only a change from a two-tiered system of voting to direct voting, though the electorate became even more restricted, due to a change in the census from 90,000 to 80,000 men, which was 10.5 percent of the men over the age of twenty-three, and only 2.66 percent of the population at large (Blok 1987, 250–51). The extension of the suffrage in the Netherlands was for a long time opposed by conservatives and liberals alike. The lower strata of society were assumed to be unfit for political participation. The arguments are well known: workers had too little time and too little education; they were only interested in material gain; and they would value only the sectarian interests of their own class. Political rights could be extended only to independent citizens with enough leisure to spend some time on politics and enough wealth to have an eye for the public interest. In the revision of the constitution of 1887, the vote was granted to all men who showed "signs of capability and wealth." The criteria to determine who was part of this category became elastic, and the electorate started to expand. After a prolonged struggle over the census and a gradual extension of the electorate, universal male suffrage was introduced in 1917, and granted to women only two years later. Arguments about the capacity to vote had not disappeared, yet the traditional argument that a certain level of taxes paid was a good measure for political capability had lost most of its validity. Socialists and confessional parties had made it abundantly clear that the liberal bourgeoisie was no longer the core of the nation, but just another part of the nation (De Haan 2003, chapter 3).

The right to vote is only a first criterion of democracy. Much depends on how the vote is practiced. As Alain Garrigou has demonstrated, the early introduction of male suffrage in France led to a protracted period of experimentation with, and fears about the consequences of the ballot. Power formally belonged to the people, yet in actuality it was limited by severe restraints on electoral procedures, and by manipulation and corruption. Initially the greatest anxiety was not the self-interest of the workers, but the gullibility of the peasants. The fact that the regime of Napoléon III was based on an electoral legitimation reinforced the fear that universal suffrage without general education would lead to the tyranny of a manipulated electorate (1992, 111–24). Especially after the debacle of 1870, universal suffrage was castigated as "the rudest political machine that has ever operated," to quote Ernest Renan (in Rosanvallon 1992, 308). However, various proposals in the early 1870s to reduce the electorate along the lines of the law of May 31,1850 were rejected out of fear that another Bonapartist regime could present itself again as the champion of universal suffrage.

This leads to another aspect of democratization: accountable government. The Second Empire was a *démocratie césarienne*, in which the government could hardly be considered accountable. The *Corps législative* lacked the right to initiate or amend laws. Laws needed a final sanction of the executive, who also had the right to convene or dissolve the parliament (Burdeau 1966, 291–93). Only after 1857 did a more liberal regime develop, but also then the supporters of Bonaparte argued that parliament was an unreliable representation of public opinion. They rejected the position of republicans and moderate liberals like François Guizot, who saw the parliament as the core of the political system and feared the extension of the electorate. Bonapartists argued that this was actually "the denial of the democratic principle and the reproduction of the oligarchic thesis borrowed by the French bourgeoisie from the English aristocracy" (Ollivier, quoted in Rosanvallon 2000, 189). Instead, the Bonapartists referred to the United States and Switzerland to argue for a plebiscitary democracy, in which the people gave direct support to the executive, the latter being the embodiment of the unified people. This antiparliamentarism became a constant counterpoint in the political culture of the Third Republic, from the movement of Boulanger of the 1880s to the National Revolution of Vichy of 1940–1944 (Rosanvallon 2000, 185).

The reverse of this combination of strong electoral legitimation and weak parliamentary control could be found in the Netherlands. There the electorate was not only limited, but also lacked the enthusiasm for participating in the elections. Candidates were in general not very eager to mobilize their constituency or to accentuate differences of opinion and, given the lack of political excitement, a substantial part of the already limited electorate refrained from voting (De Jong 1999, 72–78). Only after 1870 candidates began to acknowledge the force of electoral mobilization, to administrate potential voters, and to align to political formations on a national scale. The power of the electorate became clear with the election in March 1888. After the constitutional revision of 1887, the size of the electorate had doubled, to about 300,000 men, who granted for the first time a majority to the confessional candidates. On the other hand, the position of the parliament was much stronger than in France. The velvet revolution of 1848 had put parliament in a dominant position. Although the toppling of the Second Republic in France inspired Dutch conservatives to reinstall a strong monarchical rule— their attempts to realize this in the so-called April Movement of 1853 brought down the liberal government of Johan Rudolf Thorbecke, yet failed to dismantle the liberal constitution. Parliament became the center of Dutch politics (Te Velde 2002, 19–51).

A further aspect of democratization involves the organization of civil society. In this respect, France and the Netherlands are often presented as counter-images—with French republican politics as the heir to the absolutist state of Louis XIV and the bureaucratic centralism of Napoleon, and the Dutch constitutional monarchy as a successor to the Dutch republic. A similar distinction is drawn by Pierre Rosanvallon in *L'État en France de 1789 à nos jours*, where he presents a comparison between France and the United Kingdom. The early rise of the rule of law and the establishment of a parliamentary tradition enabled the English aristocracy to gradually adapt the institutional forms of aristocratic rule. The transformed aristocratic intermediary institutions, and the ethos they came with, were a counterbalance to the negative effects of democratic individualism in the nineteenth century. According to Rosanvallon, France lacked the development of a resilient civil society and a pluralist political culture because aristocratic rule had already lost much of its legitimacy during the eighteenth century, and was radically eradicated after 1789. After the destruction of intermediary institutions and of the ethos of the aristocracy, all social and political energy became focused on the state. In this comparative recapitulation of the Tocquevillean interpretation of the French Revolution, the Netherlands is generally considered to fall into the same category as the United Kingdom (1990, 95–99).

The question whether this distinction between a statist tradition versus a pluralist one makes sense is directly connected to the central issue of this chapter. Did the French political culture of the nineteenth century allow room for intermediary institutions in which divergent cultural practices could flourish? Was the Dutch parliamentary state built on a lively public sphere of civic associations and cultural groups with a separate standing, independent of the state? Or is this distinction too crude, and should we conceptualize the difference between France and the Netherlands as different ways to articulate and organize cultural cleavages within a specific political framework?

Articulating Difference

A natural starting-point to answer this question is the situation after 1848. At that time, both France and the Netherlands began their journey toward the full implementation of democracy, albeit along different paths, as argued above. Both the French and the Dutch historiography of the nineteenth century tend to skip over the period between 1850 and 1870. For instance, Pierre Rosanvallon's *Sacre du citoyen* dismisses the period in less than 8 out of 450 pages as "le temps de la réaction." In his handbook of Dutch history, E. H. Kossmann argues that the debates of the 1850s and 1860s gave the impression that "both the representatives and the government lacked political élan: they lacked both the words and the gestures to give a political form to the dramatic situation of their time" (1986, 226).

Yet perhaps this vagueness is exactly what is at stake in this period, both in France and the Netherlands. One way to describe the period of the Second Empire and of the gradual erosion of the liberal hegemony in the Netherlands of the 1850s and 1860s is as a time of experimentation. As Rosanvallon has argued, in France until the end of the nineteenth century universal suffrage was perceived as a sphinx (1992, 312): Its workings were inscrutable and the outcomes of the electoral process were highly unpredictable. Only in the final quarter of the century did people start to get used to the new political machinery. Politicians learned how to approach the electorate, and the common Frenchmen learned how to become voters. In a way, this was also what happened in the Netherlands, yet the point of departure was different. The constitutional reform of 1848 had not introduced universal suffrage, but it created a new political space that did not exist before. It marked the beginning of a period of "training in parliamentary forms, party politics and the scaling up of political relations," as Henk te Velde characterized it (1999, 97–175).

To understand what cultural distinctions exactly made the difference for democracy in France and the Netherlands, it is therefore necessary, first, to get a grip on the nature of the experimentation of the third quarter of the century, and, second, to understand what changed after 1870. In the first half of the nineteenth century, political conflicts in the Netherlands were generally resolved either at a local level, or by royal decrees without any democratic legitimacy. The constitutional reforms of 1848 limited the power of the king and instituted direct elections, but also introduced new legislation on the electoral process, on the relations between different levels of government, and on public education and poverty relief. Especially the last two issues forced the groups who until then had fought over the local schools and charities to organize on a national level, in order to influence the parliamentary debate. The reforms of 1848 created a new national space, in which political participants were initially unable to orient themselves (De Haan 2003, chapter 2).

Because this was a period of confusion, political trial and error, and failed coalitions, it is impossible within the limits of this chapter to give a detailed picture of the period. It involved at least three sets of problems (based on De Haan 1998, 183–217; and De Haan 2000, 35–57). In the first place, Protestants were split between a conservative reformed bourgeoisie and an increasingly radical protestant *kerkvolk* (churchgoers) led by protestant schoolmasters who rejected the compromise on primary education of the law of 1857. Initially, this was a conflict within the Reformed Church, but as the protesters against the primary school system became better organized, it evolved into a conflict with the political elite, which was predominantly liberal, both religiously and politically. As a result, in the 1860s a protestant *volksdeel* emerged, which was antimodernist and suspicious of church-leaders, liberal preachers, and the liberal state.

A second division emerged on the catholic side. Roman Catholics kept aloof as a result of the protestant signature of the Dutch nation, even though they had enjoyed equal political rights since the constitution of 1798. However, after 1848 there was a full separation of church and state, and then Catholics could restore the clerical hierarchy that had been dissolved since the seventeenth century. In 1853, the appointment of five bishops, and the naming of Utrecht (perceived by conservative Protestants as the birthplace of the Dutch nation from the Union of Utrecht, 1579) as the seat of the archbishop contributed to a growing catholic confidence—but also to a strong antipapist sentiment, which forced Catholics to close their ranks. On a local level, the catholic bourgeoisie was forced to accept the strengthened position of the local clerical leaders, but the latter lost in their turn power to the Roman curia. In contrast to the protestant body, where the disintegration of the church was the starting point for the formation of a separate part of the nation, the catholic integration started at the top of the clerical hierarchy and slowly trickled down to the common people. Due to the central place of the clerical organization in catholic public life, the *political* organization of Catholics emerged much later, in the 1920s.

The third group that underwent a reorientation were the liberals. They presented themselves as the core of the nation, continuing the project of national integration started by William I; and at the same time as the guardians of the constitutional form that the nation acquired after 1848. Their orientation toward both the content and the form of the nation reinforced their rejection of partisan politics. As a result, the emergence of protestant and catholic groups was not only perceived as a threat to the substance of liberal values, but also as an attack on the liberal form of politics. In the reaction to this double threat, the liberals fell apart, into (at least) two camps. Conservative liberals held on to their national orientation and persisted in the rejection of all forms of partisan politics. A younger generation of liberals began to accept the consequence of their own partiality in relation to the other parts of the nation, and in the 1870s they began to formulate a liberal political program, which they no longer presented as the form of the nation in which all other parts had to fit, but as a conception of the nation that could compete with protestant and catholic claims to a national existence. They no longer perceived the nation as a given form, but as a project that had to be defended and developed, notably by way of public education. This led to the much more explicitly liberal law on primary education of 1878.

There was a remarkable shift in the political culture in the Netherlands after 1870. The link between liberals and Catholics was severed under the influence of ultramontanism and the frontal attack on liberalism of the Dutch bishops in 1868, following the condemnation of liberalism by the pope in 1864. The liberal group radicalized after the death of Thorbecke in 1872 and embraced a more partisan program, culminating in the law on primary education of 1878, which shared the secularist point of view of the *loi Ferry*. Some radical liberals tried to connect with the first manifestations of lower middle class political consciousness. And in 1879 the protestant *Anti-*

revolutionaire Partij (Anti-Revolutionary Party, ARP) was founded as the first national party organization. This inaugurated the era of mass democracy, dominated by well-organized parties and charismatic leaders. In this way, after 1870 in the Netherlands a constellation of forces emerged, which in retrospect could be identified as the manifestation of age-old cleavages within the Dutch nation. This was evidently an invention of traditions, introduced to legitimize the new pluralism that resulted from the creation of a new political space at a national level by the constitutional reform of 1848.

At first sight, the French case seems very different. Initially, at least as many groups as in the Netherlands manifested themselves. But in the Second Empire an odd mixture of very different political forms emerged. An authoritarian state was combined with a democratic system of universal suffrage. The issue became more complicated in the Third Republic, because its constitutional structure was even more a jumble of principles and forms. As Theodore Zeldin has argued, this was exactly the point of the constitution of the Third Republic:

> It based itself on *débrouillage*, the art of getting by somehow. It allowed people to find a corner where they could be more or less comfortable, and where, so as not to be disturbed, they took care not to disturb others. ... It was sustained by the enormous strength of inertia; but because the rewards it yielded could not be respectably defended it compensated for its theoretical weaknesses by passionate attachment to grand principles, though little was ever done about these in practice (1973, 572).

Perhaps here is also a clue to the apparent difference between France and the Netherlands. While the liberal constitution of 1848 in the Netherlands was soon generally accepted as the framework for political alignments, political debates on cultural differences in France were immediately translated into conflicts about constitutional forms. For instance, as Claude Langlois argued, the struggle between clericalism and *laïcité* served immediately "to cement the republican camp" (1992, 150). *Laïcité* in turn was a form of secularized Protestantism, closely linked to the republican movement as it reemerged at the end of the Second Empire (Johnson 1985, 73–77; Nord 1995, 90–114). Clericalism, on the other hand, was part and parcel of French royalism and legitimism, and thus in the same way politicized. Another example of the immediate politicization of cultural difference is that of the French Jews. Their religious identity was perceived to be a private matter. In their public persona, Jews could only be republicans, (however, as the Dreyfus case showed, defenders of republican values could easily be attacked as Jews [Birnbaum 1992]).

As a consequence of the direct relation between cultural difference and political forms in France, regime changes had a revolutionary nature. As was argued in the report of the parliamentary commission of inquiry into the causes of the 1871 Commune: "We are afflicted with a superstition of power, but of revolutionary power; we ask everything of the state, it is for us the deus ex machina, and every time we are unhappy, we want a different God" (quoted in Hazareesingh 1998, 202). While in the Netherlands parliamentary debates, dominated by a very small class of bourgeois and enlightened Protestants, were relatively independent from social and cultural groups, who followed their own development within civil society, the cultural pluralism of French society was immediately translated in constitutional differences. Orléanists, legitimists, republicans, and Bonapartists were clearly connected to certain social and cultural sections of French society, but first and foremost they were protagonists of competing constitutional systems.

It would be a mistake, however, to interpret this trait of the French political culture as a sign of immutable etatism, as if one could envisage political change only via the state. What is striking about the Second Empire, and also of the Commune and the Third Republic, is the strong support for decentralization and the strengthening of civil associations. On this point, there emerged an odd coalition, or coalescence between republicans and legitimists, and even with Bonapartists. They all shared the Tocquevillean insight that only an independent civil society with strong intermediary institutions could keep the negative consequences of democratic individualism in check. The most significant sign of this changing perspective on the revolutionary heritage is the revocation, in 1864, of the ban on coalition, first encoded in the *loi Le Chapelier* of 1791 (Rosanvallon 2000, 201–5). With this measure, Napoleon III proved himself ahead of his political opponents, who bundled their forces in the struggle for decentralization in the Nancy Program of 1865, supported by republicans like Sadi Carnot and Jules Ferry, Orléanists like Victor de Broglie and François Guizot, and legitimists like Ferdinand Béchard and Claude Marie Raudot (Kale 1992, 113–14). This enthusiasm for decentralization did not result from an ideology of self-government, as it did in most liberal political theories of the mid-nineteenth century, like that of John Stuart Mill, or in the Netherlands, of Thorbecke. Legitimists only followed Tocqueville's analysis of secondary associations, because they saw it as a means to reinforce the power of provincial bodies—traditionally an aristocratic stronghold—and to weaken the power of the Bonapartist regime, based in the political center, in Paris (Kale 1992, 107). The same desire to mobilize the countryside against the capital and to reinvigorate local elites inspired the Bonapartist attempts at decentralization. According to Sudhar Hazareesingh, in his study on democratization under the Second Empire, the Bonapartist policy must even be understood as a way to form a coalition with monarchists and legitimists against the challenge of republicans (1998, 64). It is in any case beyond doubt that the conservative proposals for decentralization were not intended as a step to political liberalization. This is clear from the law of 6 June 1868, which established a more general right to associate, yet still explicitly excluded the right to form political associations (Rosanvallon 2000, 206–12).

However, once the spirit of associationalism was released, it spread to all sides. At the end of the 1860s, republicans coalesced in multifarious forms. After the introduction of the law of 1868, public lectures became more and more openly political meetings, and in 1869 turned into *réunions electorales*, which already announced the Third Republic (Nord 1995, 192–95). As Philip Nord states: "The idea and even the practice of democratic citizenship were in place before a republican Third Republic existed to give them sanction" (1995, 216).

Yet, the mistrust of citizens who freely associated to promote political goals, so characteristic of postrevolutionary France, did not disappear after 1870. On the contrary: the Paris Commune, perceived by many of its participants as "the paradise of association," (Johnson 1996) fed the idea that a politically active citizenry had to be kept in check—yet the form changed from a ceasarist blockade of effective representation to the education of the citizen as a subject of the national community.

This turn to national unity was as much a consequence of the shock of the Commune as it was a reaction to the defeat of France in the Franco-Prussian war of 1870. This created a revanchist mood, in which the regeneration of the French nation took a much more expansionist and militarist form than before. The reform of the school, proposed by Ferry, was closely related to the reform of the army and the abolishment of substitution of conscripts by the law of 1 January 1873. Both were visibly connected in the *Bataillons Scolaires*, who after 1882 participated in the manifestation of 14 July. This link was legitimated by a historical education based on the work of the patron of French historiography, Ernest Lavisse, and on *Le tour de la France par deux enfants*, subtitled *Devoir et patrie*, the schoolbook from which all French children learned the geography of the country. The revanchist element in this book is made clear by the fact that the two children whose tour the reader follows were born in the Lorraine, a region which had been lost in the Franco-Prussian war (Becker and Audoin-Rouzeau 1995, 170–71; Weber 1976, 333; Nora 1984, 247–89; Ozouf and Ozouf in Nora 1984, 291–321).

The nationalism that developed in this context balanced between inclusivist nationalism of the revolutionary tradition, stressing the rights of man and citizen, and exclusivist nationalism, which found a first expression in the unity of the people under Bonapartist leadership, but which was mobilized in the Third Republic by Boulangists and finally by the anti-Dreyfusards at the turn of the century (see Winock 1990, 11–40; Sternhell in Tombs 1991, 22–38). As a result of this development, the revolutionary notion of the nation as a unity of political will, instead of common soil, language, or culture, came under attack. Thus, the concept of *jus soli*, regulating the integration of immigrants was—in the end unsuccessfully—opposed by supporters of the tradition of *jus sanguinis* (Brubaker 1992, 98–110). Also the notion of popular sovereignty as an aggregation of individual decisions, which had until the 1870s dominated the democratic vocabulary, was now replaced by national sovereignty as an impersonal and collective force (Rosanvallon 2000, 230–35).

Explaining Difference

Let us return to the initial question: what is the relation between democracy and cultural difference? Contrary to conventional political wisdom and the harshest critics of democracy, democratization does not necessarily lead to cultural homogeneity, as other contributions to this volume show, but also to the emergence of new forms of pluralism. The basic flaw in Carl Schmitt's equation of democracy and homogeneity is that he misses the point between the organization of input and that of output in the democratic process. Indeed, democracy produces a homogeneous output in the form of binding decisions. Yet the democratic process also organizes its input by creating an institutional structure to articulate differences.

There are obviously major differences in the way in which this input is organized, but they should not be overstated. The awakening of nationalism at the end of the nineteenth century is not limited to France. At that time, a strong nationalist current emerged also in the Netherlands. But there are clear variations. In the Netherlands this kind of nationalist rhetoric was mainly the product of liberal attempts to catch up with confessional and socialist politicians, who turned out to be more capable of mobilizing an electorate with an evocative moral and an affective appeal to their constituency. The liberal turn to the nation was a short-lived attempt to get rid of its rationalistic image (see Te Velde 1992). Nationalism is much more widespread in the Third Republic and shared by everyone—except perhaps by socialists disappointed in the results of democratization so far. The most important reason for this difference between the two countries seems to be the experience of war. The call of national unity in the Netherlands was much less urgent than in France, where the nation's self-image had been shattered by the military defeat at Sedan and the humiliating peace of 1871. As a result, the democratization of the Third Republic was accompanied by a significant emphasis on cultural unity, but again it could very well be that this had less to do with democracy than with the effects of warfare.

A more promising explanatory route to understand the relation between democracy and diversity may be to take into account the nature and timing of democratization. The early introduction of general male suffrage in France gave an immediate political outlet to cultural differences, which in the Netherlands first had to be organized on a societal level. When universal suffrage was finally introduced in the Netherlands, it only confirmed the cultural dividing-lines, which had been drawn in the period before 1917. The actual existence of universal suffrage in France after 1848, in combination with an illiberal executive, enabled Napoleon III to mobilize an electorate as a counterweight against the claims to authority of parliament and civil associations, thereby eliminating most arenas for legitimate political contest. This unitarian tradition was in a way continued in the Third Republic, at the same time as it was transformed into the *démopedie* of the nation.

Timing therefore seems one of the essential ingredients to explain the differences between France and the Netherlands. In the latter case, universal suffrage was introduced a long time after the creation of a national political space in parliament. As a result, cultural differences were articulated outside the electoral core of the democratic process. In France, on the other hand, due to the early introduction of universal suffrage, all differences were immediately politicized and related to the master narrative of French political history of the nineteenth century, the struggle among the differential constitutional alternatives which had been brought forward in reaction to the Revolution. Thus also in France, democracy produced pluralism, but this was always a political pluralism. The fact that cultural pluralism has no place in French politics does not mean that its political culture is homogeneous. It probably only implies that cultural difference had to be articulated elsewhere: in literature, in philosophy, in the realm of intellectual debate. This could explain why French political culture breeds a lively cultural debate and politically "irresponsible" intellectuals, as Tony Judt among many others has argued (1992). Does this mean that the Dutch political culture bred politicized intellectuals and an intellectually impoverished cultural debate?

It means in any case that democratization neither presupposes nor invariably produces cultural homogeneity. Democracy indeed organizes and feeds certain kinds of difference. Even when democracy has a homogenizing tendency, it only does so by creating at the same time heterogeneity of a political, ethnic, cultural, or other nature, depending on the national trajectory of democratization.

CHAPTER FIVE

Ethnicity and Democracy in Europe's Multinational Empires, 1848–1918

AVIEL ROSHWALD

In Robert Musil's novel *Man Without Qualities*, a loyal subject of the Habsburg monarchy observes that "We must not forget that His Majesty's noble and generous resolve to let the people take part in the conduct of their own affairs, up to a point, has not been in effect long enough to have produced everywhere the kind of political maturity in every respect worthy of the confidence so magnanimously placed in the people by His Majesty" (1995, 181). In a later passage, the author depicts the displacement of dynastic loyalty by nationalist fervor, while optimistically remarking that:

> It would be wrong to think of the notorious Kakanian nationalist rivalries as particularly savage. It was more a historical process than a real one. The people actually quite liked each other; even though they did crack each other's heads and spit in each other's faces, it was done as a matter of higher cultural considerations, as when a man who normally wouldn't hurt a fly, for instance, will sit in court under the image of Christ Crucified and condemn another man to death.[1]

65

Musil's sardonic prose points to some of the most vexing questions surrounding the relationship among imperial authority, democratizing reform, and ethnic nationalism in the multinational empires that were to meet their doom in the First World War. Did the introduction of constitutional forms and electoral politics undermine the stability of the Habsburg, Romanov, and Ottoman empires and sow the seeds of hatred among their nationalities? Was the problem simply a lack of 'political maturity', a problem that would have been resolved in the normal course of historical progress, had the Great War not intervened to cut short the process of constitutional development? Or did the hitch lie in the phrase "up to a point," with which the character in Musil's novel qualifies the nature of popular self-determination under the dynastic regime? Was it the half-baked nature of imperial experiments in democratic reform that resulted in the worst of all possible worlds for the development of ethnic relations? Conversely, given what we know of what ensued upon their collapse, ought we to forgive these now long-dead empires their shortcomings and look upon them as inspiring, and even instructive, models of how to accommodate ethnic pluralism within the framework of a stable polity?[2]

A Lost World

It is indeed tempting to look back on the imperial "world of yesterday," to paraphrase Stefan Zweig, with nostalgia (1964). For all the current talk of globalization, pre-1914 Central European, East European, and Middle Eastern empires could boast—if they cared to—of a much greater intermixing and interaction of languages, ethnicities, and cultures than could many of the ethnically cleansed, democratic European nation-states of today. Metropolitan centers such as Vienna, Budapest, Odessa, and Istanbul hosted polyglot populations and cosmopolitan elites with strong ties to cultural, intellectual, and commercial networks that cut across political and geographic boundaries. Among the very nationalist activists who questioned and challenged the imperial power structures there were many, around the turn of the twentieth century, who engaged in intense correspondence and collaboration with their counterparts among other ethnic groups both within their own empires and in other polities. The right-wing Polish nationalist Roman

Dmowski spoke to a convocation of Ottoman opposition and nationalist groups brought together by an exiled Young Turk leader during the Hague Peace Conference of 1899 (Fountain 1980, 112–13; Hanioglu 1995, 128–29). Croatian democratic radicals looked to Czech activist Tomáš Masaryk for guidance and inspiration, while right-of-center Slavic nationalists from the Russian and Habsburg empires sought to launch a neo–pan-Slav movement.[3] Pan-Turkist ideas, in turn, were propagated in Istanbul by exiled Tatar intellectuals from the Russian empire, who drew inspiration from the pan-Slavic movement (Arai 1992, chapter 4). For their part, the imperial regimes were largely willing to tolerate the active cultivation of multiple linguistic, cultural, and religious identities among their subject peoples. In some instances, they were even ready to cede a large measure of political authority to certain regional elites—as in the cases of Hungarian self-rule and effective Galician Polish autonomy within the Habsburg monarchy, Finland's special status in the Russian empire, and the de facto independence of various Balkan states still nominally under Ottoman sovereignty in the latter half of the nineteenth century.

Indeed, many cultural and political nationalists among the empires' subject nationalities, to say nothing of outright imperial apologists, contended that the empires provided the most stable and secure frameworks for the coexistence of geographically intertwined nationalities and for the development of modern national cultures free of the fear of external aggression or internecine warfare. Austrian social democrats Karl Renner and Otto Bauer famously called for a reformed Habsburg empire that would combine the economic and political stability of the existing geopolitical structure with a system of extra-territorial cultural autonomy—loosely modeled on the Ottoman *millet* system—that would afford each nationality the opportunity to nurture its own identity without prejudice to the unity and integrity of the state.[4] Roman Dmowski was an advocate of Polish autonomy under the protective aegis of an anti-German Russian empire (Fountain 1980). Even Masaryk did not call for the outright dissolution of the Habsburg monarchy until his self-imposed exile in 1914.

But, in looking back on the lost world of European empire-states, it would be misleading to paint a rosy picture of benign, patriarchal monarchs graciously presiding over the peaceful development of multicultural societies. While Finland held on to an ever-shrinking domain of political autonomy,

Congress Poland was subject to heavy-handed tsarist repression and sporadic Russification campaigns. The Czech cultural renaissance under Vienna's rule contrasted sharply with the systematic marginalization or eradication of Slovak cultural and educational institutions by the authorities in Budapest. Administrative centralization of the Ottoman Empire by the post-1908 Young Turk regimes undercut the traditional prerogatives of Arab notables in the Fertile Crescent.

More disturbing were the outbreaks of violence against minority communities in Russia and the Ottoman Empire. Thousands of Jews died and hundreds of thousands emigrated in the course of the periodic pogroms of the last three decades before the First World War. Although mass violence was officially frowned upon by a tsarist regime suspicious of any display of popular initiative, the regime was itself deeply steeped in anti-Semitic prejudice, and Russian police authorities often seemed either unable or unwilling to intervene in timely and effective fashion on behalf of beleaguered Jewish communities (Klier 1995; Rogger 1986, esp. chapter 4; Aronson 1992). In the Ottoman Empire, Armenian separatist activities led to brutal massacres in the 1890s and again in 1909—waves of atrocities in which government and military officials were deeply complicit, official protestations to the contrary notwithstanding (Suny 1993, 98–106; Somakian 1995, 15–31). Much worse was to follow in 1915.

While it may be tempting to characterize such examples of repression and violence as desperate responses to forces and pressures that were exogenous to the essential imperial idea, this would be a misleading and artificial distinction. The Habsburg, Romanov, and Ottoman regimes were not hapless victims of socioeconomic and political modernization; they seized upon key aspects of it, selectively but deliberately, in an effort to harness the power of industry, centralized administration, and/or mass political consciousness for their own domestic and international purposes. Embedded as they were in an intensely competitive world system, the multinational great powers endeavored to keep pace with, and outdo, both one another and their nation-state rivals by channeling the energies of new social and political classes away from suspect ideologies and into loyalty to the ruling dynasties, strengthening their bodies politic by tapping into and co-opting hitherto neglected material, manpower, and emotional resources.

Official nationalism was—or so they thought—one way of doing this.[5] Right-wing Russian and pan-Slavic nationalist parties and movements, such as the Union of Russian People, were given a wink and a nod from tsarist authorities who were loath to fully and openly embrace the potentially subversive idea of popular nationalism, yet sorely tempted to employ it as a means of generating mass support for autocratic institutions and of marginalizing liberal, socialist, and separatist movements.[6] In the Austrian part of the Austro-Hungarian Empire, pan-German nationalism posed a threat to the integrity of the monarchy, and even anti-Semitism was frowned upon by an emperor who repeatedly refused to appoint the anti-Jewish demagogue Karl Lueger as mayor of Vienna before finally bowing to the will of the city's electorate in 1897. But in Hungary, Magyar nationalism was vigorously and persistently promoted by the kingdom's autonomous government, which offered ethnic minorities the rewards of upward social mobility at the price of assimilating into Magyar culture. For its part, the Ottoman government responded to its steady losses in the Balkans by mounting a pan-Islamic propaganda campaign designed to consolidate its grip on its remaining territories. Following their seizure of power in the last years before the Great War, the Young Turks, or Committee of Union and Progress (CUP), supplemented this approach with the promotion of pan-Turkist associations that were intended to awaken militantly nationalist zeal among the ethnically Turkish core population of the empire. Indeed, recent research indicates that Turkish nationalism was more than a useful propaganda option for the new government. The leadership of the CUP was itself zealously—if secretly—committed to a Turkish nationalist agenda directed against Greek and Armenian ethnic minorities within Anatolia and toward the eventual incorporation within the Ottoman Empire of the Turkic peoples of Russian-ruled central Asia.[7]

By condoning or promoting chauvinistic nationalisms among politically dominant ethnic groups, imperial regimes stoked the fires of communal hatred and interethnic conflict, contributed to the crystallization of nationalist and separatist ideologies among minority groups, and undermined their own ostensible roles as impartial arbiters among their diverse subject peoples. Conversely, to the extent that the ruling dynasties did tolerate cultural and linguistic diversity and regional autonomy, it was not as the expression of a fundamental ideological commitment to ethnocultural pluralism or popular self-determination. They did so partly as a function of the dynastic-religious bases of their political legitimacy, which, in principle, did not conflict with ethnocultural pluralism to the same extent that the post-1918 nation-state concept did. There was also a strongly manipulative element to the imperial regimes' engagement with multiethnic politics. As Steven Beller has argued, even in the case of the most liberal and tolerant of the empires—the Habsburg monarchy—the selective devolution of power to certain regional ethnic elites (Magyars in the Hungarian kingdom, Poles in Galicia) came at the expense of other nationalities within those regions and took the form of bilateral bargains struck between center and periphery rather than a systematic restructuring of power on ethno-federal lines throughout the empire as a whole. After 1867, the political aspirations of the Slavic nationalities in both halves of the empire were held hostage to the Habsburgs' historic compromise with the Magyar-dominated half of the empire. The ill-fated Archduke Franz Ferdinand was known as an opponent of this stultifying dualism, but his sympathy toward the idea of south Slav autonomy within a trialist arrangement was motivated by a desire to contain and offset Hungarian power rather than by a principled commitment to ethnic self-rule; he appears to have opposed a proposed compromise with the Czechs over the vexing administrative-language issue in Bohemia in 1904 on the grounds that ethnic peace would weaken the power of the crown (Beller 1996, 187–88 and *passim*; Williamson 1991, chapter 2; Kann 1974, 429).

The introduction of constitutional forms and representative institutions in all three empires often reflected similar calculations of how best to preserve and protect the dynastic interests and/or autocratic principles that remained central to the identities of these regimes (see Beller 1996, 80–94, 99–107, 160–74). The inauguration of electoral politics was not accompanied by the establishment of strict cabinet accountability to a parliamentary majority. Parliaments served as *de facto* forums for the politics of ethnic representation without creating commensurate roles of political responsibility or sufficient incentives for coalition building among the elected representatives of ethnonational communities. The temptation to score easy political points by attacking the representatives of rival ethnic groups was generally too great to resist. If, in the French Revolution, a tennis court served as the site for a dramatic act of political self-determination, in Austria, the elected assembly served as an arena for athletic displays—the hurling of inkwells at one another by Czech and German deputies. Conversely, even relatively sincere efforts by the regime to link democratization to interethnic cooperation and political compromise were prone to backfire. As Philipp Ther's essay in this volume points out, the broadening of the suffrage did lead to imaginative and constructive compromises over ethnic power-sharing in such crownlands as Moravia, Bukovina, and (abortively, in 1914) Galicia (see Chapter 6; see also Sked 1989, 222–24). But in the cockpit of intercommunal tension, Bohemia, liberalization of the electoral system only heightened tensions between the local Czech majority, eager to use the one-man/one-vote principle to consolidate regional power, and the German minority, unwilling to relinquish its traditional position of social, linguistic, and administrative dominance.

In the other empires, the inverse relationship between electoral democratization and the accommodation of ethnoregional interests is even more striking. In the Ottoman Empire the introduction of an elected parliament under the Young Turks was accompanied by moves to consolidate Istanbul's administrative and political grip over the provinces. The Arab Decentralization Party, which advocated a federalization of the empire, was limited to the role of an ignored opposition at best. The combination of political repression with the rigging of elections in Arab provinces provoked the most committed activists into establishing secret nationalist societies or going into political exile.[8] In Russia, the regime's grudging concession of an elected legislature in 1905 was not accompanied by a restoration of Polish or recently curtailed Finnish constitutional autonomy. Within the new duma, right-wing deputies indulged in poisonous invective against Poles and Jews. Ethnic-minority representatives tended to align themselves with ideologically compatible (liberal or socialist) Russian parties that paid lip service to various schemes of ethnofederal reform, but whose primary political agendas were themselves predicated on a highly centralized conception of democratized government (Pipes 1964, 55–56, and chapter 1).

In the absence of any promising opportunity of striking satisfactory, long-term political bargains, and without the burden of serious political and administrative responsibility, nationalist ideologues and intellectuals were free to fantasize about and debate all manner of political scenarios, either within restructured imperial frameworks or, especially after the outbreak of the

First World War, within fully sovereign nation-states. Their visions of independence could take the form of liberal-democratic societies in which culturally or historically related ethnic groups would join together in amicable civic unions. Tomáš Masaryk's program was the paradigmatic example of this humanistic form of nationalism, with its vision of a politically and culturally progressive Czech national elite taking both Czech and Slovak masses by the hand in a common march toward a westernized society rooted in Hussite spiritual values.[9] The Yugoslav project espoused by Croat activists Ante Trumbić and Franjo Supilo and the pan-Arab programs of some of Britain's allies and interlocutors in the Middle East also defined national identity in vaguely inclusive ways that held forth the promise of harmonious coexistence among a variety of historically or culturally related ethnic and religious groups (Rida 1909; Kerr 1966, 166–75; Hourani 1962, 303–6). Other nationalists conjured up appealingly simplistic visions of ethnically pure homelands free of interference from culturally alien elements. Dmowski's virulently anti-Semitic version of Polish nationalism was a case in point (see Bromke 1967; Opalski and Bartal 1992, 104–5). So was Croatia's bitterly anti-Serb Frankist movement. Just after the outbreak of war in 1914, the official party organ of this ideological forerunner of the fascist Ustaša Party remarked that "the Serbs are poisonous snakes from whom you are safe only after you have crushed their heads."[10]

Regardless of their definition of nationhood, nationalists were all too prone to identify self-determination with democracy and national liberation with the free exercise of popular will in markedly simplistic ways, avoiding confrontation with the dilemmas and paradoxes inherent in these equations. As long as they were denied access to political authority, they were free to build nationalist castles in the air without being forced to confront the potential flaws in their architectural designs. Demagogues like Dmowski were not obliged to consider the consequences a policy of institutionalized minority-baiting might have for a country's long-term political stability. By the same token, the very inclusiveness of liberal visions such as Masaryk's licensed their proponents to lay claim to lands populated by a diverse array of ethnic groups. A well-led, democratic nation-state, it was thought, could have its cake and eat it too: extend its rule to ethnographically diverse territories and instill a genuine—if ex post facto—sense of nationhood among its population. Just as in France or Britain, so too in Czechoslovakia, Yugoslavia, or Poland, strong, democratic governments allied with politically engaged and culturally creative social elites would be able to forge cohesive nations out of the inchoate masses.

During 1914–18, wartime exile widened the physical and psychological gap between some of these nationalist leaders and their ostensible political constituencies. Their actual constituencies became sympathetic journalists, intellectuals, émigré communities, and government officials in Britain, France, and the United States. What better venue for the articulation of ambitiously optimistic scenarios of interethnic cooperation in the creation of a brave new world of liberal-democratic nation-states, untroubled by the petty jealousies and internecine squabbling that imperial divide-and-rule policies had so cynically perpetuated? Yet how ineffectual a framework of operation this was for purposes of creating a solid base of popular support among the populations on whose behalf these projects were being advocated![11] By the same token, eleventh-hour imperial offers of national autonomy, such as those forthcoming from Vienna in October 1918, or the Russian Provisional Government during its brief political tenure in 1917, lacked credibility and seemed little more than signs of weakness heralding the empires' imminent collapse.

To be fair to the empires, it is hard to envisage a happy outcome to their political evolution even if their regimes had been more sincere and systematic in their implementation of parliamentary government, electoral reform, and ethnopolitical pluralism. Democratic politics leads inexorably to identity politics. The creation of representative institutions begs the question of *who* is being represented. And the answer to this was elusive within an imperial framework. The most liberal and accommodating of these Leviathans was, almost by definition, the least certain about its identity. To quote Robert Musil once again, "The Austro-Hungarian state ... did not consist of an Austrian part and a Hungarian part that, as one might expect, complemented each other, but of a whole and a part; that is, of a Hungarian and an Austro-Hungarian sense of statehood, the latter to be found in Austria, which in a sense left the Austrian sense of statehood with no country of its own" Musil 1995, vol. 1, 180). Within the framework of such a statewide identity vacuum, democratic politics readily degenerated into communal politics. On the other hand, a Metternichian refusal to countenance substantive political reform and suffrage extension would itself have been a recipe for a political explosion.

Accomplishments and Shortcomings

Counterfactual history is a notoriously dicey proposition. In reflecting on the questions raised at the beginning of this essay, it is impossible to pronounce with authority whether or not any of the multinational empires would have successfully resolved the tensions among ethnonational diversity, dynastic interests, and the democratization of politics if it had not been for the First World War.[12] Indeed, it is worth emphasizing that the Great War was itself in part the byproduct of Austria-Hungary's failure to devise a peaceful framework for the resolution of these tensions, of other states' eagerness to take opportunistic advantage of the Habsburgs' discomfiture, and of the German-backed Habsburg decision to lash out blindly in response (see Williamson 1991). The First World War was not an extraneous factor; it was precipitated by events growing directly out of the intractable political dilemmas under review in this essay. That said, it seems fair to say that, had a major war somehow been averted, any eventual unraveling of empires would have been less abrupt and less destabilizing than the events of 1917–18 proved to be. Indeed, the relatively peaceful disintegration of the Soviet Union at the end of the twentieth century serves as an alternative, peaceful model for the breakdown of multinational empire, one that (so far) has entailed less large-scale chaos than did the decline and fall of the Habsburg, Romanov, and Ottoman regimes. The Soviet case, in which Russian President Boris Yeltsin took the initiative in dissolving what had been a Russian-dominated empire, suggests that, in an age of democratization, amicable divorce may provide the surest path to the easing of differences among the partners in the polygamous marriage of multinational empire. Whether any of the pre-1914 empires would ever have accepted such a prospect outside the framework of total military defeat remains an unanswerable question.

Regardless of whether the multinational empires ever had a chance of squaring the ethnodemocratic circle, it makes little sense to look back to them for positive lessons on how to reconcile diversity with democracy. A nostalgic disposition may lead one to see in the multinational empires models of relative interethnic harmony, politically harmonious Atlantises sunk beneath the century's successive waves of ethnic, religious, and ideological hatreds. But a historicist perspective suggests that the empires themselves served as incubation vessels for nationalist conflicts. In part this was their rulers' fault; in part it was a function of the historically over-determined dilemmas they faced.

To be sure, the evils of the imperial states seem benign by comparison with the horrors that were to follow their collapse. But to limit one's analysis to a simple contrast between the images of Europe before and after 1914 is to disregard the causal links that connect those two periods to one another. We can certainly learn from studying the multinational empires of the pre-war world, but more by exploring their shortcomings than by extolling their accomplishments. To the extent that they did accommodate democratic forces and ethnic identities, it was in a haphazard, half-hearted, and inconsistent manner that aggravated tensions and intensified frustrations rather than creating solid incentives for cooperative behavior. Insofar as they held firm to dynastic and autocratic conceptions of state interest, they undermined the credibility of their own reforms and made visions of radical political change and outright nationalist separatism all the more alluring.

For their part, it was the great failing of the nationalist elites that their own conceptions of political sovereignty left even less room for the accommodation of multiple ethnic identities than did the imperial structures that they challenged. Some of the most liberal-minded nationalist thinkers and leaders were fundamentally convinced that national identity had to be shaped so as to conform perfectly to a preconceived notion of the centralized, modern state, characterized by the uniform distribution of its authority throughout its territory and governed in the name of an indivisible popular sovereignty. Their cult of centralization was partly modeled on the example of the successful nation-states of Western Europe and was, in fact, encouraged by the Allied and Associated Powers at the Paris Peace Conference. But the leaders of the new states may also have been more influenced than they would have cared to admit by the very tradition of imperial absolutism against which they had struggled. The rulers of those empires had identified centralization of power and uniform projection of territorial control as the key to survival and success in the face of both internal and external challenges, and as an essential element of their modernization programs—however short of the mark they had fallen in practice. This was precisely the outlook adopted by the nationalist elites the moment they found themselves in positions of political authority, vague wartime promises of autonomy for ethnic minorities notwithstanding.

Indeed, like revolutionaries in every era, the new nationalist elites had less patience than their imperial predecessors for contradictions and inconsistencies in the implementation of their visions. As leaders of nation-states based on the principle of self-determination, they saw no need to accommodate sectional interests, regional sentiments, and minority identities. All these were so many obstacles in the way of complete self-determination for the peoples on whose behalf the new or expanded polities of East Central Europe had ostensibly been formed. Just as the French state had molded its population into a cohesive national whole, assimilating minorities and ironing out dialectal variations (see Bell 2001; Weber 1976), so too the nationalist leaders of East Central Europe set out to forge culturally homogeneous societies out of the people in whose name they governed. But unlike the French state (which itself fell short of complete sociocultural homogenization even at the late-nineteenth and early-twentieth-century height of the endeavor), this process was expected to achieve success overnight rather than emerge as the product of centuries of political evolution. In the name of the people, the East European nationalist regimes proved more single-minded and relentless in their pursuit of political integration and cultural homogeneity than either West European models or imperial predecessors ever had been. Those who did not fit in were expected to assimilate, leave, or quietly accept second-class status on the margins of the new political framework. The minorities treaties foisted on the new states by the Western powers never did more than promise members of minority communities their basic civil rights and the freedom to maintain their distinctive cultural and educational institutions. They did not afford them legal foundations for claiming political autonomy nor did they offer them any guarantees of consociational power sharing. In any case, the treaties were, generally speaking, not observed (Fink 1995, 197–205; Finney 1995, 533–51; Macartney 1934, 220–24, chapter 7; Gadgil 1975, 71–72).

Needless to say, this approach only served to aggravate political disaffection among minorities and to exacerbate ethnic tensions. Moreover, the economic disruptions and geopolitical instability of the interwar years perpetuated the region's pervasive condition (and self-image) of "peripheral backwardness," as delineated in Chapter 3. This further doomed any prospects there may have been for building mental and material frameworks for compromise and reconciliation among competing nationalities. The resultant crises of national self-determination contributed to the rapid disintegration of democratic norms and institutions everywhere in interwar East Central Europe other than Czechoslovakia. Be it under democratic government or dictatorship, none of the East Central European states ever succeeded in establishing a long-term, stable basis for coexistence between their dominant ethnic groups and the multiple minorities that formed a large segment of each of their populations. The new, would-be nation-states were no more predestined for success in dealing with the nationalities issue than their imperial predecessors had been.

Ultimately, it was the nationalist regimes' ruthlessness—and that of their occupiers during the Second World War and the Cold War—that "resolved" the region's nationalities problems. From the internationally sanctioned Greco-Turkish population exchanges of 1923, through the German-orchestrated genocide of the Jews, the post–Second World War expulsions of ethnic Germans, the Bulgarian persecution of ethnic Turks in the 1980s, and on to the Serbian and Croatian ethnic-cleansing programs of the 1990s, state-organized violence proved the preferred method for resolving East Central Europe's hitherto intractable demographic dilemmas.[13] In the new and improved *Mitteleuropa* of the post-Cold War years, democracy has been established in the wake of a brutal homogenization of ethnic identity that has cleared the ground of the thorniest problems on which the interwar polities stumbled. Ironically, it is among the West European countries, whose ostensible unity and homogeneity had served as a model for the East Central European nation-states, that there are now those willing to accommodate ethnocultural diversity within the framework of democracy by moving away from the unitarist conceptions of sovereignty inherited from Europe's age of monarchic absolutism.

CHAPTER SIX

The Homogeneous Nation-State and
the Blockade of Democratization

Germany and East Central Europe

PHILIPP THER

The history of twentieth-century Europe demonstrated that democracy is a hard-won and fragile achievement. In order to prevent future failures of democracy one needs to ask about its preconditions and the causes for its decay or abolishment. The past provides a particularly rich empirical basis to analyze the correlation between ethnic diversity and democratization. Since the European Union is developing into a multiethnic space under the governance of a "common administration" in Brussels and of mutually dependent and entangled nation-states, this question has gained additional relevance.

As Chris Lorenz has shown in his introduction into historical methods, the comparative method is a particularly well-suited tool to generate causal explanations, to synthesize findings from different countries and regions, and to deduce models of development (1997, 231–84). The recent participation of comparative historians in theoretical debates in France and Germany indicates a renaissance of causal explanations in historiography.[1] In view of some excesses of postmodernism in the last two decades of the last century, when already the usage of terms such as *case studies, structure,* and *explanation* aroused suspicions,[2] this change should be welcomed. This is especially true for the research about the history of democracy. However, today's comparativists should be more careful about causal explanations and correlations, if they do not want to run into traps as Barrington Moore did in his book on the social preconditions of democracy (Moore 1967). Moore's sweeping attempts to correlate causes and effects over several centuries of history and his sole reliance on social structures set an example for a lot of comparative studies. The overstretched comparisons of the 1960s and 1970s can be seen as one the reasons for the postmodern reaction in the last two decades of the twentieth century.

Proving a causal relationship between democracy and ethnic diversity requires very careful definition of both terms, which actually goes beyond the scope of this chapter. Can ethnic structures really explain the success or failure of democracy, and does democracy lead to more or less ethnic diversity? For a definition of democratization, the definition as given in the introduction suffices; *ethnic diversity* needs more elaboration. This term describes a population or a society, which consists of various groups defined by political interests, language, culture, or other common denominators, which can be understood as ethnic. For academic purposes the term makes sense only if we can measure the ethnic composition of a society at a given moment and thus specify the form or degree of ethnic diversity.[3]

Ethnic diversity is a modern issue. Prior to the construction of modern nations and the invention of the nation-state in the nineteenth century, ethnicity or nationality were not regarded as primary political problems or objects of societal discourse. One of the most participatory political systems of the early modern period, the Polish *Rzeczpospolita,* was also ethnically one of the most diverse countries on the continent (see Kamiński 2000). The ruling nobility did not perceive this as a problem, however, as long as its domination over other social groups was secure. All over early modern Europe, the most important cleavages of society were social or religious, and not linguistic or "ethnic." The governments and the social elites did not care much about the assimilation of various linguistic and cultural groups, but there was a lot of "natural" assimilation, especially if it was seen as a precondition of social and economic advancement. Hence, ethnic structures were already fluid then, but the changes were not perceived as fundamentally relevant for states and societies.

In the modern period the ethnic structure of states and societies developed into a political issue of primary importance. During the Enlightenment linguistic homogeneity became a value in the name of rationality and modernity; a multitude of languages and cultures in one state was viewed as a remnant of the past. In Central and Eastern Europe enlightened attempts to create unified language were a key factor in creating a popular basis of nationalism. Now the native language influenced individual prospects at school, of social advancement, and of participation in the legal and political system. Somebody who grew up speaking Czech in Joseph's Austria or a native Pole in Prussia did not have the same preconditions for a career as a German speaker, because first he had to learn German, and needed to master it well for bureaucratic or official affairs (Hroch 1999, 35–54). Hence, the universalism of enlightenment created new inequality when it was applied in linguistically mixed areas. One's nationality now mattered much more than before, and nationality itself was increasingly defined by language and other cultural denominators. It was one of the central aims of the national movements to unify and homogenize the population they were referring to. Homogenization took on a new dynamism in nation-states; linguistic and national diversity were viewed as detrimental to the "national interest" and as appropriate to abolish.

The attempts to build homogenous nations and nation-states contrasted with the increasing mixture of populations in Europe. In the nineteenth century, political, ethnic, and religious movements and migration for work were facilitated through quickly developing lines of communication and travel (Bade 2000). Some of the migrants were integrated in the areas and societies of arrival, but many of them tried to resist assimilation and thus followed the example of residual nationalities, which became increasingly aware of their own cultural and political traditions. Hence, we should stress not only the dimensions of change in democracy. Ethnic structures were rapidly changing as well.

Toward the end of the nineteenth century, through the invention of national statistics, national and ethnic diversity became a quantitative and scientific category. The increased frequency and quality of these statistics show that the ethnic composition of a territorial state was perceived as a process, which could and should be influenced by the government. Moreover, societies became involved in discourse about the unity or diversity of their populations. In the times of positivism and social Darwinism it became a common opinion that ethnic diversity (which would then rather have been termed national disunity) was not only negative, but could also be eradicated with scientific methods.

Independent of normative judgments, the national composition of any given population was understood as a process. Therefore, instead of burdening the term *ethnic diversity* with these dynamic elements, I prefer to talk about *ethnic diversification*, or if we want to take its antonym, *ethnic homogenization*. With these terms it is clear that we are dealing with a process, and not a static category. This terminological modification is not supposed to be an exercise in splitting hairs, but has consequences for the causal explanations we intend to get from this study. Instead of factors, which influence each other, we are dealing with interdependent processes. This essay concentrates on a special aspect of this interdependence, on ethnic homogenization as a negative factor for democratization.

The history of Central and Eastern Europe in the last third of the nineteenth and the first half of the twentieth century offers excellent empirical material to show the correlation between ethnic homogenization and the blockade of democratization, and even the abolishment of democracy and the establishment of nondemocratic rule. The basis for this causal explanation will be diachronic and intraregional comparisons within the wider territorial frame of Central and Eastern Europe, i.e., the landmass of the continent east of the river Rhine. The data are derived from past research about the failed democratization of imperial Germany, population policy, nationality policy, and migrations in various European countries, and the establishment of communist rule in postwar Poland and Czechoslovakia.

The Case of Imperial Germany

When the German Empire was established in 1871, its universal male suffrage on the federal level was progressive for European standards. In the two decades prior to its breakdown in 1918 imperial Germany was commonly viewed as a laggard in democratization and as an autocratic system. What brought about this change of positions within Europe? German social history has explained the alleged *Sonderweg* (peculiar path of development in modern history) of Germany mainly by the weakness of the bourgeoisie and of liberalism, rising class conflicts, and the discrepancy between economic modernity and political backwardness.[4]

In addition to this explanation one can put up the thesis that the most important factor for the stagnating and failing democratization was the Polish question. The German Empire viewed itself as a nation-state, although it had incorporated several million Poles and other minorities of Slavic origin. Until the middle of the nineteenth century it was thought that non-German speakers could be assimilated because of the supposedly higher level of German culture. Faith in a natural or automatic assimilation was severely weakened over time, in particular in the Polish partition, but the Prussian government was still convinced that it could forge different ethnicities into one nation. In 1872, one of the first crucial laws that were passed in the German Empire explicitly forbade any other language than German in elementary and religious education. The official goal of this policy was to reduce the influence of the Catholic Church, but it was also directed against the Polish national movement.

While the conflict between state and church (the *Kulturkampf*) was ended by a compromise a decade later, none of the anti-Polish measures was taken back. On the contrary, in 1886 the empire radicalized its policy and passed a law of settlement (*Gesetz betreffend die Beförderung deutscher Ansiedlungen in den Provinzen Westpreußen und Posen*), which explicitly aimed at changing the ethnic composition of the Polish partition and encouraged Germans to settle there. The law never worked as intended because many Germans from the eastern provinces continued to migrate to Berlin and the industrialized regions in the west. Poles also had higher birth rates, and their national movement continued to mobilize Slavic speakers and imbue them with a Polish national identity. The government reacted to the failure of its policy with ever more suppression. The rights of assembly, of forming associations, and of employment in the state service were severely curtailed in order to break the resistance against assimilation. Poles and other Slavic speakers were by law prohibited to use their language at school, at court, or in business. In 1908 the German government amended the law of settlement and allowed the dispossession of Polish landowners in favor of Germans. Because this amendment clearly violated the constitution, it aroused a lot of resistance, now also from liberals (Broszat 1963, 114). The winning argument of the government was, as it had been before, the national interest of the homogeneous nation-state. In his book about the Prussian partition of Poland William W. Hagen concluded that the policy against the Poles "was one of the monarchy's defenses against social and political modernization" (Hagen 1980, 199). Social democrats and left liberals observed the correlation between the blockade of democratization and the anti-Polish policy. But any change of Prussia's electoral system was precluded, because free elections would sweep Polish parties to power in several regions of the country. Thus, while the southern states of Germany liberalized their election systems in the beginning of the twentieth century, Prussia remained unreformed. Placed in a longer perspective, the law of settlement from 1886 set a dangerous precedent for entire East Central Europe. The manipulation of the ethnic composition of the population became a generally accepted political tool, which can be termed *national engineering*. The National Democrats in Poland, the most important nationalist party, copied this policy in their program in the beginning of the twentieth century. They demanded to settle ethnic Poles in the eastern borderlands in order to preserve their Polishness against the majority of Ukrainians. When Poland became independent the government partially adopted this policy in eastern Galicia and in Volhynia (Torzecki 1993 12). This population policy can also be viewed as a logical precursor of ethnic cleansing. When the borders changed in Central and Eastern Europe, as happened several times in the twentieth century, the new masters did all they could to remove the alleged settlers and colonizers from territories where the ethnic composition had been manipulated before. Hence, settling and unsettling were two closely related and often consecutive processes.

The Case of Imperial Austria

The correlation between ethnic homogenization and a lack of democratization becomes even more evident if one compares imperial Germany with the Habsburg Empire. In the partitions of Poland, Austria had acquired large swathes of Polish lands as well. Until the end of absolutism in 1861 Austria also made some attempts to Germanize the Polish population. However, it could not keep up its policy after several wars had been lost against Italy and Prussia between 1859 and 1866. In 1867, the same year the *Kulturkampf* started in Germany, the government granted the Austrian Poles a considerable degree of autonomy.[5] Polish became the administrative language of Galicia in 1872, and the theaters and the universities were Polonized. However, this political deal between the monarchy and the Polish nobility did not include the Ruthenians—or Ukrainians, as they increasingly called themselves. The Polish nobility resisted democratization because it would have endangered its national and its social domination of Galicia. In 1908 Polish-Ukrainian tensions culminated in the assassination of the highest government official, the Galician governor count Andrzej Potocki.[6] However, with the support of the central government a compromise was reached in 1913. The Polish elites accepted greater participation of the Ukrainians and the liberalization of the election system.

With this remarkable compromise, Galicia followed the example of Moravia and Bukovina, where the various ethnicities had reached similar solutions. The basis of these compromises, or *Ausgleiche*, was that the nationalities were supposed to be represented in the local and regional diets according to their proportion in the population, and could run their own affairs on this level. The durability of the Galician *Ausgleich* was never tested because of the outbreak of the First World War, and recent literature has also raised serious doubts about the two other compromises. Because they based political representation on nationality, they would have privileged ethnic over other political allegiances, which would only deepen the gaps among the various ethnic groups.[7] Yet there is no question that the search for a solution of nationality conflicts was a major impetus for the democratization of Austria. A better representation and hence integration of the nationalities had already motivated the government to introduce universal male suffrage for the federal diet in 1907.[8] But as important as the federal level was, democracy on a local scale was fostered by the far-reaching self-governance of the cities. The point here is not to idealize the Austrian experience, but to develop a comparative scheme.

One could summarize that the acceptance of ethnic diversity supported the democratization and the evolution of the *Rechtsstaat*, a state that respects and fosters the rule of law, while this development was blocked in Germany. The conclusions from this comparison are, however, not sufficient to address a more fundamental question: Could empires democratize themselves without endangering their very existence? The First World War and the breakdown of the Habsburg Empire in 1918 have deprived historians of the possibility of answering this question. Nevertheless, the case of Austria demonstrates that democratization and democracies do not require nation-states as a frame. At least in the long nineteenth century there were multiple ways toward democracy, which has been associated much too often with nation-states. The case of imperial Austria with its various regions also shows that ethnic diversity or even conflict does not necessarily prevent democratization, but can be an impetus for democratic reforms.

East Central Europe Between the Two World Wars

The interwar period provides additional empirical evidence for the initial thesis on the negative influence of ethnic homogenization on democratization, but before we go into details a few words need to be said about the existing literature: Postwar historiography in Eastern Europe has come to conclusions very different from our thesis and contends that the existence of large minorities destabilized Poland, Czechoslovakia, and other countries in the region. This opinion was shared by prominent historians in exile like Radomír Luža (1964). He pointed in particular at the fatal role of the Germans, who were widely seen as tools of the Nazis. Although the destructive influence of German minorities on interwar Poland and Czechoslovakia can hardly be denied, there always was a subscript behind these claims. Their purpose was to legitimize the postwar order, which was based on homogenous nation-states formed as a result of "ethnic cleansing."

The denunciation of minorities as hindrances to and even foes of democracy reached its climax at the end of the Second World War and is exemplified in Winston Churchill's speech in December of 1944 about the future of Poland. The British prime minister wanted to legitimize the westward shift of Poland and the population transfers he was proposing for East Central Europe, and in particular for the Poles living in the vast Polish territories annexed by the Soviet Union. His main argument was that the "mixture of populations" had caused "endless trouble" in the interwar period, and hence that there should be a "clean sweep" (1974,7069). Churchill's speech articulated common Western opinion about democracy and ethnic diversity. The British prime minister could imagine democracy only in combination with "proper" nation-states such as Britain or France.

But were minorities or ethnic diversity indeed the cause of all this trouble? We should also point to the problem caused by "nationalizing nation-states," as Rogers Brubaker has termed it.[9] The ruling elites in Poland adhered openly to the ideal of a nation-state formed according to the French model. As a result of this, interwar Poland pursued a homogenizing policy, and implemented it with a mixture of suppression, force, and national engineering. This policy backfired terribly. Especially the Ukrainians, who formed a majority in the southeastern provinces of Poland, were alienated from the second Polish Republic. The same is true for the Jews and in particular the Germans, although their treatment was still relatively mild compared to the French policy of *"purifier, centraliser, assimiler"* in Alsace after the First World War (Kohser-Spohn 2001). Hence, ethnic diversity indeed became a problem. However, in the Polish case, one needs to distinguish between the periods before and after the coup d'état of 1926. When Poland was still a democracy and its borders internationally settled, the internal ethnic relations were not always as tense as afterwards. In the authoritarian phase the relations with the Ukrainians and the Jews deteriorated. Moreover, the overthrow of democracy was not a result of interethnic clashes, but a response to a deep political crisis. There is no direct correlation between ethnic diversity and the failure of democracy in 1926. The history of southeastern European countries like Romania and Yugoslavia confirms the experience in interwar Poland. Once more assimilating and homogenizing policies had negative effects on democratization (Banac 1984, 214–25).

Interwar Czechoslovakia stood in contrast to these cases of failed democratization. As in Poland there was some violence right after the formation of new borders in 1918, but interethnic tensions calmed down in the 1920s. Czechoslovakia was one of the few countries in Central Europe that did not pursue a strong homogenizing policy. Certain imbalances existed also there and were shown in the very name of the state, where the second-largest nationality, the Germans, were not represented at all. In the economy, the political system, and especially the state administration, there was a bias in favor of Czechs. Hence, one should refrain from idealizing Masaryk's republic, which was also a nationalizing nation-state. Yet interwar Czechoslovakia never pursued a policy of national engineering, and it did not consistently suppress minority schools, universities, or the cultural life of the Germans.[10] For a certain period in the 1920s Germans participated in the government. The political system was so stable that it actually suffered from a lack of change and the inclusion of new elites in the 1930s (Křen 2000, 179–203). As we all know there was no happy ending in the Czech case. From 1935 Hitler was able to mobilize the German population across the border. Yet the end came because of intervention from abroad—the Munich Treaty in 1938—when France and Great Britain deserted their previous ally.

Summing up, interwar Czechoslovakia can serve as the basis for a counterfactual argument. It was the absence of a homogenization policy and the acceptance of ethnic diversity that stabilized the democracy in the 1920s. However, the end of Czechoslovakia is as telling as its intermediary success. When France and England allowed the secession of the Sudetenland in 1938, they based their decision on democratic votes. They argued that the vast majority of the Sudeten-Germans had supported the secession from Czechoslovakia and cast their ballot accordingly. Although this argument was clearly driven by the need to legitimize the Munich agreement and the appeasement of Hitler, the majority of the Sudeten-Germans had indeed voted several times for their most secessionist and nationalist party.[11] Hence they had democratically decided against democratic Czechoslovakia and in favor of a notorious dictatorship. As the split of Czechoslovakia in 1993 demonstrated, multinational states and ethnic diversity can be ended through democratic elections. So democracy can also be a tool to get rid of ethnic diversity.

Postwar Poland and Czechoslovakia

The final argument about the negative correlation between ethnic homogenization and democratization can be based on the postwar period. Between 1945 and 1948 almost all of East Central Europe was ethnically homogenized. About 12 million Germans, 2.1 million Poles, and hundreds of thousands Ukrainians, Finns, and Hungarians, to name but a few nations most severely affected by the change of state borders and ethnic boundaries, were forced to migrate from the lands where they were born to their alleged home-countries (Ther 2001a, 52–58). This is not the place to deal normatively with the details of this inhumane *repatriation*, as the allied and communist propaganda termed the process. For the purpose of this chapter the focus rests upon the effects of this ethnic homogenization on the countries and societies affected by it.

In 1938 Poland and Czechoslovakia had been countries with minority populations of roughly one-third. In 1948, 95 percent of the inhabitants of Poland were Catholic Poles. In 1938, only two-thirds of the population of Czechoslovakia belonged to its two state nations. By 1948, the country was 94 percent Czech and Slovak. This homogenization process was at first initiated by Nazi Germany in 1938. After the Germans had annexed the Sudetenland and large parts of western Poland, they forced several hundreds of thousands Czechs and more than a million Poles to move out of these territories in order to build up a racially clean German *Lebensraum*. The Nazis also murdered six million Jews in the Holocaust. Hence, the ethnic composition of Central Europe was already dramatically changed by the end of 1944.[12]

When the Allies continued the ethnic homogenization after 1944 they hoped that the states of East Central Europe could be stabilized and return to democracy. However, it soon turned out that large scale ethnic cleansing was an excellent tool for the establishment of communist rule. Stalin recognized this very early and engaged the Soviet Union in the implementation of population transfers. He supported them especially in the case of the Germans in East Central Europe and of the Ukrainians in Poland, but he also compelled reluctant governments like the Hungarian to implement the Potsdam Treaty (Tóth 1997, 98–100). Between 1945 and 1948 East Central Europe not only saw an unprecedented transfer of people, but also of property. In Czechoslovakia, in October 1945, president Edvard Beneš collectively dispossessed the Germans, Magyars, and other so-called traitors. As a result of the Beneš decrees, 11,200 factories; 55,000 small businesses; 125,000 farms; 200,000 one-family houses; and almost 3 million hectares of land were nationalized (Suppan 1997, 9–32). This transfer of people and property violated principles and laws of a state ruled by law and thus weakened one of the cornerstones of the democratic system.

In Poland the impact of the transfer on the property structure was even more profound than in Czechoslovakia. The factories, farms, and houses that were situated on a third of the entire postwar territory of Poland fell to the hands of the state. Of the entire amount of 6 million hectares distributed in the Polish land reform after the Second World War, 80 percent came from previous German ownership (Słabek 1972, 262). Additionally, the government acquired the previously Jewish property stolen by the Nazis. Hence, a large proportion of the Polish economy was owned by the state by 1945.

Governments in East Central Europe used these ample resources in several ways, but in particular to strengthen their power. First, the property of forced migrants provided capital stock for social redistribution such as land reform. For example, until June 1947 the Polish government had created 48,528 new farms in central Poland, 389,993 in the previous German territories, and enlarged thousands of already existing small farms to make them more profitable. Second, the property was distributed to build up allegiances between the communists and the populace, and to reward party members for their services. As the Czech historian Zdeněk Radvanovský has shown, not only land, but also family houses, apartment, shops, and small companies were handed over to communists and to potential voters for the party (Radvanovský, 2001, 241–62). The results of the 1946 election in the Czech borderlands indicate that this tactic worked. The Czech Communist Party *Komunisticka Strana Československa* (KSČ) was particularly successful in mobilizing voters in areas that had previously been ethnically cleansed.[13] The same is true for Poland, where the communists scored their best results in the crucial 1946 referendum in those areas where the Germans had been driven out and replaced by Polish settlers.[14]

The transfer of ownership during and right after the Second World War was a major step on the way to a socialist economy. After 1948, the communists used the property of previous minorities to build up a Stalinist system. An example of this is again the land reform in Poland. In 1945/46 the government had distributed almost 6 million hectares of land. However, the recipients did not become owners in the legal sense, but got the farms, the machinery, and the cattle as usufructuaries. Soon after the falsified elections of 1947 the government began with the collectivization. Since most farmers did not have legal titles of ownership for their land, they could not put up much resistance (see Lach 1993, 62–63). This explains why the collectivization proceeded very quickly in Polish regions previously inhabited by Germans and Ukrainians. All over East Central Europe, ethnically cleansed areas became experimental areas for the transformation of social and economic structures.

However, the ethnic homogenization after the Second World War did not create homogeneous societies. The minority population that had to leave Czechoslovakia and Poland was replaced by internal labor migrants. In the case of Poland there were also 2 million Poles, who had been expelled from the previous eastern territories of Poland, and more than 1 million so-called autochthons, i.e., former German citizens who were allowed to stay in postwar Poland. Although almost the entire society was ethnically Polish, it soon became deeply divided by new conflicts about property, political partic-ipation, and culture. The lines and forms of this confrontation were as deep and as violent as in previous interethnic conflicts in East Central Europe. There were mutual denunciations, violence, and even killings (Ther 1998, 301–19). Paradoxically, the failure of integration in the 1940s strengthened the position of the communists. In her monograph on the establishment of communist rule in Poland, Krystyna Kersten concludes that the fragmenta-tion of society due to forced migration weakened the resistance in the entire country. In the former eastern territories of Germany, the degree of solidar-ity among employees was especially low and the networks of the opposition weak (Kersten 1991, 308 and 318; (Kenney 1997, 335–46). There were fewer strikes and less resistance, and the communists could control the government much earlier and more thoroughly than in other parts of the country.

One can summarize that the final abolition of ethnic diversity in Central Europe supported the establishment of communist rule. It contributed to a nationalization of property, changed the social and economic structures to-ward a socialist economy, severely weakened the legal system, facilitated bringing the opposition into line, and destabilized the societies, which be-came less capable of resisting an oppressive regime. The example of Poland also indicates that the expulsion of various minorities did not reduce inter-nal conflicts. The confrontation between various population groups shows that ethnic homogeneity turned out to be a dangerous myth and not a tool to solve social and ethnic conflicts.

Conclusion

It may be hoped that this diachronic and interregional comparison has pro-vided sufficient evidence to support the initial thesis about the correlation between ethnic homogenization and the blockade of democratization. The measures necessary to substantially accelerate the assimilation of an ethnically diverse population are incompatible with a democratic system and a state that respects the rule of law. Forced assimilation requires the selection and suppression of groups that are the target of this policy, and is incompatible with the principle of equal treatment by law. It creates a special class of citizens, requires their over-representation in the legislature and the government, and has no other potential of development than ever more-refined modes of suppression. The more the various governments insisted on national engineering, the more likely it was that democratization would not only be blocked, but even reversed. This is also the main contrast between nationalizing states on the one hand, and early modern states and modern empires, which did not attempt to manipulate ethnic structures, on the other.

Moreover, acceptance of ethnic diversity never precluded the integration of various ethnic groups. Throughout nineteenth- and twentieth-century Central and Eastern Europe, small or politically unviable minorities were dissolved, the size of large ethnic groups changed considerably over time, and many people switched national identity during their lifetime or over several generations.[15] This change of identity was especially common in moments of political crisis, in the case of changing state borders, or when it was conceived as a precondition for social advancement. Especially in ethnically mixed areas, national identities were influenced by circumstance and by the attractiveness of various options of identification. However, during the nineteenth century this individual assimilation slowed, because of increasing migration and the rising self-awareness of ethnic and national groups. It is one of the paradoxes of modern history that the unification and homogenization of newly constructed nations and nation-states was accompanied by ethnic diversification. Democracy did not fare well in countries and societies that could not tolerate this paradox.

In imperial Germany the decreasing acceptance of ethnic diversity in regard to several Slavic minorities, Alsatians, and Danes, and in particular the Poles, blocked and damaged democratization. This negative development stands in contrast to imperial Austria, where the need to mediate among various nationalities and to solve conflicts among them was an important impulse for more democratic representation and a strengthening of the legal system. Additionally, the case of Austria shows that empires can democratize and that democracy is not bound to the frame of the nation-state. In the interwar period the negative influence of nationalizing policies on democratization can be demonstrated with the cases of Poland, Romania, and Yugoslavia. The history of Czechoslovakia shows that the acceptance of ethnic diversity was a precondition for a thriving democracy. The postwar period confirms this thesis under opposite circumstances. In Poland and in Czechoslovakia the radical homogenization of the population was a major factor in the establishment of communist rule.

However, so far this conclusion has touched only upon one dimension of the relationship between democratization and ethnic diversification. The question how democracies can cope with ethnic diversity can only partially be answered. The example of interwar Czechoslovakia provides some evidence for the thesis that the more ethnically different groups are integrated in the political system the more a democracy is stabilized. This conclusion is underlined by the history of the United States and of many postwar democracies in Europe. But what does this precondition of integration mean for concrete minority policies? History has shown that universalism or the application of equal rights can also create new inequality. If minorities are treated as equal citizens today, does this indeed create equality and would it be perceived as equal treatment by the minority itself? The discrepancy between actual minority politics and their perception was one of the main internal reasons for the breakdown of interwar Czechoslovakia. The German minority was in fact less discriminated in the state of the Czechs and the Slovaks than anywhere else in Central Europe or in France. By the standards of the time the Germans fared well in Czechoslovakia. But at the same time they were insufficiently integrated on a symbolic level, and hence never identified themselves with Masaryk's republic as *their* democracy. And if ethnically diverse groups receive special treatment, as in the American model of affirmative action, how does the majority of a society react to this? The problem for historians is that the experience of democracy in ethnically diverse societies is relatively short, in particular in Europe, where most democratic countries were ethnically homogeneous until the import of foreign labor and the end of colonialism in the 1960s. Since then democracy has been thriving regardless of an increasing ethnic diversity in most of Western Europe. However, all countries of the European Union were based on nineteenth-century concepts of nation-states. The major challenge seems to be to develop this ideology in a way that the democratic systems of these countries can cope with an increasing ethnic diversity in the future.

A couple of conclusions can also be derived from the repeated failure of democracy in Central and Eastern Europe. One of the primary reasons for the tragedy of the interwar period was the implementation of *one* western model of democracy. When Poland, Romania, and Yugoslavia turned into nationalizing nation-states, they did this not just because of their urge to unify their nations internally. They also pursued these homogenizing policies because they adhered to an administrative system according to the French model. Hence, there were various motivations for centralizing states and homogenizing populations. The problem was not only a supposedly eastern European version of nationalism—which simply does not exist—but also the Western model and its inflexible implementation. In view of the fact that most of the non-European world is still ethnically mixed, one can only warn against repeating this mistake and implementing democratic systems formed in and according to the needs of ethnically homogenous countries and societies. Democratic systems need to be adapted to degrees and various forms of ethnic diversity.

CHAPTER SEVEN

Democracy and Multinationality in East Central Europe

The External Factor

ANDREW C. JANOS

One may well argue that the study of politics became scientific when the Aristotelian *polis* turned into a Copernican "system," interdependent and integrated both vertically and horizontally. In this two-dimensional system, vertical integration refers to the structure, scope, and exercise of public authority; horizontal integration to principles and practices that engender solidarity and legitimize the spatial and geographical boundaries of the state.

The enterprise to which the title of this chapter refers is to raise questions concerning the relationship between the horizontal and vertical integration of political systems. Democracy is one particular way in which authority is being exercised. To invoke a piece of Aristotelian wisdom, it refers to a form of government in which the few who govern are accountable to the many (1957, 69). On the other hand, nationality, whether of the "mono" or "multi" variety, is a category that is likely to have some bearing on the horizontal integration and the spatial-demographic boundaries of the state. Hence the questions raised and the study proposed represent justified curiosity. For where national groups prefer to form their own political community rather than live in a multinational state, or vice versa, they will question the legitimacy of the arrangement, and in this manner disrupt the consensus on which the smooth functioning of democratic institutions must rest.

This chapter will approach this particular relationship by making comparisons over space and time. Spatial comparisons will be made between the countries of Western and Eastern Europe, or, more accurately, between the countries of East Central Europe and the northwest "triangle" of the Continent. Chronologically, the essay will compare ethnopolitics during three waves of democratization in East Central Europe: one during the "long" nineteenth century, the heyday of classical nationalism; another following the First World War, quickly aborted by the rise of totalitarianism under German and soviet auspices; the third following the demise of the Soviet Union (1989–92). All three of these waves of democratization were set in motion by the West, albeit each time with different instrumentalities, objectives, and intensity. Comparing them will illuminate the role and dimensions of the *external factors* of power and influence, all too frequently ignored by contemporary studies of democratization and nation building.

The Terms of the Discourse

In order to lay out the terms of discourse, we will have to start by clarifying the concepts of *ethnicity* and *nationality*. As will be used here, ethnicity refers to a two-dimensional concept. As objective reality, ethnicity relates to the existence of perceptible social markers—such as language (accent, dialect, family name), cultural practices (often rooted in religion), or physical features (race)—generally acquired upon birth or by early socialization. These markers, however, become *social facts* only when actors—be they bearers of the markers or outsiders—begin to perceive them and attach to them social significance as standards of inclusion and exclusion.

Defining *nation* is somewhat more problematic, for throughout much of European history it has been used with two significantly different meanings. Derived from the Latin *nascere*, in reference to birth, it has been used either to designate people born at the same location or as a synonym for *gens*, referring to parentage and bloodline. The contemporary distinction between *civic* and *ethnic* nations reflects this essentially medieval usage. However, a closer examination of modern texts suggests that the derivatives of the term nation—national, nationality, nationalism—are almost always used with ethnic connotations, a standard to be followed in this essay as well.

As students of ethnography and political sociology are struggling with these definitions, they are also divided on a number of issues related to the concepts hiding behind the terminology. One of these divisions concerns the relationship between the objective and the subjective dimensions of ethnicity and the malleability of ethnically based social and political identities. The main dividing line on this issue runs between *primordialists* and *instrumentalists* (alternatively *contextualists*). The former believe that the relationship between ethnic marker and ethnic awareness is natural, and is predicated upon intuition, instinct, and impulse; that the relationship between social markers and ethnic awareness is change-resistant, natural, instinctual, and devoid of calculations of cost and benefit. On the other hand, contextualists hold that ethnic markers acquire relevance in particular situations and that they will be brought forward and mobilized either by human intervention or by impersonal social forces. One of the side benefits of this study will be an opportunity to participate in adjudicating this issue.

The conceptual problem of the external factor raises questions concerning the proper understanding of the *social system*. Classical sociology has generally defined the social system in terms of the division of labor or culture often enclosed within political boundaries. Its paradigm told us that if we wanted to understand, say, French or Bulgarian politics, we should start our inquiry by exploring the structural and cultural configurations of the underlying French or Bulgarian societies. More recently, however, social scientists have found this paradigm too narrow and confining. Thus, they have started to refocus attention on the global division of labor, configurations of power relations among states, and on the global relevance of the material culture of a number of leading or hegemonic societies in a modern world system (see, among others, Wallerstein 1974; Wallerstein 1984; Nurkse 1962; and Mann 1988). All this meant a realization that changes in the economic structure of Country A may provide better explanations for political changes in Country B than do structural changes in B itself.

To be more specific, when talking about the external factor we are speaking of economic and political factors, which may have an impact on domestic institutions and behavior by exerting either influence or power. As to the former, it operates through demonstration effects that are independent from the volition of those taken as a model. Most prominently, we are dealing here with the demonstration effect of the consumer cultures of "advanced" or "pioneering" societies on consumption patterns and aspirations in less developed countries; alternatively with the demonstration effect of institutional innovations that, on account of their success in one particular environment, become objects of imitation in another. Still more obviously, and directly, external factors may operate through the political will and resources of one state mobilized to shape the institutions, personnel, and policies of another. These external forces may be incidental, related to a particular political move, or they may be institutionalized in the form of a stable, hegemonic, or patron-client relationship. Our study of three waves of democratization in East Central Europe will provide us with an opportunity to focus on the contrasts among these types of external forces at work.

The Nation-State and Democracy: The Influence of the Western Model

There is a near-complete consensus ranging from the classics to modern historians and social scientists that links the historical rise of representative government to the technological revolutions of Europe in the postmedieval period. A revolution in the means of production created surplus and a class of risk-taking entrepreneurs, whose experience made them natural opponents of hereditary privilege. Meanwhile, revolutions in the technology of warfare—the invention of gunpowder and advances in metallurgy—diminished the social utility of warrior aristocracies and undermined justifications for their privileges. Finally, revolutions in the technologies of communication and transportation expanded the potential scope of both markets and centralized control over administration. Overall, these revolutions changed the balance of man-to-nature relations: rather than being slaves of the forces of nature, people suddenly saw themselves as masters of the material world. Then, slowly but inexorably, this new sense of personal efficacy spilled over into social and political relations, encouraging the belief that people can not only control the forces of nature but their own personal destiny and government as well. By the eighteenth century the view became widespread that political authority must reflect, and be subject to, finite and discernible human purposes. As these beliefs matured, all over Atlantic Europe the terms of political participation were changed by legislation or revolution, first to include the proprietors of the new means of production, then, far more haltingly, the rest of society as well. In the classical case of Britain, the electoral reform of 1832 extended suffrage to a larger class of proprietors and taxpayers; the reform of 1867 included new classes; the legislation of 1882 made male suffrage universal; and, finally, the parliament acts of 1918 and 1927 brought women into the political process.

The causal nexus between the technological revolutions and the horizontal integration of societies is more complex. Three linkages here stand out in importance. First, as the capacity to produce surplus increased, producer-entrepreneurs developed an interest in expanding trade beyond narrow, regional boundaries. This objective was shared by the rising educated, and the declining traditional, classes who had an interest in expanding the size of public administration and hence in the expansion of the territorial boundaries of core states. Second, improvements in agricultural production—commonly described as the agricultural revolution—diminished the number and ratio of people necessary for the production of comestibles. As a corollary, more people became available for alternative pursuits, including navigation and military service, which increased the size of navies and armies. As the numbers of men under arms increased—from tens of thousands to hundreds of thousands between 1700 and 1800, then to millions by the end of the nineteenth century, and to tens of millions during the two world wars—demography became an important asset in international politics and another force behind the desire for territorial expansion. Third, there was the already-mentioned growth in the political awareness of the masses that made it more and more important for elites to be in touch with mass constituencies. This, in turn, required mutually intelligible codes of communication. It was for this reason, then, that a common language gained importance and began to serve as a logical roadmap for territorial expansion driven by both economic and political considerations.

Ironically, in view of its widespread acceptance, this ideal-typical model of nation building does not adequately summarize the historical experience of Britain and France, the two pioneers of European nationhood. In brief, the territorial expansion of these states, whether driven by markets or absolutist governments, did not follow linguistic markers and could not be construed as instances of national unification. In the case of Britain, the modern nation with a common supraregional identity emerged after the territorial expansion of England into the Celtic provinces of Wales, Eire, and Scotland (see Dietz 1932; Nairn 1977). In the case of France, the rise of the modern nation-state followed the expansion of Île-de-France into neighboring, feudal domains—Bordeaux (in 1451), Grenoble (1455), Dijon (1477), Aix (1501), and Rouen (1534)—whose inhabitants originally spoke mutually incomprehensible local tongues: Occitan (with regional variations in Provence, Gascony, and the Auvergne), Basque, Breton, Picardian, Flemish, and Corsican (Potter 1955, 1–6). But in both cases, territorial expansion was rapidly followed by the abolition of tariffs and other barriers to trade, the building of an up-to-date transportation system, and, in the case of France, a highly centralized system of administration. This, in turn, was followed by the adoption of the core region's language in the newly incorporated peripheral regions. In France the process was hastened by the creation early on of a highly centralized educational system. But in neither one of the countries was linguistic homogenization strenuously resisted. Indeed, it can be described as a spontaneous process in response to economic opportunities provided by the rise of supraregional markets, by the expansion of overseas trade and colonial administration (in the case of Britain), by employment opportunities in the centralized bureaucracy (of France), and, overall, by the aura of great power status that both of these countries acquired in the process of state building. In Britain, as Ernst Haas so tellingly observes, a diverse population and its local leaders willingly acquired a common language and supraregional identity, because "being British was seen as being a member of the world's premier trading nation, of a nation devoted to manufacturing quality goods and rendering reliable service, a nation being able to back up its overseas commitments and interests with adequate military force when this seemed required" (Haas 1997, 108). As to the experience of France, John Stuart Mill's words had a ring of validity when he argued that "nobody can suppose that it is not more beneficial to a Breton or a Basque of French Navarre to be brought into the current ideas and feelings of a highly civilized and cultivated people to be a member of the French nationality than to sulk on his own rocks, the half savage relic of past times" (1963, 549).

The rise of Britain and France may be seen as the first acts in the drama of the rise of the modern nation-state that played itself out under a unique conjuncture of events and without following a blueprint. But the impact of the economic and political success of these pioneering countries was nothing short of stupendous, for their example, as indeed their very existence, cast a long shadow across the European continent. The impulse to imitate was particularly strong among Germans and Italians, who felt the impact of French military might and who, unlike the inhabitants of France and the British Isles, were members of large and relatively homogeneous ethnolinguistic communities though divided by political boundaries. German and Italian nationalism were thus nurtured both by the demonstration effect of the new form of state and by the thrust of foreign military power into their territories during the Napoleonic wars. In 1870–71 the project of national unification was accomplished. But unification was not tantamount to democratization. While some of the institutions of Britain and the political rhetoric of France were adopted, both Italy and Germany were divided societies plagued by great disparities of wealth and power among their diverse regions. This contributed to the rise of hybrid political orders in both countries, in that the institutions of representative government were forced to share the public sphere with powerful bureaucracies, either acting on their own or under the effective control of the monarchy.

Whatever perils the nationalism of Italy and Germany entailed to international peace, these countries became great powers upon unification, strengthening the belief across the Continent that political unification *cum* cultural and linguistic homogeneity represented the highest level of political development that any society could attain. In Eastern Europe, to be sure, the rise of Germany brought not just new evidence for the universal relevance of the nation-state model, but also a sense of the clear and imminent danger of great power hegemony. Italy's example, less threatening than Germany's, was romanticized more. Thus, Serbian nationalists designated their small country as the *Pijemont* of South Slavs, Romanian liberals adopted the name of the *carbonarii* (*carvunării*) used by the Italian nationalist underground, and Hungarian nationalists were singing popular songs about Garibaldi as the liberator from Austrian rule. Still, the most favored model was France, a country less threatening by the middle of the nineteenth century and somewhat distant, so that these East European nationalists became the correspondents of

Michelet, Montalbert, and Lamartine as they were pondering the prospects of liberation and national unification (see Campbell 1971, esp. 103–55; Body 1972). Poles, Bulgarians, Czechs, and Slovaks were not far behind.

The problem was that, while the model was enthusiastically embraced, there were substantial differences between pioneers and followers, and between the western and the eastern parts of the Continent. Let us start with their economies, which, in comparison with England and France (as indeed with Germany and Italy) were underdeveloped, in that they had not participated in the great initial thrusts of the agricultural and industrial revolutions. While the slow diffusion of agricultural innovations from the northwest toward the south and east of the Continent had created clearly discernible differences in per capita productivity by the year 1800, the new material standards created by the industrial revolution of the core region (1780–1830) created a new material culture that was being diffused much faster in the form of aspirations than the technologies necessary to sustain it. This imbalance hindered any effort to catch up by undercutting propensities for saving among agrarian producers and the mercantile classes on the geographic peripheries. The story of the progressive reproduction of backwardness has been told elsewhere (Janos 1989; also Janos 1982). Here it is sufficient to remember that the premature adoption of western patterns of consumption by underdeveloped regions cut deep into the social margins of saving. This bankrupted traditional elites, both landed and commercial, and these elites, together with the upwardly mobile class of educated people, tried to find income and security via employment in the state. To be sure, in the small states of East Central Europe there was no state to turn to in the early nineteenth century. So, one after the other, these refugees from the unproductive traditional economic structures turned out to be the foremost protagonists of independent statehood. While all of these refugees from the economy rallied around the banners of liberalism, under the circumstances this liberalism acquired a cast quite different from that of its western counterparts. If western liberals had set out to liberate the entrepreneur, and eventually all citizens, from the tutelage of the state, the priority of the easterners was the liberation of the state from foreign tutelage. Once this goal was accomplished, the liberal rebels seized the apparatus of the states and turned them into revenue-raising instruments that would lift these new political classes to the level of material well-being enjoyed by their counterparts, the middle classes of France and Britain. In the process, they could justify their privileges by claiming to be the builders and protectors of national political communities. Strikingly, the builders of these new national states were often recruited from diverse ethnic communities. The new Romanian elite, for instance, included a large contingent of Greeks and Slavs, which prompted the German Foreign Minister (later Chancellor) Bernhard von Bülow to give us the nasty *bon mot* that Romanian was not a nationality but a profession. Derogatory in intent, this statement contained a great deal of sociological truth that was applicable to other East European countries as well, above all to Hungary. There, the first generations of nation builders included large percentages of Germans and Slavs, some of whom became star members of the cast in narratives of building the national state. But whatever their composition, the sustenance of these classes by public revenue required expenditures that evoked popular grumbling and which could be collected only by corrupting the institutions borrowed from the model countries of the West. Before 1914 parliaments did exist and function all through the region, but political machines built around centralized systems of public administration exercised strict control over the electoral process, thus corrupting the essence of representative government.

There was, however, yet another major difference between East Central Europe and the West, and this was the demographic fragmentation of populations among large numbers of ethnolinguistic groups. It was not just that there were many more ethnic groups per unit of space in this area than in the West, but that the diverse groups intermingled with each other geographically, producing a pattern in which different ethnic groups had to coexist with each other not just at the regional, but also at the municipal level. The most obvious examples of this were Transylvania; the Hungarian Bácska-Bánát (later, the Yugoslav Voivodina); Bosnia-Herzegovina; contemporary Slovakia (with its Slovaks, Hungarians, Germans, and Ruthenians); Bohemia-Moravia, with Germans and Czechs living side by side; the Krajina and Slavonia within the larger entity of Croatia; and the ethnic mosaics of Bukovina and Bessarabia, just to mention the most conspicuous examples of regional multiethnicity. This ethnic heterogeneity was perceived by contemporary nation builders with a degree of apprehension, above all by the Hungarians, who had started their project long before the revolutions of 1848, and then, by the terms of the *Ausgleich* of 1867, received a free hand to finish it. For some time, these misgivings were allayed by the example of France, which seemed to suggest that a multitude of linguistically different groups could be—with some effort—molded into a single French nationality.

But the French analogy turned out to be false and misleading. With hindsight we can cite three reasons for this. First, compared to France and Britain, the latecomers had neither the economic momentum nor the prestige of great-power status to provide incentives for voluntary linguistic assimilation or for the adoption of a double identity (as some Hungarians hoped in a memorable debate on this subject in the 1840s) (Barany 1968, 380–421). Second, and perhaps still more significant, was the fact that, precisely because of the earlier success of Britain and France, ethnolinguistic identities had not only gained in salience, but became virtually sacralized by future participants as the basis for the claim of political self-determination. Finally, unlike the potential assimilees of Britain and France, those of the East Central European states had adjacent kin states with national ambitions of their own that would act as magnets for conationals living under adjacent foreign jurisdictions.

One can harbor but little doubt that among the latecomers and imitators of initial nation-building projects this diversity diminished the horizontal integration of political communities and that its prevalence also detracted from the impulse to sustain democratic governments. In countries with large minority populations (like historical Hungary, where in 1900 only half of the population wanted to be counted as members of the ruling Magyar nation), the problem was not only how to distribute the contested social product, but also how to maintain the boundaries of the existing state, while at the same time maintaining some semblance of representative government. But the problem was not restricted to the Hungarian multinational state (enjoying a large measure of institutional autonomy within the Austro-Hungarian Monarchy). It was also shared by some of the ethnically homogeneous countries of the region, whose populations had their ethnic kin living outside the territorial boundaries of the national state. In these instances, the purpose of unification with conationals living outside their political boundaries put a strain on the functioning of parliamentary government by providing the bloated bureaucratic states with a proper pretext for pursuing their exploitative policies in the name of a commonly held, sacred objective.

In sum, economic backwardness and the ethnic fragmentation of the region interacted to foil incipient projects of democratization that were undertaken to gain respectability in the eyes of the economically advanced countries of the West. One can hardly doubt the relevance of both ethnicity and scarcity in explaining nondemocratic outcomes, but for the analyst the task remains to assign relative weight to these corrupting factors. This task is not easy, but it was attempted by the Hungarian premier István Tisza (1903–5, 1913–16) when he pleaded against the introduction of universal suffrage in the place of a census that had restricted voting to a mere 6 percent of the population. Under universal suffrage, he argued that

> entire regions of the country would be inevitably lost to the [Hungarian] national cause. Two- to three-hundred Hungarian deputies [of the then 413] in the House of Representatives would face 150 to 200 non-Hungarians, and a substantial part of the former would be controlled by the internationalist socialist movement. The rural constituencies would be stirred up by dema-gogues of all kinds. The serious representatives of a responsible national policy would be reduced to a handful.
>
> *Budapesti Hirlap*, October 5, 1905

If we can believe Tisza—and there are good reasons to trust his judg-ment—class and ethnic tensions had about equal weight in discouraging the ruling establishment from extending the suffrage. While the enfranchise-ment of non-Magyars raised the potential threat of diminishing the state—as happened after the lost war in 1918—the political empowerment of the lower classes would have raised the threat of expropriating land and capital on which policies of development were to rest. Historically, such prospects have not been favorable to reformism and have been more likely to result in civil war and dictatorship than in working democracy. If Count Tisza was not Disraeli's stripe of conservative, it was because Hungary in 1905 was not what Britain had been in 1867.

Aborted Second Wave and Totalitarianism

We should make it clear at this point that the East Central European proj-ects of nation building did not take place in an external political vacuum. The new states were being built in a continental environment dominated by a concert of great powers bound together by a common interest in extra-European expansion, and, closer to home, by the orderly liquidation of one of their "sick" members, the Ottoman Empire, facing the rebellion of its subject peoples. Operating through a consensual system upheld by the balance of power, the concert had a domestic agenda for the new states. It emphasized the importance of legality and domestic tranquillity (to protect international trade and investment), but did not make democracy a requirement for recognition and certification of their *bona fides*. How could it have?—since some of the great powers of the time, most notably Russia, shunned democratic institutions, and the institutions of Austria and Germany were not flawlessly democratic either. Thus, English gentlemen in their clubs and French intellectuals in their coffee houses would rail about the lack of political civility within the partnership of great powers. But as long as these partners paid their external debts, protected British trade, and did not massacre their own subjects, the concert treated the functioning of their political systems as a purely domestic matter.

This would change after the First World War. The war destroyed the old concert and the resultant vacuum was filled by a new international regime nominally under the aegis of the League of Nations (though in reality upheld by the victors of the war). Led by France and Britain, this international regime implied new territorial dispensations. In the place of Austria-Hungary, there emerged now a number of successor states: Czechoslovakia, Yugoslavia, Hungary, territorially expanded Romania, and Poland, together with Albania and Bulgaria, within boundaries drawn prior to the war. In deviation from earlier standards, and in an attempt to replicate the democratic principles of the League, as well as the domestic institutions of the victors, the agenda also included domestic political requirements, expecting the new states to have democratic governments based on universal suffrage. This was duly introduced across the region in 1918–20.

But this international regime had major flaws. First and foremost, although boundaries were drawn in the name of national self-determination and of creating ethnically homogeneous states, given the complexities of ethnic maps (and the security interests of the victors), these objectives had not been attained. The total population of the seven countries that now constituted East Central Europe (Albania, Bulgaria, Czechoslovakia, Hungary, Poland, Romania, and Yugoslavia) was reported in 1921 to number 82,551,000. Of this number, 21,330,000, or about 26 percent, were still living detached from the bulk of their conationals by political boundaries, in states they could not call their own (Seton-Watson 1962, 494–97). However, this percentage figure does not recognize differences between Czechs and Slovaks, or among Serbs, Croats, Slovenes, Bosnians, and Macedonians, all of which were lumped together by the early censuses under the Czechoslovak and the Yugoslav labels and which were ambivalent about their titular status in their new countries. If we recognize this fact, we must add at least another six million to the number of potential ethnic malcontents. This would raise the proportion of "minorities" to a whopping 38.7 percent of the total population of these "national" states (Seton-Watson 1962, 494–97), though it would still not account for parts of diaspora minorities like Jews and Gypsies—the former not generally recognized as an ethnic group, the latter purposely undercounted.

In an attempt to correct these discrepancies between the principle of national self-determination and the realities of multinationality, Articles 86 and 93 of the Versailles Treaty (and appropriate articles of the subsidiary treaties of peace) recognized a list of minority rights that the signatories had to guarantee. The minorities had to be granted citizens' rights, and allowances were to be made for the free practice of religion, as indeed for the freedom of teaching their spoken languages, albeit not necessarily from public funds.

However, the fact of the matter was that, from its inception, this international regime was too weak to enforce its agenda for the newly created states. Of the victors, Italy rebelled early against the regime, and the United States withdrew in disappointment over its imperfections. This left the French and the British as enforcers, a two-power alliance that was not sufficiently strong economically to provide the necessary material underpinnings for democracy, nor the military power to enforce violations of their dispensations on an ongoing basis. As a result, the agenda of the victorious powers was subverted by purely formal compliance with its tenets. Universal suffrage was introduced in 1920 in every state of the region. But the rigging of elections continued by new means: stealing and stuffing of ballot boxes, intimidating voters, banning of political parties of the Left, or by electoral laws that assigned bonuses to turn small pluralities into huge majorities. When such measures failed to produce safe numbers for the governments of the day, the universality of suffrage and the powers of parliament were whittled away. Thus Hungary returned to a more limited suffrage and the system of largely open voting in 1922, Albania in 1924, Poland in 1926, Yugoslavia in 1929, and Bulgaria in 1934. Minority rights were treated in the same cavalier manner, for under the guise of equality the landed property of minorities became subject to redistribution, exclusion from state services became common, and educational institutions associated with minorities became the subject of stringent and discriminatory regulation. Between 1918 and 1938 the number of schools of minorities declined radically.[1]

By 1938, the only country of the region where the electoral process remained free from manipulation and that recognized the legality of political parties (including the communists and the parties of the minorities) was Czechoslovakia. But even here certain outer limits were set to political and national agitation. This was accomplished by the passing of a series of statutes: the Administrative Laws of 1920 and 1922, which greatly diminished the autonomy of local governments; and the Law of Protection of the Republic (1923), which banned a great number of acts "committed or intended against the state." These restrictions were further augmented by the Statute on the Security of the Republic (1933), giving the police broad powers to investigate and bring charges against minorities and "autonomist" Slovaks and Ruthenians, to suspend their newspapers, and to curtail the activities of political parties on suspicion of subversion (Slapnicka 1975, esp. 141; Mamatey 1973, 99–167). It was thus with some justification that some scholars have described the regime as an "authoritarian democracy" (Bosl 1975, 139), though it would perhaps be more accurate to describe it, as we have described the German and Italian regimes, as a regime in which competencies in the public sphere were more or less evenly divided between parliamentary institutions and a heavily centralized bureaucracy. In this arrangement, parliament legislated and the electoral process remained uncorrupted. But the centralized bureaucracy inherited from Austrian rule retained a high degree of autonomy with respect to economic policy, defense, and the management of the less developed, eastern half of the Republic.

If in the 1920s democracy and minority rights existed only in form and not in substance, in the 1930s they became further weakened before becoming extinct altogether. Historical convention tends to attribute this erosion, and the simultaneous rise of openly authoritarian, one-party regimes, to the Great Depression. However, a more careful examination of facts and dates will reveal that the old quasi-parliamentarism (and in Czechoslovakia a working multiparty system) survived the crisis itself and that its demise started only in 1935 at a time when the economies were emerging from the depression and had begun to grow at respectable rates. The politics of one-party regimes became more conspicuous not because of growing economic desperation, but because of the progressive decline of Franco-British power on the Continent and the rise of Germany and Italy, first as new models that could be followed both by the radicals and the conservatives of the Right, then as hegemonic powers whose very existence became a significant calculus in the domestic politics of the lesser nations. Organized mass parties of the fascist type made impressive electoral gains in 1935 (Sudetenland), 1937 (Romania), and 1939 (Hungary). One-party regimes were set up in Romania (1938), Slovakia (1938), and Croatia (1941). In Poland (1937) and Hungary (1938) the governing parties acquired fascist trappings, but these coexisted with quasi-parliamentary institutions till the demise of the regimes (in 1939 and 1944 respectively). Much the same can be said about Yugoslavia under the Radical National Union government of Milan Stojadinović (1935–38). In Bulgaria no attempt was made to create official mass organizations with fascist trappings, but political parties were banned while the old quasi-parliamentary regime continued without them.

Under these regimes and, after 1939, under German hegemony, the status of minorities was revised along racial and radical nationalist lines. Ostentatiously and rhetorically racist, the wartime client regimes assigned a special status to the German and Jewish minorities, the former exempted *de jure* from the competence of local jurisdictions and obligations (including service in the local armies), the latter gradually deprived of all rights, eventually becoming subject to expropriation, concentration, and extermination. The net result of this regime is well known. It was the loss of some five million from the total population of the region and from its numerous minorities. Yet next to its genocidal impulses, German policy could also show considerable pragmatism. It could launch the massive resettlement of unwanted population groups—Poles from western Poland, Serbs from Croatia—while simultaneously encouraging tolerance toward the nationals of one client state—Hungary, Slovakia, Romania—now living on the territory of another as the result of the recent redrawing of the region's boundaries. Still more remarkably, and opportunistically, the racial teachings of German national socialism were practiced with considerable flexibility. While denounced in

Mein Kampf together with the rest of the "scum" whose sight presumably hastened Hitler's racial awareness (1971, 123), Hungarians, Croats, and Slovaks now became part of a larger "Aryan family." And in the last, manpower-strapped years of the Second World War, together with the Bosnians, Albanians, and the earlier-detested Ukrainians, they provided recruits for SS regiments that were once seen as the paragons of Nordic virility.

All this, and the vain hope for a new wave of democratization, were swept away by the rise of soviet hegemony after 1945. No friends of "bourgeois democracy," the soviets permitted the holding of relatively free elections in Czechoslovakia (1946) and Hungary (1945, 1947), only to nullify their results in 1948 with soviet-backed communist seizures of power. In all other countries of the region elections were rigged in the favor of communist-led coalitions. On the road to "people's democracy" and "democratic centralism," the soviets also annulled boundary changes that had been ordained by Germany and, in violation of their own universalistic ideology, sponsored radical measures of ethnic purification directed above all against the German minorities of East Central Europe. Lesser campaigns of cleansing—of the Turks of Bulgaria, the Albanians of Kosovo, and some of the Hungarians of Slovakia—were not directed but tolerated by the soviets. By such measures, the ethnic picture of East Central Europe was further "simplified." The proportion of officially declared national minorities declined from the interwar high of 26 percent to approximately 13.4 percent in 1980 (*The Statesmen's Yearbook* 1994). Once again, these numbers exclude "state peoples" like Croats, Slovenes, Muslims, Macedonians, and Slovaks, who now lived in federal states with which they did not identify, and these figures most likely still ignore large proportions of Gypsies, either by undercounting or by counting them as part of dominant ethnic groups.[2] Then, as now, the largest nondiaspora minority groups consisted of Hungarians (8 percent in Romania, 11 percent in Slovakia, and 2.5 percent in Serbia), Albanians (in Serbia-Montenegro, Macedonia, and Kosovo), the Greeks of Albania, and the German minority groups in Romania, Hungary, and Poland, where they resurfaced as ethnic groups after the fall of communism (*The Statesman's Yearbook* 1994).

Yet after having sponsored or tolerated rather brutal policies of ethnic simplification by purification, the soviets imposed a rather conciliatory and sophisticated ethnic regime on their satellites, based largely on their own experience with building and managing a large multinational state. In this model, peoples—whether majorities or minorities—were allowed, indeed encouraged, to cultivate their own language, folklore, and literature, and to construct their own historical narratives as so many "contributions to human progress"—as long as these activities did not run counter to imperial objectives and peace among the members of the bloc. Thus, while in 1945 soviet soldiers had been exhorted to "kill one German and then another" (Ehrenburg 1967, 26–27), the ideology was flexible enough to turn East Germans into model citizens of the bloc by reciting to them later that "Hitlers come and go, but the great German people will remain" (Naimark 1995, 76). In the same spirit, the remainder of German communities in Hungary and Romania were given cultural recognition, and the Hungarians of Transylvania territorial autonomy. Yugoslavia, and with some reluctance Czechoslovakia, were to follow variants of the soviet model for federalism. Problems remained with some of the diaspora peoples, above all, with Jews and Gypsies. As to the former, Stalin wavered between recognition, assimilation, and intimidation (while his successors accepted the option of emigration). As to the latter, assimilation became the official policy pursued with declining vigor with the passage of time.

Ironically, once Stalin died and his successors began to liberalize their control mechanisms over the lesser members of the bloc, many of the region's socialist leaders used their newly won freedom to diminish the status of minorities. They either chose a strategy of assimilation masquerading as benign neglect or returned to old historical narratives emphasizing the special contributions to progress of the majority nationality. In a few cases there was also blatant ethnic discrimination, as in the purge of Jews from the Polish intelligentsia (1968) or the violent anti-Turkish campaign of the Bulgarian government in the mid-1980s. But still, till the very end, in the majority of cases the universalistic rhetoric of the communist movement provided a thin veneer of civility in public discourse and policy.

The Third Wave: Ethnopolitics and Democracy under Western Leadership

In the recent spate of both academic and popular writing, developments in postcommunist East Central Europe have been described as a transition to democracy and capitalism. Whatever the justification for the use of a term evoking accomplished fact and success, it is important to bear in mind that these processes themselves are part of much broader changes in the international arena where East Central Europe has experienced a transition from soviet to western hegemony. While the term *hegemony*, with its implications of inequality, evokes an image of continuity, the character and agenda of this new international regime are vastly different not only from those of its soviet predecessor, but also from those of nineteenth-century liberalism. Compared to the latter, it is not only a harbinger of liberalization and democratization, but also of a new idea of political community in which ethnicity and sovereignty are subordinated to broad principles of universal obligations and rights. This new idea of political community challenges the Westphalian model of the nation-state with its emphasis on particularistic identities. Indeed, it not only negates, but, in the words of President Clinton, "combats, as a moral duty, tribalism . . . this oldest demon of human society" (*San Francisco Chronicle*, April 16, 1999, A1, A16).

The question is, then, why the West, comfortable in its prosperity, decided to be an active player in these borderlands of the Continent formerly under soviet rule. In the official pronouncements of the 1990s we encounter a great deal of idealistic rhetoric. But upon closer examination we find that the motivations for exerting power and influence in this part of the world were not altogether different from those of the previous hegemon, the Soviet Union. To be sure, and contrary to allegations frequently made, economic considerations were not paramount. When balancing costs and benefits of the recent past—mainly in balances of trade that have consistently favored the West—the advantages still appear to be minuscule, while the political risks have been substantial. On the other hand, much as in the case of the Soviet Union, considerations of collective security were significant. There was a well-justified perception of a need to forestall political chaos in this region adjacent to the cold-war West, with fears of disorderly mass migrations from East to West. There was also an unspoken fear of the revival of Russia and a desire to meet such a contingency on more favorable geostrategic terms. Last but not least, and once again as in the case of the soviets, there was a strong ideological impulse of self-validation among the social-liberal governments ruling most of the West, an impulse to demonstrate the universal viability and relevance of liberal social, political, and economic projects both to potential enemies abroad and to conservative skeptics at home.

Whatever the motivations, after the first wave of enthusiasm, the ambitious political agenda of the West ran into the resistance of powerful emotions rooted in the legacies of both the communist and the precommunist period in the East. For one thing, the states of the region were expected to surrender their sovereign rights just at the time when they were recovering from decades of soviet usurpation, long denounced by the West itself as an egregious insult to national sentiment. For another thing, the very logic of building new postnational communities required a new emphasis on minority rights, which went hand in hand with denouncing the privileges and asserting the culpability of ethnic majoritarianism. At times this bias is quite palpable in liberal rhetoric. In the words of one protagonist, the liberal project requires the rejection of "the myth of ethno-cultural neutrality" in favor of a new model of political community in which ethnic minorities can "demand certain group specific rights for the accommodation of their distinct identities" (Kymlicka and Opalski 2001, 6). As to ethnic majorities, liberals are not averse to advocating forceful measures of reeducation, censorship, the banning of textbooks that serve to articulate "national victimhood," and other measures "that may run counter to oft-expressed liberal principles" (Kaufman 2001, 216). At variance with both classical nationalism—in which majorities were assigned all the rights—and socialist internationalism—in which both majorities and minorities could create positive narratives of their accomplishments and identity—this model has become the most salient reason for the politics of majoritarian backlash. The discourse of backlash gains further impulse from the fact that the precise boundaries of minoritarian entitlements and grievances are hard to standardize and are said to depend "on the nature [and circumstances] of the minority group" (Kymlicka and Opalski 2001, 6). Free from legalism, the scope of these rights becomes subjectivized: whatever aggrieves a targeted group may *ipso facto* become a grievance. If defined and enforced by outsiders, this mode of community building will appear to the formerly dominant ethnic groups not only as a violation of the principle of equality, but also contrary to the majoritarian essence of democracy. Indeed, in some liberal discourse, this majoritarian essence is subject to nagging doubts. As one American student of the Balkans writes: "The liberal inclination is to leave political competition unconstrained and let the most popular politician win. The trouble with this formula is . . . that a national chauvinist [may] come to power" (Kaufman 2001, 216). Clearly, for the liberal democratizer, this is an agonizing dilemma, but voicing it will allow local populists and national radicals to denounce the universalist project as a sham and to portray themselves as the true guardians of free speech and democracy (Sajó 1997, 44–49).

While collective memory and the terms of past ethnic discourse have provided powerful catalysts for opponents of the Western project, they are by no means the only fountainheads of political resistance. Just as in the past, ethnic conflict may be fed by economic adversity, and in the postcommunist context, such adversity is widespread. Here again the legacies of communism and precommunism have a perverse way of reinforcing each other. On the one hand, dismantling the communist legacy of centralization has resulted in the "creative destruction" of production units that, in turn, is responsible for output collapse, trade deficits, and unemployment. This fallout is then aggravated by the precommunist legacy of backwardness and by the ever-present feeling of relative deprivation fed by obvious material differences between East and West. Soon enough, national and economic frustrations together turn into economic nationalism: the suspicion of foreign capital, entrepreneurship, and free trade that, in the form of protectionism, anticapitalism, and antiglobalism, are the centerpieces of populist and nationalist economic programs.

While these legacies and dilemmas have produced a considerable backlash to the Western project of liberalizaton and democratization, the intensity of the backlash is not uniform across the region. Nor are its extent and intensity random. To the contrary, it shows a definite pattern of correlation with both economics and demography. As to economics, the degree of "creative destruction" suffered by East European economies correlates closely with the country's degree of development *before* the advent of communism.[3] While on its face this seems to be counterintuitive, the explanation is that sectors of the economy once designed with an eye to the laws of the market have found it easier to adapt to their postcommunist milieu than branches of the economy built to produce for the soviet war economy or for consumers in communist societies with their artificially depressed expectations concerning the quality of products. Thus as Table 7.1 suggests, the larger the proportion of industries built under state socialist auspices, the greater has been the distress caused by output collapse and unemployment.

TABLE 7.1

Extent of Communist Industrialization and Per Capita Output Collapse
(in percentages)

	Industrialization[1]			Output Collapse (1994)	Unemployment (1993)	Distress Index[3]
	Pre-Communist (1938[2])	Communist (1980s)	Difference			
Czech Republic	59.6	66.9	7.3	19.0	3.2	22.2
Poland (1950)	37.1	52.0	14.9	8.9	15.4	24.3
Hungary	35.7	47.0	11.3	16.6	13.0	29.6
Bulgaria	18.3	50.9	32.6	27.7	16.0	43.7
Romania	28.4	57.1	28.7	27.0	9.0	36.0
Slovakia	35.9	61.8	25.9	22.1	13.5	35.6
Yugoslavia	17.6	42.4	24.8	n.a.	n.a.	n.a.
Slovenia	35.9	46.9	11.0	5.6	14.4	20.0
Croatia	22.5	38.5	15.9	16.0	17.2	33.2
Serbia	16.1	43.8	27.7	50.0	25.0	75.0
Bosnia-Herzegovina	17.1	50.6	33.5	n.a.	n.a.	n.a.
Macedonia	14.3	51.5	37.2	47.0	28.6	75.6
Montenegro	8.1	36.5	28.4	n.a.	n.a.	n.a.

[1] Percentage Contribution of industry to GDP
[2] Figures for Yugoslavia are from 1953
[3] Percent Output Collapse + Unemployment
SOURCES: Ivan Berend and György Ránki, *East Central Europe in the Nineteenth and Twentieth Centuries* (Budapest: Akadémia, 1977); M.C. Kaser and E. A. Radice, *The Economic History of Eastern Europe 1991-1975* (Oxford: Clarenden, 1975). For Yugoslavia: *Statisti?ki Godisnjak. Savezni Zavod za statistiku* (Beograd, 1989), 101-103. For output collapse: European Bank for Regional Development *Report (1994)*, (Brussels, 1996), 185.

The demographic profile of East Central European countries is likewise variable. Due as much to historical accidents as to more recent projects of ethnic engineering, some countries of the region—the Czech Republic, Hungary, Poland, and Slovenia—are more homogeneous than ever before. While at least two of the above four have diaspora minorities, none of them entered the postcommunist period with substantial minorities from adjacent kin states. To be sure, the presence of diaspora minorities—Roma and Jews—have engendered irritating antiminoritarian manifestations and public discourse. But as of 2004, radical populist parties have not been able to seize the helm of governments, and the mainstream parties have shown sufficient diligence in passing legislation that gives broad recognition to cultural, linguistic, and political rights. This has not been the case in the rest of the countries of the region, where ethnic strife flares up time and again, often laden with territorial implications. An attempt to summarize the record of this strife and the status of minorities appears on Table 7.2.

As one can expect from the foregoing, and as Table 7.3 illustrates, the variables—the level of economic development and the ethnic fragmentation of societies—do correlate with the trials and tribulations of the democratization project in the 1990s, even though, just as in earlier periods, it is

TABLE 7.2

Rival Minorities and Ethnic Conflict

Country	Minority (% of Pop.)		Treatment*	Record
Albania	Greeks (Tosk-Gheg Division)	3	4,5,6	ethnic violence
Bosnia-Herzegovina	Serb	31		ethnic violence; foreign intervention
	Muslim	45		
	Croat	19		
	"Other"	5		
Bulgaria	Turks	9	1,3,4,5	
	Pomaks	3		
	Roma	4		
Czech Republic	Slovak	0.2		
	Roma	0.1		
Croatia	Serbs	6	1,4,5,6	
	Roma	0.2		
Macedonia	Albanians	23	5	ethnic violence; foreign intervention
	Turkish	4		
	Serb	2		
	Roma	2		
Poland	German	1.3		
Romania	Hungarians	8	1,2,3,6	
	Roma	2.5		
Serbia	Albanians	17	1,4,5,6	ethnic violence; foreign intervention
	Hungarians	3		
Slovakia	Hungarians	11	1,2,3,6	
	Roma	2		
	Other Slav	1		
Slovenia	Croat	3		
	Serb	2		

* Explanation of coding on "treatment":
1 = defining citizenship in ethnic terms
2 = denial of use of language in education and local administration
3 = assimilationist pressure
4 = exclusionist pressure; expulsions
5 = electoral discrimination by gerrymandering
6 = institutional exclusion.

SOURCES: Stein 2000; McIntosh 1995; RFE/RL *Newsline* 1997–2000; Department of State 1999, "Ethnic Relations in a New Era," 45–58.

TABLE 7.3

Correlates of Democracy and Civil/Political Rights

	Democracy Index	Civil–Political Rights	Economics	Ethnic Homogeneity
Czech Republic	1.38	1.50	++	+
Hungary	1.44	1.67	++	+
Poland	1.44	1.78	++	+
Slovenia	1.88	1.69	++	+
Bulgaria	3.8	2.44	—	–
Slovakia	3.8	2.75	+–	–
Romania	3.9	3.56	—	–
Croatia	4.2	3.94	+–	–
Albania	4.5	4.06	—	–
Bosnia-Herzegovina	5.0	5.57	—	–
Macedonia	3.9	3.36	—	–
Yugoslavia	6.0	3.72	—	–

*Table 7.3 is reproduced here with the permission of the editors of *East European Politics and Society* from Andrew Janos's article in their journal, vol. 15, no 2 (Fall 2001), p. 244. The author also wishes to acknowledge the research assistance of Andrej Krickovic.

SOURCES: Boris Shor, "Nations in Transit: 1997 Freedom House Ratings," worldbank.org/ html/trans/mayjune97, 2–4; for civil and political rights, nine-year averages, see Freedom House, Freedom in the World, Philadelphia, 1999.

Explanation of coding:
Democracy/Civil Rights: 1 = highest; 7 = lowest
Economics: + = GDP high, ++ = GDP and precommunist industrialization high
Ethnic Homogeneity: + = homogenous

impossible to measure the relative weight of the two variables accurately. For the measurement of the dependent variable, democratization, we can use the index figures provided by Freedom House as averaged out by Boris Shor over time. Countries rated plus (+) on both independent variables also score highest with respect to democratization. Those countries that score minus (–) on both economics and ethnic homogeneity rank lower, while two countries, with mixed symbols, score in between.

From the Present to the Future

The symbols and figures on Table 7.3 show discernible variations among the countries of the region, above all, between the countries located in the northwest and the southeast tiers, the latter including Albania, Bulgaria, Romania, and the successor states of the former Yugoslavia. We should note, though, that in the new millennium (more precisely, after the Kosovo war of the spring of 1999) these distinctions became far less obvious and robust. Indeed, if we examine the countries of the region in purely institutional terms, we will find that as of this writing (in the fall of 2004) the peoples of all twelve countries of East Central Europe (plus the Kosovo province with its unsettled international status) live under democratic governments, whose rules and procedures have been deemed "free and fair" by a bevy of international observers. Meanwhile, the status of ethnic minorities in countries like Slovakia, Romania, and Bulgaria have notably improved, at least to the point that they are not subject to institutionalized and regular harassment. Indeed, their representatives have been co-opted as junior partners into ruling quasi-liberal coalitions. Macedonia—recently the scene of a nasty ethnic war—has found, under foreign tutelage, a formula for the momentary coexistence of Albanians and Slavo-Macedonians. There is now a democratic government in Serbia as well, elected without resorting to the fraudulent methods of the Milošević years. Mainly under pressure from the European Union, most countries introduced special programs for the benefit of the Roma, largely modeled after similar programs for disadvantaged minorities in the advanced societies of the West.

But not everything is in perfect order in the former communist countries of East Central Europe. For one thing, just as in the 1990s, multinationality remains a problem to be dealt with rather than one that has been resolved. This is most obvious in Bosnia-Herzegovina, Macedonia, and Kosovo, where the inhabitants of different nationalities still live next to each other with daggers drawn or, at best, uneasily sheathed. The situation is better in Slovakia and Romania, but even there, despite having been participants in parliamentary coalitions, Hungarians are grumbling about being forced to live in less-developed societies and under less well-managed governments than their kin live in the "mother country."

The politicians who have been the architects of these improvements have reasons to congratulate themselves for their accomplishments. Yet political realism dictates caution, and celebrations of democratic consolidation—based on such simplistic measures as the turnover of governments in two consecutive elections—are, to say the least, premature.

This is so, even though today perhaps all governments of the region meet this particular test. But the student of postcommunist government must be keenly aware of potential differences between form and substance, between overt behavior and underlying attitude. Indeed, for a keen political eye it will not be hard to discern these differences through a close examination of political rhetoric and public opinion. If we examine the latter, we can hardly escape the conclusion that political forms are correct because of the calculations of costs that deviance from hegemonic norms would incur. In most countries the principal calculus of compliance is economic. Even though sulking about their lot, the majority of the publics and of the elites sense that they have no viable alternative to entry into, or cooperation with, the European Union—but sulk they do. In polls conducted by the U.S. Department of State in 1999, 65 percent of Hungarians, 49 percent of Czechs, and 47 percent of Poles felt that the quality of their lives had deteriorated since 1989 (U.S. Department of State 2000, 5). The same survey found that 73 percent of Czechs, 79 percent of Hungarians, and 71 percent of Poles said that transition to democracy and capitalism had adversely affected their daily lives and been harmful to interpersonal relations (U.S. Department of State 2000, 5). (No data were collected in the Balkans, perhaps because they would have been still more distressing.)

Needless to say, these attitudes easily spill over into political life, where previous polls conducted by Richard Rose showed that even in the four best positioned countries of the northern tier, only 41 percent of the respondents professed strong commitment to democratic institutions, 43 percent were apathetic or cynical—saying they could see no appreciable difference between the communist and postcommunist institutional orders—while 16 percent expressed the view that the old regime was preferable to the new one (Rose 1997, 102). While much of this negativism is due to the disappointment of vastly exaggerated economic expectations, at least some of it is rooted in the moral and cultural re-ranking of ethnic groups and mutual suspicion between ethnic majorities and minorities. In any case, these opinions have been manifest in both public and elite behavior. While institutional norms are adhered to quite strictly, electoral campaigns and rhetoric tend to be vicious. In the last two years the Serbian electorate effectively boycotted presidential elections preventing orderly succession. In Hungary, where otherwise procedure reigns supreme, parties competing in recent electoral campaigns have regularly designated each other as communists and fascists. Indeed, so glowing have been these reciprocal hatreds that one may raise some doubt as to whether electoral outcomes would have been accepted in the absence of effective oversight by the West.

We must realize that in East Central Europe today we see political systems that are unique in the history of the region. In the precommunist past, governments broke their own rules and were the products of electoral corruption to protect themselves from popular discontent and from what they perceived as anarchy. Today we see procedural correctness and relative stability, which are largely the functions of external constraints. One can trust that a proper label will be soon found for this political type by a discipline that thrives on terminological innovation. Behind it, though, will lurk the sharp distinction made by Max Weber between political orders based on expedience versus those based on legitimacy. In dealing with the future of democracy and ethnopolitics in East Central Europe the question is not only when and how democracy will be consolidated, but whether and when it will acquire sufficient legitimacy to stand on its own, absent external tutelage.

CHAPTER EIGHT

Regions, Religions, and Ethnicity in Non-Western Europe

BRUNO NAARDEN

Since the days of Aristotle there has been a persistent tendency in western thinking to connect the distinguishing features of a people with their preference for a certain political system. This should make it easy to construct a link between ethnicity and democracy, or between ethnic diversity and the poor functioning of democracy, but actually it doesn't. For centuries European political theorists thought that certain types of people were fit for either despotic, monarchical, or republican government—democracy was excluded because it did not really exist anywhere and anyway was dismissed as a sort of mob rule. When after 1918 democracy became dominant in Europe, it was a weak and highly debatable form of political authority; when finally, after 1945, it reached a state of maturity, stability, and respectability, the conviction that every political system must have specific ethnic or national traits of its own disappeared. Such a belief in national characters, still rather common around 1900, seemed, half a century later, contaminated with racial prejudice and extreme nationalism. It was considered to be indecent. Moreover, it was not obvious from the beginning that ethnic diversity should be at variance with the principles of western political democracy. After all, this type of government is based on individual citizenship, a variety of political parties, and a multiform civic society. Democratic politics do not presuppose a homogeneous ethnic community. Whatever the advantages of national unity or social harmony may be, from a political-philosophic point of view ethnic diversity should not be an obstacle to democracy, but a perfect home for it.

However, political developments in Latin America and in postcolonial Asia and Africa support the idea that democracy was perhaps not the best rule for all peoples under all circumstances. In a vigorously democratic country like the United States it became doubtful whether society indeed formed a melting pot—creating Americans out of all immigrants. Unexpected political turbulence in some west European states was associated with large-scale immigration from Muslim countries. The eclipse of communism unleashed bloody conflicts in the Balkans and the Caucasus. Democratic reforms in many eastern European countries progressed slowly and inefficiently. All these examples seemed to confirm the impression that the cultural and social-psychological makeup of specific groups of people could undermine democracy or hamper its establishment. Since it did no longer seem profitable to approach this complicated subject with obsolete concepts like *race* or *national character* a new analytical tool was needed, and found in *ethnicity*, which seemed useful because it was at the same time vague and neutral.

Ethnicity has become *en vogue* in the past two decades. However, when democratic deficiencies are only the result of deep-seated mental attitudes, we can discard our hopes of any substantial improvement in the near and probably also the far future in many countries. A number of scholars and commentators think that it is definitely not helpful and perhaps insulting when outsiders put the blame for the political misfortune of nations or ethnic minorities on their collective psychology. Other observers however fully accept as almost irreconcilable dissimilarities between large groups of people, though they do not approach the issue from the vantage point of this book: In their opinion a weak propensity for democracy is not primarily related to ethnic diversity, whether or not this is a striking feature of a region, but can best be explained by the differences among civilizations and especially among religions.

In this essay, ethnicity as an explanatory factor of the Yugoslav civil war will be readdressed, citing two cases. First, a critical assessment is given of the opinion that the weak propensity for democratic change and economic reform in a number of East European countries can be blamed on Orthodox Christianity. Second, and in more detail, we will examine specifically the Yugoslav case. An effort will be made to understand, and to refute, the arguments of those statesmen, politicians, and commentators who discard the ethnic factor as a major cause in the violent dissolution of Tito's state.

Religion in Central and Eastern Europe

The idea that the character of civilizations is determined by religion and that "the fault-lines between civilizations will be the battle lines of the future" gained academic respectability with Samuel Huntington's *The Clash of Civilizations* (1996), in spite of the severe criticisms it provoked. According to some scholars and journalists, after the disappearance of the Iron Curtain a much older but no less formidable frontier had again become visible in Europe, the more than thousand-year old religious boundary between Rome and Byzantium, between Western-Latin Christianity and Eastern-Greek Orthodoxy. In their view, Orthodoxy is a religion of rigid rules and rituals. It is a church entirely lacking in social engagement, which slavishly submits to any type of political authority. The Orthodox regions were never oriented toward the West, as the argument runs, and as a result, they were left untouched by feudalism, the Gothic age, Humanism, the Reformation, and the Age of Reason, all defining aspects of our civilization. This is why the current processes of modernization and westernization are making such faltering progress in Orthodox Europe. It also explains the success of the transition from communism to a market economy and democracy in Catholic countries like Poland, Hungary, or the Czech Republic—which seemingly had been a part of Western Christianity.[1]

The one-sidedness of such historical explanations is rather appalling. They present Western and Central Europe as a unity, which it hardly ever was. Actually the border between Western and Eastern Christianity only played a minor role in the five centuries between the fall of Constantinople (1453) and the fall of communism. The disparities between Eastern and Western Christianity never generated a bloody and destructive series of wars like those that arose within Western Christianity in the sixteenth and seventeenth centuries. The Reformation and the Counter-Reformation had disastrous repercussions for Germany, the Czech lands, Slovakia, and Hungary. The famous discussions about the relationship between capitalism and religion generated by Max Weber and R. H. Tawney also primarily contrasted the prosperity of the Protestant northwest in early modern Europe with the decay of the Catholic southern and central parts of the continent.[2] The Catholic kings of Spain, Portugal, and France severely undermined the power of their states by expelling economically active religious minorities. Neither Muslim sultans nor Orthodox tsars ever did this.

Such facts make it difficult to generalize about the positive incentives for modernity of Western Christianity and the negative ones of Orthodoxy. The economic gap with northwestern Europe caused by the discovery of America and the establishment of the trans-Atlantic trade route proved difficult to bridge for the south and the east of Europe, and made the transition from absolutist to parliamentary rule far more complicated. In respect to religion, the central part of the Continent was still aligned with the West, but in respect to poor social and political circumstances, Central and Eastern Europe were almost equal. Serfdom was characteristic not only for Orthodox Russia after 1500, but also for the states that currently make up Central Europe. It did not exist, however, in Greece, Bulgaria, Serbia, and Montenegro. These Orthodox countries lost their political independence for a long period, but the same is true for Catholic states like Poland, the Czech lands, Hungary, and Croatia.[3] Also in the realm of culture the differences with the Orthodox East are less pronounced than is often assumed. Although central Europe took part in the Renaissance and Humanism it did not profit much from it; while the Enlightenment, Romanticism, and other, subsequent movements in western spiritual life also affected the Orthodox regions.

The historical relationship between church and state in the East is not basically different from that in the West, where most governments until the middle of the nineteenth century anxiously tried to retain power over religious affairs. The separation of church and state, which is now often presented as the essence of western political culture, occurred quite late and in most cases was never fully completed. Religion in Central and Eastern Europe did undergo something of a revival following the fall of communism, but Eastern Europe has been as affected as the rest of the modern world during the twentieth century by the processes of individualization and secularization. It is very unlikely that the mental attitude of more than 250 million East Europeans is still so strongly influenced by religious traditions that they refuse to support democratic reforms.

Nevertheless, it is obvious that countries like Poland, Hungary, the Czech Republic, Slovenia—and to a lesser extent also Slovakia, the Baltic states, and even Croatia—have adapted to new realities of postcommunism faster and more thoroughly than the former communist states in the eastern and southeastern parts of Europe—it is for this reason that central Europe is generally accepted as an area fundamentally aligned with the West. We tend to forget, though, that the concept of Central Europe is relatively new, and that its existence was only recently acknowledged. For chancellor Metternich Asia started outside Vienna at the *Landstrasse*, the road to Budapest (see Taylor 1964, 11; and Palmer 1972, 286). When in 1867 Emperor Franz Joseph was compelled to share his empire's power with the troublesome Magyars, his negotiator, Count Friedrich von Beust, reportedly promised his Hungarian counterparts: "Keep your barbarians under control and we'll do the same with ours." This meant that the Austrians would deal with the Poles, Czechs, and Slovenians, leaving the Hungarians to handle the Croats, the Slovakians, and some of the Serbs and Rumanians (see Dittrich 1992, 421–22).

At the same time other Germans put the idea of a Central Europe forward. When their country became the hub of the most famous *Dichter und Denker* in Europe it could challenge French hegemony in the realm of culture, stimulate the national awakening of the Slavic peoples, and also claim to be the real center of the continent. According to the historian Leopold von Ranke free and civilized Europe belonged to all German, Roman, and some Slavic peoples because it was the result of feudalism, the Renaissance, and the Reformation. Orthodox regions and especially Russia could be considered as non-European.[4] Until 1918, however, *Mitteleuropa* remained primarily a German idea. Its realization was precluded by the disagreements concerning the formation of a Greater or Lesser Germany, the nationalism of the non-German peoples, who feared German domination, and the outcome of the First World War.[5]

In the period that followed, non-Germans, like the Czech Tomáš Masaryk, became the proponents of a Central Europe formed by democratic, independent, and western-minded nations, but this concept met with little enthusiasm in the West. Although after the collapse of the Ottoman and Habsburg empires independence was granted to a variety of small countries, these new states were seen as a mixture of squabbling races and a danger to peace on the continent. At that time, hardly any distinction was drawn between Central Europe and the Balkans. Twenty years later, during the Munich crisis of 1938, Neville Chamberlain and members of his cabinet still referred to Czechoslovakia as an unstable, strange, and far away country, as "a very artificial creation with no real roots in the past." Contemporary British opinion on Poland and Hungary was equally negative.[6]

It was scarcely acknowledged in the West that in the beginning of the twentieth century these countries were already more highly developed and more modern than the more eastern and southeastern parts of Europe. The achievements of the Russian and Ottoman empires had been less impressive than those of the German powers. The regimes of the Habsburgs and Hohenzollerns retained authoritarian and reactionary traits, but during the nineteenth century they gradually accepted the rule of law; their civil service generally became more competent and less corrupt; and they paid more attention to mass education, economic improvement, and parliamentary rule. However, the lead that central Europe enjoyed over eastern and southeastern Europe was of little benefit in the years between the wars. And the worst-affected country was the most western of all, Germany. We have to conclude that during a very long period, religious boundaries were not deemed relevant, Central Europe was only an idea, and the differences of this presumed specific region with the West seemed more remarkable than its similarities. Why then is the present situation in the Czech Republic, Hungary, and Poland far more favorable than in most other former communist countries?

The successes of economic and political reform achieved by the Poles, the Czechs, and the Hungarians in the postcommunist period can perhaps be better understood by examining the more recent past. Already in 1920, Hungary had been compelled to relinquish two-thirds of its territory, with the result that one in three ethnic Hungarians ended up living outside Hungary proper. Hungary, Poland, and Czechoslovakia almost lost their important Jewish minorities during the Second World War. Further, Poland was ethnically cleansed as a result of Stalin's redrawing of frontiers and the resultant mass migrations. After 1945, the Czechs and Slovaks kicked out their

German fellow citizens. As a result of all these shifts, these states had become characterized by an ethnic homogeneity that was quite exceptional in the eastern part of Europe. This made it less difficult to stage revolts against soviet domination on a truly national scale. Hungary in 1956, Czechoslovakia in 1968, and Poland in 1980–81 aroused enormous sympathy in the West. They were hailed as sort of western outposts under foreign occupation.

During the 1970s and 1980s, the West became extremely susceptible to the opinion of intellectuals in these countries, who again presented Central Europe as a separate region that had been forcibly ripped by the Soviet Union from the bosom of the West. This situation was once aptly described as the "captive nation syndrome often accompanied by a glorification of dissent" (Nation 1995, 30, 32). Authors like the Czech Milan Kundera warmed up the almost forgotten ideas of Leopold von Ranke. Kundera conveniently claimed that the communist regime was "eastern" and repugnant, while the native culture of Central Europe should be seen as "western" in all respects.[7] Kundera and others succeeded in putting Central Europe back on the map. This was perpetuated after the fall of the Berlin Wall, when the three countries of the region not only made rapid advances in the process of transition, but also joined NATO, and, together with the Baltic States, were the first former communist countries to be admitted to the European Union.

Although the idea that Central Europe had already existed for centuries as a separate and almost completely western region was largely fiction, we may assume that belief in it became an important psychological factor. In comparison to countries like Russia, Ukraine, Bulgaria, Armenia, or Macedonia, opposition in Hungary, Czechoslovakia, and Poland could be more intense because it was fuelled by the rejection of communism as something totally alien and specifically nonwestern. Moreover, and more important, this spirit of rebellion was in fact nation-wide, given the ethnic homogeneity of these countries. These anticommunist rebellions, and the moral support they received from the West, further reinforced the perception among the Poles, Hungarians, and Czechs that they were essentially western nations—therefore their urgent desire "to come home," to return to Europe. The possibility cannot be excluded that, after 1989, this mentality contributed substantially to the development of a social-psychological climate in which economic and political changes were able to proceed at a faster pace than in other former communist countries.

Yugoslavia Before Its Dissolution

If we want to understand why certain analysts paid so little attention to the ethnic factor when discussing the causes of the downfall of communist Yugoslavia, it is instructive to have a look at the historic background. In the past, ethnic diversity and the absence of a working political democracy were seen rather as an advantage than as a problem of this country. In the beginning of the nineteenth century all native peoples on what later became generally known as the Balkan Peninsula were mostly called Greeks because of their religion. Initially Western Europe had shown more respect for the Turks as a dominant and strong race of rulers than for the peoples they had subjugated. This changed when these peoples started their exciting struggles to free themselves from the Ottoman yoke and when the European great powers became more and more involved in the area. A whole plethora of famous intellectuals and artists was inspired by the rebellious Greeks and Serbs, and gradually the European public learned to differentiate among "suffering Bulgarians, wild Albanians, martial Serbs and proud, brave Montenegrins." At that time their Orthodox faith provoked sympathy as fellow Christians suffering under Muslim rule (see Todorova 1997, 62–115).

There was much about the numerous peoples and regions of the Balkans that appealed to the imagination. In addition to an eventful history, they were characterized by a colorful folklore, violent revolutionary movements, secret societies, ethnic and religious contrasts, agricultural poverty as well as by bloody political conflict and instability. The Balkans appeared to be a region that had somehow managed to escape the tedium and bourgeois values that were gradually taking hold elsewhere in Europe. Dozens of adventure and gothic novels, thrillers, detective stories, comedies, operettas, and films about the area appeared around the turn of the century. They reached broad sections of the general public, and served to confirm the image of the peninsula as a charming, mysterious, semi-Asian corner of Europe.

Although ethnic differences and conflicts were regularly addressed, the majority of authors did not present these as the main cause for the peculiar and dangerous circumstances in the region—The general public was not interested in a rational diagnosis of the Balkans—that strange and unknown part of Europe would lose its special attraction if logical explanations for its exotic and eastern nature were offered—the literature did however often portray a marked contrast between the corrupt world of the capital cities, with their numerous political intrigues, and the purity, nobility, and heroism of the people in rural and mountainous areas. In their view the real, original Balkans—which were presented as "Europe in its cradle," as a "genuine un-spoiled Europe"—lay outside the cities, which were negatively influenced by western modernity (see Goldsworthy 1998). Great Britain and the Nether-lands broke off diplomatic relations with Serbia for several years, following the horrifying murder of the Serbian king and queen in Belgrade in 1903.[8] Existing prejudices were confirmed by the wholesale slaughter carried out by the Serbs in Kosovo in 1913, as well as by the assassination of the successor to the Austrian throne in Sarajevo in 1914. Disgust for Serbia or Balkan vi-olence was by no means a general phenomenon, however. The atrocities and ethnic cleansings during the two Balkan wars did not greatly upset the ma-jority of the newspaper readers in Western Europe. "Victories, charges with fixed bayonets, it was all great fun, but nobody realized how little was needed to kindle the flare-up in the Balkans into an inferno that would engulf the entire world" (Bartstra 1960, vol. 4, 299). When this happened in 1914 it si-lenced all criticisms of Serbia in the countries of the Entente. The Serbs were applauded as "the thoroughbreds of the Balkans," as "magnificent spec-imens of humanity" and as "the guardians of the Gate" of civilized Europe (Anzulovic 1999, 77–78, 121ff).

When in 1918 Yugoslavia had become an independent state, the rest of Europe remained well aware of the undemocratic character of its political life and the predominant role played in it by the Serbs. Neither did the ex-tremely bloody ethnic conflicts during the Second World War escape notice. In the perilous years between 1918 and 1945, however, there was not much incentive to study Yugoslavia objectively. It seemed far more important to back the strongest group and enlist its support to fortify one's own position in the international arena. After the Second World War it was no longer Serbia or Croatia, but Communist Yugoslavia that became such an attractive object of international competition. When Tito did not bow to Stalin, Yu-goslavia became the outcast of the soviet bloc and the favorite of the West. Over a period of four decades, it was the only communist country with which we were able to maintain significant and relatively intensive contacts. Its image in the West was mostly extraordinarily rosy.

It did not really matter that everyone knew that Yugoslavia had a one-party rule, with an unrivalled dictator at the pinnacle of power. Tito was considered to be "the friendliest dictator in the entire world" (Schroevers 1961, 24), while party and people were "fearlessly blazing new trails towards the fulfillment of their ideal" (Speyer 1951, 127). To some this remarkable national unity was the result of the rather liberal form of communism introduced after the rupture with the Soviet Union (see Newman 1954), while others believed that the Slavs' ancient "collective instincts" were at work in contemporary Yugoslavia. No less important was that the communist regime appeared to have found a workable and lasting solution to the nationalities issue. The ancient squabbles between Serbs and Croats had become quite harmless. Communist ideals had replaced ethnic nationalism and the inroads of modernization into peasant society had eroded the traditional culture of ethnic groups (Eekman 1955, 143–44, 175, 186, 200, 211, 218).

According to many observers assessments of Yugoslavia could not be based on western standards alone. Before the Second World War, the parliamentary system that had been copied from Western Europe had never worked properly in this region. western democracy seemed unsuited to the mentality of the population and would have been quite unable to unite the various ethnic groups. Even commentators who did not forget the cruel and bloody aspects of Yugoslav history, and who found its inhabitants' lethargy, slovenliness, and dirty habits intensely irritating, saw the advantages of the irrational inclinations of the Yugoslavs. These included their excessive sense of independence, their tough nonconformism, their amazingly original artistic sense, and especially their natural humanism and innate love of their fellow man. Yugoslavs rather gave than received. *Social* democracy was said to be better developed in Yugoslavia than it could have been in western *political* democracies, where "bureaucratic semi-dictators mitigated by ingrained parliamentary vices" held sway (Den Doolaard 1954, passim). "In Yugoslavia people actually believe in the dream that they have found paradise." Affluent western countries may have their five-day working week, but Yugoslavia had its "paradise," its "poor destitute paradise" (Schroevers 1961, 113–14).

Once it became clear that dreams of the future could no longer be projected onto the Soviet Union, many "political pilgrims" headed for Cuba, China, and Yugoslavia. Yugoslavia retained its charm as a poor and backward—thus cheap and exotic—tourist destination, but in addition, it began to be seen as a model and an example. This view was not restricted to left-wing intellectuals; it began to be shared by trades unionists and politicians. In particular the "breathtaking boldness" (De Rijk 1980, 7) of Yugoslavia's experiments with worker participation in industrial management seemed to point the way for many more highly developed capitalist societies. Even a number of western business companies were keen to promote "participative management" and professed their respect for Yugoslavia, where this concept was first developed (see Broekmeyer 1970). Eventually, most western academic specialists became convinced that labor participation in management simply did not work in Yugoslavia.[9] In general however until 1980 the image of communist Yugoslavia remained predominantly positive. Although the country's problems were not completely glossed over, for a long time they appeared to be less serious or more soluble than those in the rest of communist Europe. In the divided but stable world of the Cold War, the Balkans were no longer seen as a powder keg. It seemed that the old clichés about a barbaric, violent, exotic, and semi-Asian Yugoslavia were wearing rather thin.

For a long time, Tito's state was seen as a relatively westernized country. Its internal ethnic, religious, linguistic, and cultural heterogeneity no longer seriously hampered its development. As a result it had become a country broadly comparable to such other Mediterranean nations as Greece, Spain, or Portugal, if not more prosperous. For people who hoped that détente and gradual convergence between the capitalist West and the communist East might end the dangerous division into two hostile blocs armed with nuclear weapons, Yugoslavia was the only country where the desired mixture of two systems seemed to have been realized already. For more than thirty years it occupied a position between East and West, as well as a central place in Europe, and not only in a geopolitical sense. Although the main part of Yugoslavia had always remained outside the culture of Western Christianity, between 1948 and 1980 it played the same role as the area we now call Central Europe presently does. Wistfully looking back after Yugoslavia had disintegrated, some experts concluded that Tito's state had been "politically, culturally and ideologically almost akin to Central Europe." Stojan Cerović, the renowned journalist employed by the Belgrade weekly *Vreme*, who wrote these lines, also commented that in many ways communist Yugoslavia was closer to Europe than the republics that succeeded it, "however much these may take pride in their democracy and European orientation" (see *Europa* 1992, 31).

After Tito's death, in 1980, the political and economic situation in Yugoslavia worsened dangerously. Although ethnic nationalism was rapidly gaining ground, most experts initially associated it with attempts to achieve greater openness and democracy, and considered it a sign of burgeoning pluralism rather than one of impending disintegration (see Ströhm 1976; Hackett 1980; Broekmeyer 1985; Allcock 1992). When in the second half of the 1980s it became clear that the crisis of Yugoslavia could be fatal, the attention of the West was no longer specifically focused on that country, but on the remarkable developments in the soviet bloc. After 1989, Yugoslavia found it more difficult to obtain support from the European Community than did such former east bloc countries as Poland, Czechoslovakia, and Hungary, which had taken over Yugoslavia's position in the center of the European political stage. This further encouraged the separatist tendencies of Croatia and Slovenia. These Catholic countries, which had formerly been part of the Habsburg Empire, took extra pride in their European roots. Tudjman's party saw its victory in the 1990 elections as the decisive step for the inclusion of Croatia in Central Europe, "the region to which it has always belonged," except in the most recent past, when Croatian territory was subjected to "an Asiatic form of government." The same rhetoric was employed in Slovenia: "We Slovenes have difficulty identifying ourselves with the pro-Asian or pro-African Yugoslavia. We cannot identify with such a Yugoslavia . . . , because we embodied the way of life that was created in Central Western Europe." At the same time the Serbs showed a marked propensity to distance themselves, as Christian Europeans, from the "barbaric" followers of Islam in Yugoslavia, who in their turn tried to present themselves as really "European" Muslims (Bakić-Hayden 1995, 917–31).

Disintegration of Yugoslavia: The Ethnic Factor

When Yugoslavia started to fall apart in a series of wars, a wide range of explanations and views was offered to explain the West's reluctance to interfere. Western proponents of more drastic action complained that in the political discourse the old image of the dangerous Balkan powder keg had returned, and for very obvious reasons: the ethnic heterogeneity of Yugoslavia could be used as an excuse for nonintervention. They indignantly cited the former American ambassador to Yugoslavia and later Secretary of State Lawrence Eagleburger, who had said that "until the Bosnian Serbs and Croats decide to stop killing each other, there is nothing the outside world can do about it"

(Holbrooke 1998, 23). The elderly but still influential American diplomat, celebrated historian, and widely recognized expert in East-West relations, George Kennan, was also criticized. He had written in 1993 that centuries of Turkish rule in the Balkans had created a separate world, "which had continued to the present day to preserve many of its non-European traits." Nationalism in the Balkans still "drew on deeper traits of character inherited, presumably, from a distant tribal past" (*The Other Balkan Wars* 1993, 7). In 1994, the American historian and leading specialist on Yugoslavia, Ivo Banac, indignantly concluded that "Western aloofness and indifference to the area itself and to any action or involvement in it" derived from the view of authorities, such as Kennan, that the Balkans diverge too widely from western civilization (Todorova 1997, 185).

The architect of the 1995 Dayton Peace Agreement, Richard Holbrooke, also referred in his memoirs to the "misreading of Balkan history" as one of the factors that might explain the failure of the West in Yugoslavia. "Thus arose," writes Holbrooke, "an idea that 'ancient hatreds' made it impossible for anyone outside the region to try to prevent the conflict" (Holbrooke 1998, 21–22). The American diplomat emphatically distanced himself from the ethnic prejudices about the Balkans. He refused to condemn Serbs, Croats, or Bosnians as a group and blamed the Yugoslavian wars on political leaders and their hysterical nationalism. Holbrooke shared this "politically correct" view with many other authors on the Yugoslavian tangle.

Journalists, scholars, and others who disagreed with the view that it was pointless to intervene in the mutual conflicts of the barbaric and irrational southern Slavs tried to unmask this "myth of Balkan Man" as a patently transparent excuse for doing nothing. They had impressive arguments at their disposal. First, there is constant confirmation of the observation that the resort to violence belongs to general human nature and is not restricted to particular ethnic groups.[10] Second, it has often been pointed out that modern wars are almost always accompanied by crimes and atrocities against the civilian population. "The mass murders of Croats by Serbs in Vukovar in 1992, or the mass murders of Muslims by Croats in Ahvinici in 1993 are not the symptoms of a specific Balkan culture—neither are the mass murders by Germans in Lidice or by Americans in My Lai symptomatic of the degree of civilization in Germany or the United States. . . . It is the culture of war that prescribes such killings, and committing 'war crimes' is therefore inevitable" (Tromp 1995, 118–31).

To this may be added that there was more to the wars in Yugoslavia than disciplined obedience of soldiers. Disobedience was no less important, in fact it may well have been even more significant. There was wholesale evasion of national service: 150,000 to 200,000 young men either went into hiding or emigrated. Although many were coerced into joining up, and it was common for men to be violently press-ganged into service, at the start of the war against Croatia, the Yugoslavia army was eighteen divisions short. The only action that the army could take against cities, such as Vukovar, was to subject them to protracted artillery barrages; in order to capture such towns and to carry out ethnic cleansing, it was necessary to use irregular troops (Udovićki and Ridgeway 1997, 109, 142, 188, 195, 203).

These criminal bands were responsible for the widespread ethnic cleansing of the civilian populations of Croatia, Bosnia, and Kosovo, which made these wars so extremely violent. Already in June 1991, when it became clear that the normal process of conscription would not yield sufficient numbers of recruits, the army decided to train paramilitary forces in special training centers and to deploy them in battle. The Croat and Bosnian armies also used units of this type to carry out their dirty work. In all, some forty to sixty units of this type were active. A number of writers on this topic emphasized the "lower class" origin of such soldiers: criminals, marginal figures, the *Lumpenproletariat* of the towns, and especially boys from poor peasant families with no work and no future, who were used to handling weapons. Joining these bands gave them a purpose in life, considerable power, and booty. Enrichment by terror is often seen as the sole motive of these men (Udovićki and Ridgeway 1997, 141; Silber and Little 1995, 246; Bennett 1995, 164; Judah 1997, 186–87).

Though a much larger group played no part in the battles or in ethnic cleansing, it was this bulk of the population that, as active demonstrators or passive voters, supported the policies of Milošević or Tudjman. They represented the power base of these politicians; and they made the violent dismemberment of the Yugoslavian state possible. Their behavior is often explained in terms of "a switch in mass psychology" brought about by the virtually absolute political control of the media, together with all the other techniques of mass mobilization of the population that communist regimes had always used. The new rulers in postcommunist Croatia and Serbia now successfully used these tools. Television had an almost hypnotic effect. The primary objective was to demonize the enemy. Impartial observers were staggered by the one-sidedness of the news coverage. Nevertheless, 60 percent of the viewers considered such propaganda to be completely true. The "dizzying repetition of pseudo-patriotic terminology" had a "shamanistic" and "paralyzing" effect on a population that was "trapped in radically deteriorating economic, cultural and social conditions." Almost ten years of confinement in the "media gulag" had made these people completely apathetic (Udovićki and Ridgeway 1997, 108–29).

Such observations supported the view that the various population groups had managed to rub along quite well for the greater part of the twentieth century in spite of their considerable differences in language, religion, culture, and regional development. At the start of the 1990s, a coincidence of circumstances brought them into conflict: the crisis and downfall of the communist system, economic decline, the loss of Yugoslavia's exceptionally favorable international position and, primarily, manipulation by unscrupulous politicians. These rulers wanted their own state, with a population as homogeneous as possible. The necessary ethnic cleansing was left to criminal and antisocial elements that are present in any population, and was facilitated by the dehumanizing effects of war. Authors who hold this point of view tend to emphasize the cosmopolitan and multicultural character of cities such as Sarajevo and Belgrade, and that in most rural areas, different ethnic groups managed to live peacefully alongside one another (though mostly not in the same villages) for long periods of time. During the 1980s, the number of people in multiethnic regions, such as Bosnia-Herzegovina, Croatia, and Voivodina, who felt that they were first and foremost Yugoslavs, supposedly grew substantially. "Such Yugoslavism indicated the existence of a reservoir of support for the country's cohesion at approximately the same time that ethnic tensions and economic problems throughout Yugoslavia were becoming more serious" (Cohen 1995, 49). No referendum was held about whether or not Yugoslavia should continue to exist, possibly in the form of a new confederation. It is by no means certain that the majority of people would have been opposed to the retention of the unified state.[11]

The Persistence of Ethnic Mentalities

The facts and opinions set out above make it clear that the Yugoslav conflict cannot simply be described as the inevitable consequence of ancient ethnic animosities. The dissolution of the Yugoslav Federation was an extremely complicated development.

First, let me return to the phenomenon of Yugoslavism mentioned above. It is very difficult to measure its strength. But it remains a fact that a maximum of 6.6 percent of citizens ever registered themselves as "Yugoslav" and that this "high" point was reached in the 1991 census. These individuals were generally the children of mixed marriages (Hall 1994, 9). As long ago as the nineteenth century, Serbs and Croats were expressing ideas and feelings about their strong mutual relationship, and about the desirability of unity. However, *Yugoslavenstvo* was a relatively recent phenomenon, and could not be compared to the much older and highly charged "emotional poignancy of *Italianitá* or *Deutschtum.*" Subsequently, neither the kingdom nor the communist republic was able to create a form of Yugoslavism that was attractive and convincing to all of the country's citizens. In Tito's days quite a number of Croats, Serbs, and Slovenes partly identified themselves also as Yugoslavs, but very few among them actually gave up their own, pre-existing ethnic identities. Among Macedonians, Bosnian Muslims, and Muslim Kosovars, ethnic consciousness even increased in strength during the communist period (Lederer 1969, 39).

According to Andrej Simić a modern nation has a common ethical code that gives its citizens a clear idea about what is good, decent, natural, or God-given. This code, which Simić dubbed a *moral field*, only governs behavior within the group. Different countries inhabit different moral fields, while mutual behavior between countries falls into the *amoral* realm (1991, 31). Sabrina Ramet applied Simić's concept to Yugoslavia and concluded that the Yugoslav veneer (the mythology of the partisans, or the projects for worker participation in management), which the communist regime had used to paper over the gaps of ethnic diversity, was too thin and wore out too quickly. "The Titoists failed to create a common moral field in which all the Yugoslavs would be included. Instead moral fields remained coincident with ethnic communities, heightening the risks and dangers of political disintegration" (Ramet 1996, 321–22). Andrew Wachtel remarked that in the last decades of the communist regime only the city dwellers, and especially the well-educated young people among them, were less susceptible to ethnic nationalism. "An autocratic party with strong ties to the church and to traditional values would be able to garner significant support for a program based on Serbian nationalism, particularly in the countryside, the provinces and among the lumpen-workers of Belgrade. Anti-Croat, anti-German propaganda would work as well" (1998, 196).

At that time, such developments were blocked by the existence of a communist one-party state, but fifteen years later this obstacle disappeared and events swiftly followed their predicted course. Wachtel suggests that Milošević and Tudjman were only successful in manipulating public opinion because their propaganda ran parallel with views that were already held by large sectors of the population, or with ideas that had long lain dormant. This means that not the skills of very unscrupulous political leaders were decisive, but the mentality of large sectors of the population. This even applies to the gangs that were guilty of the most vile forms of ethnic cleansing. In some studies they are not only presented as a random bunch of criminals and riffraff of the kind that occur in all societies, but mention is also made of their primitive nationalism and ethnic racism. They delighted in expressing this in their speech, behavior, exotic costumes, and enthusiasm for "turbo folk rock" and other forms of "ethno-kitsch." Some authors also point out that many of these individuals were from *došlaci* families, immigrants from mainly mountainous areas that had emigrated to other regions or cities in post-1945 Yugoslavia. They were reputedly more receptive to ethnic paranoia than the people who had lived in the same place for generations (Denitch 1994, 74–75, 153; Van de Port 1994, 311; Glenny 1996, 5, 8, 10, 107–8, 168, 170).

It is no simple matter to evaluate the true merit of such interpretations. Literature on the crisis in Yugoslavia is highly controversial and often colored by the easy wisdom of hindsight. Recent research did not thoroughly study for instance the mentality of the inhabitants of mountainous regions of the Balkan Peninsula. However, a number of serious historical and ethnographic studies, which appeared decades before the dissolution of Yugoslavia, did describe the clans or the extended families of Serbs and Montenegrins, their martial behavior and their code of honor, part of which is their tremendous hospitality. Ottoman conquest had resulted in the destruction of the native aristocracy, thereby compelling Serbian and Montenegrin peasants to adopt new social structures, such as tribes or clans. The large-scale displacement of populations as a result of warfare is a particularly characteristic feature of Serbian history. Even though the Serbs later tended to exaggerate the scope and drama of these events, this may nevertheless be the root cause of their militant attitude and folk culture. The Montenegrins adopted these characteristics because the only way in which these mountain-dwellers could hold out against the Turks was by permanent military mobilization.

The harshness of their impoverished and constantly threatened existence produced a society with markedly egalitarian values and the glorification of the males' abilities as warriors. Extended families were ruled by a system of patriarchal authority, with women and children at the bottom of the pecking order. Infanticide, patricide, and fratricide occurred on a regular basis. In certain parts of southern Serbia, the practice of *lapot*, the public liquidation by the hand of their own children of parents who had become redundant persisted into the twentieth century. Montenegro, like Albania, also had a tradition of blood feuds. The Serbs' and Montenegrins' long history of extremely violent raids and rebellions is well known, as are their activities in *haiduk* gangs or as mercenaries in the pay of Byzantium, the Ottoman Empire, Venice, the Habsburg Empire, and Russia. They believed that their lengthy folk poetry endorsed their militant lifestyle. These poems kept alive the hatred for the Turks, the traditional enemy, and the memory of such regions as Kosovo that had once been inhabited and administered by Serbs. They also inspired acts of manly heroism. To set such an example the Montenegrin poet, prince, and bishop Petar Petrović Njegoš wrote *Gorski vijenac* (*The Mountain Garland*, 1847) in which he sanctified an eighteenth- century mass murder of fellow-countrymen who had converted to Islam. It was not so much their religious apostasy that was condemned by Njegoš, but rather their betrayal of ethnic values that had to be revenged. *Gorski vijenac* is still considered to be an essential element of national epic poetry and one of the most important literary creations of the Serbs and Montenegrins.[12]

On the other hand, we have to admit that the waves of ethnic cleansing in the Balkans during the nineteenth and twentieth centuries were mostly not spontaneous initiatives undertaken by the local population, but state-sponsored campaigns inspired by western nationalism. Nevertheless, it can at least be concluded that the mentality and culture of a people like the Serbs certainly did not help to moderate the violent developments in the Balkans. It is no coincidence that Gavrilo Princip, the man who assassinated Archduke Franz Ferdinand in 1914, had learned Njegoš's poem by heart. At that time, most Serbs lived in rural areas, with a lifestyle that had not changed in generations. Even Princip, a young intellectual, had this type of background. The Montenegrin peasants lived in a harsh and cruel world, and were always armed. They were still around during the youth of Milovan Djilas, who was just seventeen years younger than Princip, and his memoirs contain accurate descriptions of these soldier-brigands. Djilas, who is primarily known in the West for his opposition to Tito and his interesting critical studies of communism, also knew The Mountain Garland by heart and wrote a reverential study about Njegoš. As a communist leader he was not without cruelty. He personally cut a prisoners' throat, showed himself to be a passionate proponent of executions without trial, and made black racketeering and similar offences punishable by death (Anzulovic 1999, 61–63; Broekmeyer 1985, 50).

Of course, examples of such unusual characters shed little or no light on the behavior of all Serbs or Montenegrins, although we know that portraits of Njegoš adorned many a farmhouse wall, and that even humble shepherds continued to read his poetry (Den Doolaard 1954, 50). We have to assume that in the twentieth century traditional lifestyle was moderated by urbanization, industrialization, the mechanization of agriculture, increased social mobility, contact with western tourists, and trips abroad. Moreover, the authorities imposed over their ethnic values, myths, and customs a specific Yugoslavian and communist culture. However, studies of Serbian and Montenegrin villages carried out by Boehm and Halpern during the 1960s, reveal the persistence of ancient social patterns and ethnic sentiments. Even where the size of peasant households almost halved between 1860 and 1960 this did not amount to a real dissolution of the extended family and its customs. The ancient songs about Kosovo were still known (or had been rediscovered) by young and old. Most families continued to hold the annual celebrations in commemoration of the ancestors (the *slava*), although this sometimes occurred in the guise of the May Day celebrations. Ethnic patriotism among villagers hardly diminished. They showed an "ongoing sense of pride" and a need to identify themselves with the tradition of heroic struggle. They retained lively recollections of the tragedies that had taken place during the war. Sound fieldwork carried out by the anthropologist Mart Bax drew attention to the *mali rat* (the little war), the long-established and virtually uninterrupted traditions of rivalry, vengeance, and murderous violence in Medjugorje, the well-known Bosnian place of pilgrimage (Bax 1992, 3–25; Bax 1995).

The increasing similarity between urban and rural societies resulted partly from the "urbanization of the villages" but also from the "peasantization of the towns," caused by the massive movement of rural populations to the cities. Therefore, this development has been described as "rurbanization." While the influence of magical practices and religious customs was reduced markedly and life became more rational, individualistic, commercial, and luxurious, many people did not find modernity very satisfying. During the 1960s they started to rediscover their own past. At the time, this nostalgic movement seemed quite innocent. It involved the opening of museums, the building of local monuments, and the more frequent singing of ancient songs, but "kinship and ethnicity, never discarded and now reinforced, remained vital" (Boehm 1983, 73–75; Halpern and Kerewsky Halpern 1972, 26, 43, 64, 66, 74, 110, 118, 123–24).

This revival of traditional standards and values in the Serbian population, together with renewed interest in their own culture and history, took place twenty years before the nationalistic "backlash" by Serbian intellectuals in the 1980s, which features so prominently in virtually every book on the disintegration of Yugoslavia. The communist state itself had even earlier given up its attempts to create a single, unified Yugoslav culture. The regime made a virtue of necessity and presented cultural variety as a token of the robustness and stability of the political system (Wachtel 1998, 174). Although "unity in diversity" remained the predominant ideology, in practice the autonomy and mutual rivalry of the various Yugoslav republics increased enormously. All government posts were carefully assigned in accordance with an ethnic key. At the same time, however, the modest individual prosperity that had been so laboriously achieved began to unravel, and life became increasingly uncertain. As mentioned above, these developments made some people more aware of the fact that they were Yugoslav, first and foremost, but we can take it for granted that the majority of their countrymen were inclined to the opposite reaction. In that case, the Serbian intellectuals made no attempt to push the people in a new direction. They simply reflected the widespread ethnic consciousness that had returned or had remained half-hidden all the time.

Nevertheless the activities of the intellectuals were of crucial importance, since they smashed the communist-Yugoslav taboos. In Tito's days the novelist Ivo Andrić, who won the Nobel Prize for Literature, had been elevated by the regime to the status of a national cultural icon. It didn't really matter that he was not a communist and that his work dealt primarily with the painful, tragic, and often violent aspects of a society riven by ethnic differences. His work was acceptable, because in books such as *The Bridge over the Drina*, (1959) he also incorporated a nation-building message, which told readers that rifts in society would eventually be overcome and wounds inflicted would be healed. In this period, virtually all Croat and Serbian writers conveyed this type of Yugoslav ideology. From the 1970s on, however, many of them developed into nationalists, primarily devoted to the destruction of supraethnic values. That was the end of the communist ideal of brotherhood and unity. From then on, one's own people came first (Wachtel 1998, 156, 174, 176. See also Bakić-Hayden and Hayden 1992, 18–20).

Tables were turned and times changed in the Yugoslav cultural and political landscape. To use Simić's terminology, a new *normative zone* had been created. It could be used to determine who was *good* and who was *bad*. The entire gamut of ethnic traditions, symbols, attitudes, political views, and mythological interpretations of the pas, was restored to its former glory. Culture and power, the elite and the common people were united with one another by favorable sentiment concerning their own ethnic group and by unfavorable views concerning outsiders. For the Serbs the objective became a larger, more powerful Serbia, while the Croats and the Slovenes aimed at a state of their own. The minorities who opposed this development were politically and socially marginalized. Anyone expressing a dissenting view encountered an increasingly unpleasant reaction. "Obstinate otherness," the need to be fundamentally different from other ethnic groups, became openly widespread, especially among Serbs, and was a major element in the fatal developments that occurred prior to 1991, and thereafter. It favored the fomentation of a hysterical mood in response to the perilous position of the Serbs in Kosovo. This in turn helped to bring Slobodan Milošević to power (Wachtel 1998, 197–200; Anzulovic 1999, 99–146; Judah 1997, 75–80; Van de Port 1999).

Large-scale and intensive political manipulation was required to achieve a situation in which all parties were prepared to resort to force. However, this would not have achieved the desired effect if the citizens had been less receptive to the ethnic-nationalistic message. During the 1980s the one-party state was in an advanced state of decay and the erosion of the totalitarian system in Yugoslavia meant that its subjects could no longer be compelled to toe the line. Strong public support was needed if the country was to discard this system and switch to an entirely different political situation.

Appeals to ethnic solidarity proved to be an extremely effective means of winning over a majority of voters in Serbia, Croatia, and Slovenia. In other words: in the Yugoslav case ethnicity proved to be a fast and reliable vehicle to transport a population from ramshackle totalitarianism to an authoritarian democracy.

The release of accumulated ethnic tensions in Yugoslavia in eruptions of excessive violence was by no means unique in the history of this peninsula. The fact that this has occurred at regular intervals to some extent justifies statements about "ancient hatreds" and "deeper traits of character presumably from a distant tribal past" (*The Other Balkan Wars* 1993, 7). In a sense, it also supports the "Balkan Man" school of thought. However, such generalized qualifications tend to gloss over both the complexity of the region's past and the elusive phenomenon of ethnic identity. Many western observers have seen merciless nationalism as the true characteristic of the Balkans. History shows, however, that this phenomenon usually "has only ever been sustainable for brief periods by governments before it begins to soften, then fragment and finally decays" (Glenny 1996, 241–42). In other words, from time to time, violence-prone Balkan Man suddenly pops up all over the place, only to disappear again later. During the intervals between these upheavals, the various ethnic groups live relatively peacefully with or alongside one another.

For this reason, the notion that ethnicity is purely a question of a rigid tradition, unalterable dependence, and deep conviction on the part of numerous, clearly demarcated groups of people, needs to be amended. The enormous contrasts and fluctuations that characterize the history of the Balkans result from the complex distribution of different population groups throughout the area, from the Ottoman heritage, and from the incomplete westernization of the region (Vucinich 1965, 120–21; Vucinich 1963, 61–114; Stavrianos 1993, 184–222). Ethnicity was very strongly rooted in some groups, but others were only faintly aware of it, or only paid lip service for utilitarian reasons. Dishonesty, deception, lies and deceit were all permissible tools in the struggle to survive in a hostile outside world. In practice, ethnic and religious boundaries were sometimes frayed and vague. Religious syncretism was much more common than doctrinal piety. Among the Serbs existed a striking mixture of heathen magic and Christian practices. The church served as the most important repository of national culture, but its saints could also offer protection to Muslims, Catholics, or Gypsies. The literature repeatedly makes reference to the fact that, as a religious institute, the church played a rather insignificant role in the spiritual life of Serbs and Montenegrins during the nineteenth and twentieth centuries. Village churches were unobtrusive and small, and they were not regularly attended. Village priests had little authority, and people were as distrustful of the senior incumbents of the state church as they were of worldly authorities. An opinion poll conducted in 1985 showed that no more than 11 percent of the people of Serbia, Montenegro, and Voivodina defined themselves as believers (Allcock 2000, 366–76; Duyzings 1999, 1–36).

In times of violent change, increasing uncertainty, and danger, people seek any means of protection and tend to "go with the flow." Large groups of citizens are immediately prepared to renounce the symbols and practices of a discredited regime or leader, and to offer their support to a new patron, preferably the most powerful one available. "In modern conditions of mass media this means that they will carefully emulate what the 'most' authoritative voice—His Master's Voice—tells them to think and believe." This results either in a greater emphasis of dependence on traditional ethnical values or a more ostentatious display of adherence to a given religion. This conduct does not necessarily have much to do with these people's genuine feelings or religious conviction: "The more menacing the power, the thicker the mask." Such chameleon-like behavior has been a regularly recurring feature in the history of Eastern Europe. Sudden changes at the top of the political pyramid were associated with the continuation of despotism, poverty, and dependence. It was essential to make the correct political choices, and to do so quickly (Duyzings 1999, 35–36; Dittrich 1991, 19, 29).

Ethnicity and Democracy

It seems, therefore, that many inhabitants of the Balkans are capable of considerable adaptive flexibility. However, anyone who supposes that this characteristic would enable the rapid reconstruction of healthy, multicultural societies in Kosovo, Bosnia, and Macedonia under international supervision would probably be in for a disappointment. The ability to use ethnic and political mimicry is directly related to the destruction and violence that characterize so many Balkan conflicts. Nothing is more important in this world of pretence and sham than the national symbols, ethnic marks, and religious beacons. It is these things that delineate and fill the "normative zone." They provide direction and clarity. It is imperative that both this abstract territory and the nation's actual physical territory be clear and pure. They must be free of any confusing or contaminating elements. This is why Serbs are not permitted to live on Croat land and why all mosques on Serbian soil must be destroyed. Many individuals were willing and able to demonstrate their loyalty to their fatherland by assisting with the cleansings. This has seldom been carried out as thoroughly as in the most recent of the Yugoslav conflicts.

These wars were much worse than many previous eruptions of ethnic violence, primarily because they lasted considerably longer. The Balkan wars at the start of the twentieth century were bloody, but the first lasted only for a couple of months and the second for no more than a month. In terms of their nature, duration, and scope, only the events of the Second World War were of a comparable order of magnitude. Coming to terms with the tragic events that occurred between 1941 and 1945 would have required a lengthy and thorough historical investigation. Such studies were initially impeded by the communist regime, and subsequently by the nationalist hysteria that succeeded Tito's administration. However, the Second World War taught all Yugoslavs that ethnicity could be a very perilous thing indeed. Half a century later the ongoing fear of a possible repetition, coupled with the need to be permanently alert to such developments, had the effect of a self-fulfilling prophecy. Now people have to come to terms with the repetition of these events as well. This is an enormous barrier to the restoration of normal social and political relations.

In my opinion it is not necessary to decide for or against the existence of Balkan Man, or for or against the existence of "ancient ethnic hatreds." What is vitally important, however, is to realize exactly what we want these terms to mean. The distinctive history of the Balkans has led to the development of sharp ethnic contrasts. It has also given rise to a mentality (or mentalities) in large sections of the population that differ in some respects from the western or European frame(s) of mind. In attempting to visualize this, we usually fail to allow for their enormous range of variation and for the fact that they are in a state of constant flux. We mostly rather easily resort to generalizations about peoples and regions in Central and Eastern Europe.

The selection of Eastern Christianity as the main cause of everything that is presently wrong in the East is only the latest product of a long western tradition of prejudiced opinion about this area. As has happened often before, one particular element of reality was disproportionally enlarged because it had to function as a comprehensive explanation for actual and complex developments.

Although ethnicity can be presented as an attractive substitute for religion, it does not make much sense to replace one mono-causal explanation with another. The assumption of a connection between ethnic diversity and corrupt forms of democracy will always remain something of an educated guess, because it is not possible to prove a direct and causal relationship between issues that belong to completely different categories. In the past ethnicity has been pointed to as a nasty obstacle to political unity in the multinational empires in the eastern half of Europe, but also as one of their most charming characteristics, producing such a variety of languages, literatures, folklore, national dress, and music forms. Cultural diversity after all was the hallmark of a truly European civilization.

The prominence of ethnicity as a determining factor in society is always dependent on a variety of circumstances, which makes it relevant to large numbers of people. Ethnicity sometimes plays the leading part on the stage, but often it is only a subordinate participant in the historical process. It should not be used as the latest fashionable passkey to a complete understanding of the past, present, and future of the eastern half of Europe. It is only when we try to describe and analyze this region as accurately and candidly as possible that we may hope to free the way for reconciliation with the past and the establishment of true democracy in the former Yugoslav republics.

CHAPTER NINE

Democracy and Ethnicity

Acculturation by Politicization

FRANK ANKERSMIT

Immigration is one of the greatest challenges that western democracies have encountered in the course of their histories, and the main problem when dealing with this problem is how it should be defined. Since democracy recognizes all its citizens as equal, democrats will naturally tend to define the problem in social or cultural terms. In this chapter a case is made for a primarily political approach of the issue.

For the past few decades western democracies have been confronted with the problem of an ever-increasing number of citizens of foreign origin in their midst. It has taken these democracies quite some time to recognize the problem and still more time to define the nature of the problem. In fact, most discussions on ethnicity, the multicultural society, and so forth focus on the question of how the problem should be conceptualized—which of course renders the problem pretty much insoluble: how can we solve a problem as long as we are in the dark about its exact nature?

Indeed, one could argue that there is no real political problem at all by virtue of the fact that, from the point of view of democracy, the multicultural society cannot and should not be a problem. The constitutions of our western democracies are silent about the cultural origin of individual citizens; the machinery of democratic government is formally indifferent to the origins, religious beliefs, and cultural background of its legal residents. Some of these constitutions (such as the Dutch one) even explicitly forbid discrimination on the basis of sex, cultural background, and color of the skin, or of religious affiliations. In this way the very question of the relationship between democracy and ethnicity is itself profoundly unconstitutional and undemocratic. And the same would then even be true of this conference on democracy and ethnicity. It discusses a problem that could not and should not be a problem in a well-ordered democracy taking itself seriously.

Emancipation and Civic Equality

Should we leave the issue there and simply refuse to deal with the problem of democracy and ethnicity? This would be too hasty, which becomes clear when we ask ourselves the historical question of how this ban on discrimination became a keystone of our democracies and inscribed into our constitutions. For this certainly has been the result of a historical evolution. Though the legal equality of all citizens was theoretically proclaimed for the first time by the French revolutionaries of 1789, it has taken all western democracies quite some time to realize this equality in practice. One need only think here of nineteenth-century census suffrage, of the exclusion of women from the ballot, or of the exclusion of slaves from the procedures of democracy in the United States before 1865. In all these cases a process of emancipation was needed in order to secure civic equality.

However, no such emancipation struggle was required to secure civic equality for our allochthonous fellow-citizens. Legal equality was self-evidently and non-problematically granted to immigrants—in this way they could effortlessly profit from what had been achieved in the emancipatory struggles of nineteenth- and early twentieth-century Western Europe. Indeed, it was rightly and universally recognized that what had been acquired with so much difficulty for slaves, for the indigent, and for women should be granted to these new citizens as well, as a matter of course.

But suppose now that someone proposed the understandable if perverse rule that rights should be granted to a category of people only on the condition that they actually have fought for them, or may be expected to be ready to fight for them. We could object that this rule—that one can only enjoy what one has been ready to fight for—could not possibly be applied to the case of the immigrant, for how could he have fought for his rights? The emancipatory movements of the past could succeed because slaves, workers, and women were part of the existing society already. Only because of this could these movements constitute both a threat and a moral challenge to the existing order; only because of this could they compel the ruling classes to consider compromise. But immigrants could never be such a threat, for the simple reason that they came to their new country from another country. And the citizens of one country can pose no threat to those of another country (unless these two countries are at war, of course). The idea of an emancipatory struggle by immigrants themselves for their legal rights is simply nonsensical by the very nature of the case. Such rights can only be granted, and not be fought for: the immigrant of a previous time is simply *recognized* by the authorities of his adopted country as one of its own regular citizens at a later time. This act of recognition is both morally and legally the only decisive procedure here. And what makes this recognition of the immigrant's legal rights fundamental, is the fact that only *it* can transcend the incommensurability, or *différend* to use Lyotard's appropriate terminology, of foreign and autochthonous citizenship.

Political Emancipation and Social Struggle

Here the problem of immigrants has played a strange trick on western democracies. For as the volume of immigrants increased dramatically over the past two to three decades and tended to concentrate in Europe's metropolises, where gradually a process of ghettoization set in, their living conditions became very similar to those of the nineteenth-century industrial proletariat. So the social predicament that ignited a hundred and fifty years ago the emancipation struggle of the industrial proletariat is ominously identical to what has been the final outcome of mass immigration. And however much our governments sincerely and earnestly have tried to counteract this return to a dismal phase in our social histories, the result has been disenfranchisement rather than emancipation.

This unsettling result is a complete reversal of the kind of social and political evolution that the West has experienced since the eighteenth century. The customary pattern ran from destitution and despair via a bitter and prolonged and social struggle to ultimate liberation and emancipation. Now, however, we seem to move in precisely the opposite direction, from emancipation and the adjudication of equal rights into the kind of predicament that used to motivate our bourgeois and proletarian ancestors to fight the several anciens regimes of western history. History has been turned upside down.

This may explain our bafflement and helplessness when confronted with this enigmatic social derailment; truly we cope here with a problem that is wholly new in the course of western history and there are no obvious historical precedents suggesting how to deal with it. We should, therefore, not be surprised that the challenge of the problem sometimes has elicited strange and contradictory reactions from the existing polity. The social-democratic answer is an example: as one might have expected from socialists, they tended to model the problem of immigrants on that of the nineteenth-century worker proletariat—and this certainly was a good beginning. But whereas Marxism and socialism in its many variants were very much aware that the conflict between labor and capital was a social and political conflict transcending any juridical formulation of it, in practice the socialists' approach to the immigration issue rarely went beyond an insistence on equal rights and an almost paranoid condemnation of all that even remotely reminded of discrimination. This is most surprising since socialists themselves would have been the first to recognize that an appeal to rights would have been wholly useless in their own heroic struggle with the capitalist bourgeoisie— all the more so since rights and duties belong to the political arsenal of liberalism, and socialists have always known that this weapon can turn, and has successfully been turned against them. Not an appeal to rights, but the quite real threat of social revolution succeeded in satisfying the socialists' claims. So the paradox is that socialists hoped to improve the immigrants' predicament by an appeal to the kind of instrument that they could have known better than anybody else to be useless under the given circumstances.

No Politicization by Immigrants

And this brings me to what seems to me to be the crux of our so sadly ineffective dealings with the problem of the multicultural society. Though there have been cultural minorities in our western democracies for more than three to four decades by now, and though these minorities share a number of social and political interests (which are too obvious to be stated), nevertheless in no immigrant country have political parties been organized to promote these interests. Already in 1974 Daniel Lawrence saw three ways for immigrants to improve their situation: first, by incorporation into the existing class structure; second, by organization along ethnic lines; and third, and preferably, by organization "around the common badge of color," which becomes an instrument of political pressure.[1] However, not in France, in the United Kingdom, nor in Germany or the Netherlands, nor anywhere else do we find political parties that have been founded by immigrants aiming at the politicization of immigrants and at the improvement of their situation by political means (attempts have been made to that effect in the Netherlands,[2] but they have been wholly unsuccessful[3]). This is a truly amazing fact. If only because of its strange combination of universality and counter-intuitiveness we would expect that at least somewhere some such party would have struck root to become the obvious focus of the immigrant vote.

One can only guess at the explanation of this absence of political parties for immigrants and ethnic minorities. Perhaps these ethnic minorities live at such a great mental and cultural distance from each other—Turks amongst the Turks, Moroccans amongst Moroccans, and Asians amongst Asians— that a political party furthering their shared collective interests makes no sense to them.[4] Perhaps, because of their experience with politics and politicians in their countries of origin, immigrants are just as much disillusioned with politics as so many of us are—though obviously for different reasons.[5] Or, perhaps these ethnic minorities are just as much confounded by the insistence on (equality of) rights as the socialists were. For how could they possibly improve their situation by an appeal to rights? They already have all the rights that majority citizens possess, so the discourse of rights is neutral between the members of minority groups and their new fellow-citizens. It might be objected now that in actual practice the application of law is not neutral and often favors native citizens at their expense. This may be true; but even if it is, this only accentuates the practical inadequacy of the rights discourse in this kind of issue.

Even more important, we must recognize that nothing may more strongly paralyze one's awareness of one's interests than the discourse of rights. Interests are, so to say, rights in *statu nascendi* and move to the background as soon as they have developed into rights in the proper sense of the word. So as soon as one starts to use the rights discourse, conflicts of interest automatically disappear beyond the horizon. In this way, it can be argued that emancipatory struggles can truly be fought in terms of interests only, and not in those of rights. Interests may question existing power relationships, rights tend to fossilize them.

The Shortcomings of Acculturation

It will be obvious what this implies for the relationship between ethnic minorities and their adopted nation. Namely, that they can only become a true and authentic part of their new world by developing a truly *political* relationship to it, by becoming aware of the *political* dimension of their attempt to find the right place in their new country and of how their specific interests had best be expressed *politically*. Hence, the suggestion that integration could be realized by acculturation—as is recommended in the Netherlands, for instance, by Paul Scheffer[6]—puts the cart before the horse. Cultural integration undoubtedly is an important phase in the development of integration, but for two reasons not the right thing to start with.

In the first place, what is acquired by immigrants in terms of cultural integration will tend to remain something relatively external to them, merely a lesson that has been learned but that has not been internalized. In the second place, a politicization of how they relate to their new world will make them aware of their own specific interests—and there is no stronger glue to tie people to their *Umwelt* (social environment) than such an awareness. Not rights, but interests make us into citizens of the country in which we live; interests involve us with others and with society; rights allow us to live apart from them (and are meant to achieve just this). A society where rights have taken the place that is proper to interests is a disintegrating society. Hence, there is no better instrument to integrate new citizens into their country of adoption than politics and to put one's trust into a free and open-minded articulation of the conflict of interests. To put it into one formula: we should aim at acculturation by politicization. There is no road to acculturation without or apart from politicization.[7] It is most satisfactory that the Dutch government has recognized the domain of politics as a spearhead of integration.[8] Nevertheless, it need not surprise us that few have advocated this strategy until now. For it may well be argued that a politicization of immigrants will elicit an exacerbation of the conflicts unfortunately already existing between allochthonous and autochthonous citizens.[9] Hence, the effort of the existing parties to give ample room in their midst to allochthonous citizens who are politically interested.[10] In this way, it is believed, it will be possible to subsume the political dimensions of the acclimatization of citizens of a foreign origin within the matrix of already existing political issues,[11] whereas the emergence of political parties focusing exclusively on the interests of immigrants will only foster radicalism and intransigence. That may well prove to be the case; but in all likelihood we shall have to pass through such a stage of radicalization and increased intransigence sometime, somehow—this is the lesson to be learned from the emancipatory struggles of the past. Whether we like it or not, it is part of the *condition humaine* that all that really counts in life can only be secured after a struggle with others—and oneself, as I would like to add. What is simply given to us, leaves us unchanged.

Moreover, as has been recognized by Hilhorst (2001) and others, allochthonous representatives typically find themselves in an impossible position as long as they stake everything on what may be achieved via the already existing traditional parties. For their very presence there is meant to suggest that the traditional party will take care of the interests of allochthonous citizens. However, as soon as they actually do so their political associates often accuse them of preferring partial interests to the national interest (see also Note 8). As a consequence, allochthonous representatives tend to avoid the problematic dimension of the multicultural society—and the net result is negative rather than positive.[12] So the choice seems to be between continued ghettoization and an ever-postponed true citizenship of immigrants on the one hand, and on the other, the readiness to face once and for all the truly political dimensions of the problem of multiculturalism. This certainly is a nasty problem, but the attempt to avoid it will never contribute to a real solution.

Democracy and Ethnicity

Returning to the issue of democracy and ethnicity that I briefly referred to at the outset of this discussion, one more argument can be given in favor of the politicization of the relationship between immigrants and their country of adoption. It makes sense to follow Michel Albert in distinguishing between Anglo-Saxon and continental European variants of democracy (Albert 1993). As I have tried to show elsewhere (Ankersmit 2002, chapters 4 and 7), the difference between them can be explained by the fact that each variant was intended to solve a wholly different kind of political problem. Anglo-Saxon democracy should be related to the Glorious Revolution of 1688 and to the American Revolution of 1776. The main aim of these revolutions was to establish government by consent and to develop a system of checks and balances against royal or presidential autocracy. Continental democracy, on the other hand, came into being in the years after 1815 and *its* main aim was to achieve the possibility of fruitful and creative compromise in politically strongly polarized nations.

Continental democracies have been quite good at bringing about political pacification and reconciliation (having been constructed specifically for the purpose). One might well say that they have been the most powerful political machines ever devised for creating social and political peace—they undoubtedly have been more successful in this than Anglo-Saxon democracies since the Second World War. This success justifies the expectation that continental democracies are relatively well equipped to deal with the political polarization that would result from the politicization of the social problems of immigration. From this perspective, continental democracies can afford the risks of such political polarization—especially in that the advantages to be expected from it will far outweigh the potential dangers.

One of these advantages is that politicization will invite immigrants to take control of themselves, whereas they now remain the more or less passive object of public debate. We have become accustomed to a discourse about immigration as if the problem were similar to a problem of tax legislation or of the infrastructure and as if immigrants were a kind of passive substratum about which we can decide just as well in one way or another. Think, for example, of the discussion about to what extent immigrants can reasonably and fruitfully be forced to cultural integration. I am ready to allow the propriety of such discussions as long as the issue is approached in the relatively careful and tactful manner that presently is still customary. But, once again, we had better start at the other end, and begin with politicization—and then acculturation will follow as a matter of course. For compromise in a continental democracy always minimally requires discussion partners to recognize what the world looks like if seen from that partner's perspective. And a more powerful vehicle for the transmission of cultural values cannot be imagined. One can only become the citizen of a new country after having passed through a phase in which one's own cultural values and those of one's new country have both been objectified, and after they have been considered from a perspective beyond those two cultural perspectives. One can move from one set of cultural values to another such set only after having passed through a perspectival vacuum, as it were, not directly. And it is politics and political compromise that compels that move.[13] Moreover, a politicization of the multiculturalism issue will make the minorities more aware of each other, of their shared interests, invite them to transcend their cultural differences, and thus stimulate cooperation amongst themselves and with the political forces in their country of adoption. And this will, in its turn, promote a clearer definition of the issue—though political polarization undoubtedly is the price we will have to pay. But, as Machiavelli already knew, the cause of freedom is served better by conflict and polarization than by shelving problems that have to be faced sooner or later anyway.

The three greatest crises in western history since the Middle Ages have been the great religious civil war of the sixteenth and seventeenth centuries; the struggle between democracy and royal or totalitarian autocracy from the eighteenth to the twentieth century; and the conflict between labor and capital in the nineteenth and early twentieth centuries. Though it may be too early to tell, it seems that the challenge posed by the multicultural society is a likely fourth great crisis. All these struggles have intrinsically been political struggles and could be solved only after having been recognized as such.

For example, the religious civil war could only be ended after it was seen as political rather than religious. (One might argue that the disaster of communism has been the attempt to solve social problems with (very brutish) social instead of political means.)

Politics may give us *truth*—*truth* in the Heideggerian sense of that much-discussed word; truth in the sense of *aletheia*, the Greek etymology of the word meaning an uncovering of the object of knowledge, of a taking away all that hides it and prevents our access to it. This is what politics can most successfully do. Politics can take away the veils hiding the world in which we have to live, to think, and to act—and make us aware of the conflict of interests underneath these veils. Political truth is to be found in the conflict of interests—nowhere else, and certainly not in the discourse of rights. Rights are derivatives from interests and therefore can never sufficiently protect them. This is why politicization is absolutely necessary when we are confronted with serious social or collective problems that will not go away spontaneously—such as those of the multicultural society. And, obviously, this is Machiavelli again.

Reference Matter

Notes

1. See Greenfeld 1992; Hobsbawm 1994; Moore 1967; Lipset 1960; Luebbert 1991; Rueschemeyer 1992.
2. See the works of John Breuilly, Ernest Gellner, Eric Hobsbawm, Hans Kohn, Antony D. Smith, Peter Sugar.
3. See Skocpol 1979; Tilly 1975; Schulze 1994.
4. Rokkan and Urwin 1982. The central notions in this volume were more or less developed by Eisenstadt 1981.
5. See the websites of Freedom House and the UNDP; and Fish 1998, 217, 225.

1. Lévi-Strauss 1952, chapter 3; Lévi-Strauss 1983, preface. Lévi-Strauss's argument however is that diversity is good, and must be saved and protected.
2. See Kenrick and Puxon 1972, 33–35; Bogumila Michalewicz, in Williams 1989, 129–39.
3. "Which Australian Candidate Has the Hardest Heart?' in *The New York Times*, November 9, 2001.
4. Noiriel 1988. But compare Braudel 1988, 215, who claims that two-thirds of mixed marriages end in divorce.
5. Touraine 2001, 229–30. Compare *The New York Times*, June 13, 2002, where a "Bulletin from Durban, South Africa," presents Indians living there as oppressors who pay low wages and treat Africans with disrespect.
6. Cohen 1998, 297 and 289, shows that in 1981, 43 percent of the French felt that notions of Right and Left were valid, and 33 percent considered them out of date. By 1996, only 32 percent still considered them valid, 62 percent out of date.
7. *Libération*, June 10, 1991: "There are no more French, that means nothing any more. All races are mixed," declares one habitué of the annual concerts of *SOS*

Racisme, who attended his seventh concert on Saturday, June 8. This ended in violent fights "between gangs of rival projects and groups of young Blacks and beurs."

8. Patrick Weil in *Pouvoirs* 47, 1988; Mitterand in *Le Monde*, December 12, 1989, and June 23–24, 1991.

9. Nor do alleged collective identities work well: in Southern California, some Hispanic candidates in Hispanic districts cannot afford to address their public in Spanish, because the multiplicity of accents, dialects, and forms of language would get them into trouble.

10. Plutarch, paragraph 329. Compare Lévi-Strauss 1983, 49: "The peoples studied by ethnologists grant the dignity of a truly human condition to their members only, and make no distinction between the others and animality."

CHAPTER FIVE

1. Musil 1995, 577. "Kakania," of course, was Musil's sardonically scatological pun/nickname for the imperial and royal (*kaiserliche und königliche*—K und K) state of Austria-Hungary.

2. Among the pre–1914 imperial ancien regimes, the Habsburg monarchy has been the most frequently eulogized. In interwar literature, Czech novelist Jaroslav Hašek (1930) poked fun at the stodgy police-state mentality of Habsburg officialdom in *The Good Soldier Schweik*. Joseph Roth (1995) depicted the decline and fall of Austria-Hungary amidst the squabbles of its nationalities as a European tragedy (most famously in *The Radetzky March*). Among historians, criticism of the Habsburg monarchy's autocratic sclerosis was the norm during the interwar years. The seminal work of this genre was by a Hungarian-Jewish progressive intellectual and political activist, Oscar Jaszi (1929), who had briefly held office as minister of nationalities in Hungary's short-lived liberal government of October 1918–March 1919. Critiques of Austria-Hungary gave way after 1945 to a more positive reassessment of its qualities as a transnational *Rechtsstaat*. One popular historian contended that, "in an important sense, the Habsburg system was more rational than anything seen in Europe before or since" (Crankshaw 1963, 4. See also May 1951). Alan Sked (1989) makes a case for the Habsburgs' continued potential for success as of 1914. For a fuller exposition of the relevant Habsburg historiography, see Beller 1996, chapter 1. Beller counters the more positive interpretations of late Habsburg history with a critical view of the monarchy's (mis)handling of nationalities problems, ranging from its rejection of the proposed Kremsier constitution of 1849 (which would have created a systematized, federal framework for national autonomy within a still-unified Habsburg monarchy) to the ill-fated occupation and annexation (in 1878 and 1908, respectively) of Bosnia and Herzegovina. The most exhaustive English-language overview of Habsburg nationalities policies in the post-Metternichian era remains Kann 1950. For a comparative view of empires, focused on the Russian case, see Lieven 2000. Rather in the

vein of the Habsburg apologists, Lieven rejects what he sees as a facile contrast between good, modern democracies and evil, atavistic empires, arguing that "in its time empire was often a force for peace, prosperity and the exchange of ideas across much of the globe . . . White democratic nationalism in Europe's colonies of settlement generally far outdid aristocratic and bureaucratic empire in its devastation of indigenous peoples" (414).

3. Banac 1984, 96; Vysny 1977, chapters 3–7; Bradley 1961–62, 184–205, esp. 193–97; Ferenczi 1984, 7–127.

4. Bauer 1907, 23–95; Bottomore and Goode 1978, 102–17; Blum 1985, chapters 3 and 5; Kann 1950, vol. 2, chapter 20.

5. On the concept of official nationalism, see Anderson 1991, chapter 6.

6. Pipes 1992, chapters 2–4; Kappeler 1993, chapter 4; Weeks 1996, 129–30 and *passim*; Hosking 1997, 146–47.

7. The idea that Turkish nationalism formed the dominant, if secret, agenda of the CUP's leadership is a matter of growing scholarly consensus. See Hanioglu 1995; Arai 1992; Zürcher 1984; Landau 1995. For a dissenting view, see Kayali 1997.

8. Khoury 1983, chapter 3; Dawn 1991; Tibi 1997, 109–14; Hourani 1962, 280–85; Zeine 1958, chapter 5; Kayali 1997, 69–70, 174–81, and chapter 4.

9. Skilling 1994, 6–7, 35–37, 101–3, and chapter 3; Pynsent 1994, 180–82; Kalvoda 1986, 17–32; Szporluk 1981, chapter 4. For a critical view of Masaryk's desire to have his universalism and eat his ethnocultural cake too, see Schmidt-Hartmann 1990.

10. The newspaper's name was *Hrvatska* (Croatia). The quotation is taken from Spence 1981, 63.

11. I develop this theme more fully in Roshwald 2001, chapter 5.

12. For an overview of the long-term impact of the Great War on European nationalities politics, see Dunn and Fraser 1996.

13. Naimark 2001. For a stimulating rethinking of the relationship between state and society in twentieth-century mass violence, see Mazower 2002, 1158–78.

CHAPTER SIX

1. *Annales ESC* 57, no. 1 (January-February 2002), 27–146. Under the heading, "L´exercise de la comparaison," the *Annales* dedicated several articles to show the possible assets of the comparative method. One year later, there is also an ongoing debate in the leading German journal of social and comparative history on how to open the comparison for transnational approaches. See *Geschichte und Gesellschaft* 27, no. 3 (July-September 2001), 463–98, and vol. 28, no. 1 (January-March 2002), 145–69.

2. Some postmodernists saw in comparative studies the embodiment of all faults of modern social sciences and social history. Marie Pauline Rosenau (1991) stated: "The very act of comparing, in an effort to uncover similarities and differences, is a

meaningless activity because postmodern epistemology holds it impossible ever to define adequately the elements to be contrasted or likened"(105).

3. This is, however, difficult if one tries to avoid an artificial ethnicization of history. See for this problem King 2001.

4. The most prominent proponent of this explanation in Germany is Hans-Ulrich Wehler. See Wehler 1995, 1250–95.

5. In the same year the Habsburg Empire was thoroughly reorganised and turned into the dual monarchy of Austria-Hungary. Because Hungary reached a large degree of autonomy and developed differently afterwards, this article concentrates now on the Austrian half of the empire.

6. For the Polish-Ukrainian conflict in this period, see Partacz 1996.

7. See, for the various compromises, Stourzh 1985, 213–29; Glassl 1967; Křen 1990, 323–25. Compare for the outcome in the Bukowina, Rachamimov 1996, 1–16.

8. The older literature about the Habsburg Empire is generally much more sceptical about its prospects for democratization. That is partly because it did not yet pay much attention to the local and regional level. For an example of the older literature, see Kann 1974.

9. In his 1996 book about nationalism, Rogers Brubaker offers a good compilation of Polish minority politics and a theoretical framework for understanding the nexus among external homeland, minority, and "nationalising nation states." For the case of Poland, see 84–103.

10. Kučera 1999. This also puts into question Brubaker's triangular model (Brubaker 1996).

11. For the Czechoslovak elections of 1935, see Rothschild 1974, 120 ff.

12. For the overall social and mental effects of World War II and the Holocaust, see Gross 1997, 17–40.

13. For the establishment of communist rule in Czechoslovakia, see Kaplan 1981. For the correlation with the expulsions, see Kučera 2000.

14. Paczkowski 1993. In the referendum the voters had to make key decisions about the political system and the external borders of Poland.

15. This was shown in two case studies about the Polish-German and the Polish-Ukrainian borderlands: Ther 2001b and Ther 2001c.

CHAPTER SEVEN

1. For an extensive study of Romanian, Czechoslovak, and Yugoslav policies, see Macartney 1937; for Poland, see Horak 1961 or Vakar 1956; for the Ukranian minorities, see Magocsi 1997.

2. By 2000, the number of Gypsies, now generally referred to as the Roma, grew to approximately 4.5 million regionwide partly as a result of high birth rates, partly as a result of correcting earlier methods of census taking. This figure would make

them about 3.5 percent of the population of contemporary East Central Europe. See Barany 2002, 277.

3. I have made this point more emphatically and in greater detail in Janos 2001.

CHAPTER EIGHT

1. The influence on politicians of the 'Rome-versus-Byzantium' interpretation is reflected in the remarks of the general secretary of NATO, Willy Claes, who in 1994 excluded Orthodox countries from integration into Europe because of their 'Byzantine' character, 'Oriental world view', and 'latent mentality' (see Goldsworthy 1998, 49). Elements of the interpretation can also be found in scholarly literature—see, for example Schöpflin 1989, 10–15; and Timothy Garton Ash, "The Puzzle of Central Europe," *The New York Review of Books*, March 18, 1999. For an opposing view, see Raymond Detrez, "Over de grootspraak van Europa" (About Europe's Bragging), in *Nieuw Wereldtijdschrift*, June 2000.

2. Even Max Weber (the leading writer on this issue) did not dare to put into words the idea that a religious mentality could directly influence the economy. He described the relationship between both phenomena as a *"Wahlverwandtschaft"* (elective affinity). See Tellegen 1968, 33–37.

3. After the subjugation of the Czechs by the Habsburgs in the seventeenth century, and the decline and fall of Poland in the eighteenth century, the whole eastern half of Europe, from north to south, was seen in the West as a backward region where poverty and despotism were indissolubly bound together. At about this time, the concepts of *l'Europe orientale* (Oriental Europe) started to appear in travelers' tales. Europe now had some sort of a semi-Asia right in its own backyard (see Wolff 1994).

4. For Ranke's views, see for instance Malia 1999, 127–30.

5. For a good study written before the subject became again fashionable, see Droz 1960.

6. For a number of remarkable British utterances about these countries, see Burgess 1997, 54–55; Haslam 1984, 190; Davies 1982, vol. 2, 393.

7. Kundera 1984. For an excellent criticism of such views, see Dittrich 1987.

8. See Jelavich and Jelavich 1993, vol.8, 191; Smit 1958 vol 2, 723–24.

9. Of the overwhelming amount of literature on this topic I only mention Soergel 1979; Schrenk 1979; Meister 1970; Lilge 1978; and Boonzajer, Flaes, and Ramondt 1974.

10. This is born out by sociopsychological experiments. See Meeus and Raaij-makers 1984; Milgram 1974; Zimbardo 1969, 337–47; Zimbardo 1973, 243–56.

11. In March 1991 such an event did take place in the Soviet Union, which had comparable political economic problems and similar ethnic conditions. Eighty percent of the voters (almost 149 million people) voted and 76.4 percent voted in favor

of retaining the union. Nevertheless, on December 8, 1991, the presidents of Russia, the Ukraine, and Belarus declared the dissolution of the Soviet Union. Thus the specific actions of nationalist politicians meant that this state suffered the same fate as Yugoslavia. See, for example, Gorbatsjov 1999, 143.

12. See Gesemann 1979; Grmek 1993; Boehm 1983; Halpern and Kerewsky Halpern 1972; Vucinich 1979; Agoston-Nikolova 1994; Popović 1988; Anzulovic 1999 45–68; Miller 1999.

CHAPTER NINE

I would like to thank Halim El Madkouri for his most valuable comments on a previous version of this chapter.

1. Lawrence 1974, 156. For an account of the popularity of each of the three strategies mentioned by Lawrence amongst individual minorities, see Cadat and Fennema 1996, 655–81. It is of interest to observe that those who adopt Lawrence's third strategy do not vote for minority parties but for those of the established parties that are most explicit in their promises to further the interests of minorities in general. See Tillie and Fennema 2000, 71.

2. In 1990 in the Netherlands a party for Dutch citizens of foreign origin failed to meet the quota and then disappeared from the political scene.

3. The situation is somewhat more complicated at the local level: on the occasion of the elections for the municipal council in Amsterdam in 1998, the *Partij voor de Mensenrechten* (Human Rights Party) and *Toekomst '21* (Future '21), which were both led by immigrants, obtained a mere 5 percent of the immigrant-vote in Amsterdam. For Rotterdam, Utrecht, and Den Haag, the percentages are, respectively, 3 percent, 25 percent, and 10 percent. See Tillie and Fennema 2000, 35 ff. In Belgium, the *Arabisch Europese Liga* (Arabic European League) caused considerable commotion, but failed at the local ballot box.

4. "The distance between ethnic minorities mutually is larger than that between each of these minorities individually and autochthonous culture" (my translation). See the report by the minister for Big Cities Policy and Integration, *Integratie in het perspectief van immigratie*, Den Haag 2002.

5. Communication of Halim El Madkouri, consultant at the Instituut voor Multiculturele Ontwikkeling in Utrecht.

6. See P. Scheffer, "Het multiculturele drama," *NRC-Handelsblad*, January 29, 2000. This essay provoked a lively discussion not only in this newspaper, but in others as well.

7. In order to avoid possible misunderstanding I wish to emphasize that this plea for integration by politicization is not a plea for a legislation for cultural minorities: I fully agree here with Brian Barry's argument against such a degenerated variant of pluralism. See Barry 2001, 299–305. What I have in mind, instead, is to stimulate integration by inviting our fellow foreign citizens to make clear in a politically appro-

priate way what the common, national interest looks like if seen from *their* point of view. This, and only this, is the correct basis for immigrant political parties.

8. Report by the minister for Big Cities Policy and Integration, *Integratie in het perspectief van immigratie*, 53 ff, 64.

9. In the Netherlands the argument was used by members of rightist ultra-orthodox Protestant parties when the right of foreign residents to participate in the elections of municipal councils was discussed in Parliament in 1979. See Tillie and Fennema 2000, 12.

10. The intensity of this effort should not be exaggerated—at least for the Netherlands. For example, only 21 percent of the interviewed members of municipal councils effectively undertook action to increase the number of allochthonous town councillors for the municipal elections of 1998. See Leijenaar, Niemöller, and Van der Kooij 1999, 97. Because of conflicts concerning the composition of lists of candidates for the municipal councils, participation of immigrants has now even come to a standstill. See *De Volkskrant*, January 23, 2002.

11. Illustrative is that autochthonous party functionaries unanimously condemn their allochthonous party associates if they allow themselves to be guided by ethnic considerations. The argument then always is that this should be at odds with the requirement that a representative must always vote free from instructions by his or her rank and file. See Tillie and Fennema 2000, 12. But it is, in fact, not so easy to discern what is right and wrong in this argument within a system of proportional representation as obtains in the Netherlands. Anyway, the argument would make no sense in a party having the promotion of the interests of cultural minorities as one of its top priorities—and which would therefore be, as such, an extra argument to stimulate the foundation of such parties.

12. Hilhorst 2001, 25; Tillie and Fennema 2000, 12. An additional problem is that sometimes, political authorities of the allochthonous countries of origin do not hesitate to put pressure on representatives, thus jeopardising the independence of their political choices. See also Fennema and Cadat 2000, 12: "The most important problem . . . they (i.e. the allochthonous municipal council members) struggle with is their double loyalty. They are elected because of their ethnicity, but once elected they have to renounce that ethnic background" (my translation).

13. This advantage has also recently been emphasised by Madkouri (*De Volkskrant*, January 2002, 7) when he answers the question of the results of fifteen years of *political* integration as follows: "The positive effects quickly demonstrated themselves. The number of citizens of foreign origin seeing the Netherlands as its own country steadily increased. And so did trust in Dutch politics and in the Dutch state." See H. El Madkouri, "Rol van allochtonen in politiek verdient evaluatie" (my translation).

Bibliography

Aberbach, Putnam, and Rockman 1981: Joel Aberbach, Robert Putnam, and Bert Rockman, *Bureaucrats and Politicians in Western Democracies* (Cambridge, MA: Harvard University Press, 1981).

Acton 1862: John Acton, *Essays on Freedom and Power* (London: Thames and Hudson, 1862).

Agoston-Nikolova 1994: Elka Agoston-Nikolova, *Immured Women: Representations of Family Relationships in Balkan Slavic Oral Narrative Poetry* (PhD diss., Groningen University, 1994).

Albert 1993: M. Michel Albert, *Capitalisme contre capitalisme* (Paris: Éditions du Seuil, 1993).

Alesina and Spolaore 1997: Albert Alesina and Enrico Spolaore, "On the Number and Size of Nations" (*Quarterly Journal of Economics* 112, November 1997).

Alesina, Spolaore, and Wacziarg 1997: Albert Alesina, Enrico Spolaore, and Romain Wacziarg, *Economic Integration and Political Disintegration*, National Bureau of Economic Research Working Paper Series (Cambridge, MA: National Bureau of Economic Research, September 1997).

Allcock 1992: John Allcock et al. (eds.), *Yugoslavia in Transition: Choices and Constraints* (New York and Oxford: Berg, 1992).

Allcock 2000: John Allcock, *Explaining Yugoslavia* (London: Hurst, 2000).

Almond and Verba 1963: Gabriel A. Almond and Sidney Verba, *The Civic Culture: Political Attitudes and Democracy in Five Nations* (Princeton: Princeton University Press, 1963).

Anderson 1991: Benedict Anderson, *Imagined Communities: Reflections on the Origin and Spread of Nationalism*, rev. ed. (London: Verso, 1991).

Anderson 2001: Richard D. Anderson Jr. et al., "Conclusion: Postcommunism and the Theory of Democracy," in Richard D. Anderson Jr. et al., *Postcommunism and the Theory of Democracy* (Princeton: Princeton University Press, 2001).

Ankersmit 2002: Frank R. Ankersmit, *Political Representation* (Stanford, CA: Stanford University Press, 2002).

Anzulovic 1999: Branimir Anzulovic, *Heavenly Serbia: From Myth to Genocide* (London: Hurst, 1999).

Arai 1992: Masami Arai, *Turkish Nationalism in the Young Turk Era* (Leiden: Brill, 1992).

Aristotle 1957: Aristotle, *Politics and Poetics*, translated by Benjamin Jowett and Thomas Twining (New York: Viking, 1957).

Aronson 1992: Michael Aronson, "The Anti-Jewish Pogroms in Russia in 1881," in John D. Klier and Shlomo Lambroza (eds.), *Pogroms: Anti-Jewish Violence in Modern Russian History* (Cambridge: Cambridge University Press, 1992).

Bade 2000: Klaus J. Bade, *Europa in Bewegung. Migration vom späten 18. Jahrhundert bis zur Gegenwart* (Munich: C. H. Beck, 2000).

Bakić-Hayden 1995: Milica Bakić-Hayden, "Nesting Orientalisms: The Case of Former Yugoslavia" (*Slavic Review* 54, no. 4, 1995).

Bakić-Hayden and Hayden 1992: Milica Bakić-Hayden and Robert M. Hayden, "Orientalist Variations on the Theme 'Balkans': Symbolic Geography in Recent Yugoslav Cultural Politics" (*Slavic Review* 52, no. 1, 1992).

Balibar 1992: Étienne Balibar, *Les frontières de la democratie* (Paris: La Découverte, 1992).

Banac 1984: Ivo Banac, *The National Question in Yugoslavia: Origins, History, Politics* (Ithaca, NY: Cornell University Press, 1984).

Barany 1968: George Barany, *Stephan Szechenyi and the Awakening of Hungarian Nationalism* (Princeton: Princeton University Press, 1968).

Barany 2002: Zoltan Barany, "Ethnic Mobilization Without Prerequisites: the East European Gypsies" (*World Politics* 54, no. 3, April 2002).

Barry 2001: Brian Barry, *Culture and Equality: An Egalitarian Critique of Multiculturalism* (Cambridge, MA: Harvard University Press, 2001).

Bartstra 1960: Jan S. Bartstra, *Handboek tot de staatkundige geschiedenis van de landen van onze beschavingskring van 1648 tot heden* (Den Bosch: Malmberg, 1960).

Bauer 1907: Otto Bauer, *Die Nationalitätenfrage und die Sozialdemokratie* (Vienna: Wiener Volksbuchhandlung, 1907).

Bax 1992: Mart Bax, "Medjugorjes kleine oorlog. Barbarisering in een Bosnische bedevaartsplaats" (*Amsterdams Sociologisch Tijdschrift* 20, June 2, 1992).

Bax 1995: Mart Bax, *Medjugorje: Religion, Politics, and Violence in Rural Bosnia* (Amsterdam: VU Uitgeverij, 1995).

Becker and Audoin-Rouzeau 1995: Jean-Jacques Becker and Stéphane Audoin-Rouzeau, *La France, la nation, la guerre: 1850–1920* (Paris: Editions SEDES, 1995).

Bell 2001: David A. Bell, *The Cult of the Nation in France: Inventing Nationalism, 1680–1800* (Cambridge, MA: Harvard University Press, 2001).

Beller 1996: Steven Beller, *Francis Joseph* (London: Longman, 1996).

Benda 1927: Julien Benda, *La Trahison des Clercs* (Paris: Grasset, 1927).

Bennett 1995: Christopher Bennett, *Yugoslavia's Bloody Collapse: Causes, Course and Consequences* (London: Hurst, 1995).

Berend 2002: Ivan T. Berend, *History Derailed: Central and Eastern Europe in the Long Nineteenth Century* (Berkeley and Los Angeles: University of California Press, 2002).

Berend and Ránki 1977: Ivan T. Berend and György Ránki, *East Central Europe in the Nineteenth and Twentieth Centuries* (Budapest: Akadémia, 1977).

Berg-Schlosser and Mitchell 2000: Dirk Berg-Schlosser and Jeremy Mitchell, "Introduction," in Dirk Berg-Schlosser and Jeremy Mitchell (eds.), *Conditions of Democracy in Europe, 1919–39: Systematic Case Studies* (Houndmills: Macmillan, 2000).

Bibó 1986: István Bibó, *Valogatott tanulmányok*, vol. 1, *1935–1944*; vol. 2, *1945–1949* (Budapest: Magvetö Kiadó, 1986).

Birnbaum 1992: Pierre Birnbaum, *Les fous de la République. Histoire politique des Juifs d'État de Gambetta à Vichy* (Paris: Fayard, 1992).

Blok 1987: Lodewijk Blok, *Stemmen en kiezen. Het kiesstelsel in Nederland in de periode 1814–1850* (Groningen: Wolters-Noordhoff/Forsten, 1987).

Blum 1985: Mark E. Blum, *The Austro-Marxists: 1890–1918* (Lexington: University Press of Kentucky, 1985).

Body 1972: Paul Body, *Jozsef Eotvos and the Modernization of Hungary* (Philadelphia: American Philosophical Society, 1972).

Boehm 1983: Christopher Boehm, *Montenegrin Social Organizations and Values: Political Ethnography of a Refuge Area Tribal Adaptation* (New York: AMS Press, 1983).

Bolton and Roland 1997: Patrick Bolton and Gérard Roland, "The Breakup of Nations: A Political Economy Analysis" (*Quarterly Journal of Economics* 112, November 1997).

Boonzajer Flaes and Ramondt 1974: Rob Boonzajer Flaes and Joop Ramondt, *Autoriteit en democratie. Arbeiderszelfbestuur in rijke en arme Joegoslavische onderne-mingen* (Rotterdam: Universitaire Pers Rotterdam, 1974).

Bottomore and Goode 1978: Tom Bottomore and Patrick Goode (trans. and eds.), *Austro-Marxism* (Oxford: Oxford University Press, 1978).

Bourgeois 1897: Léon Bourgeois, *L'Education de la Démocratie française. Discours pro-nouncés de 1890 à 1896* (Paris: Cornély, 1897).

Bradley 1961–62: John F. N. Bradley, "Czech Pan-Slavism Before the First World War" (*The Slavonic and East European Review* 40, 1961–62).

Bradley 2000: John F. N. Bradley, "Czechoslovakia: External Crisis and Internal Occupation," in Dirk Berg-Schlosser and Jeremy Mitchell, *Conditions of Democracy in Europe, 1919–39: Systematic Case Studies* (Houndmills: Macmillan, 2000).

Braudel 1988: Fernand Braudel, *The Identity of France* (New York: Harper Perennial, 1988).

Broekmeyer 1970: Marius J. Broekmeyer (ed.), *Yugoslav Workers' Self-Management: Proceedings of a Symposium Held in Amsterdam, January 7–9, 1970* (Dordrecht: Reidel, 1970).

Broekmeyer 1985: Marius J. Broekmeyer et al., *Joegoslavië in crisis* (The Hague: Staatsuitgeverij, 1985).

Bromke 1967: Adam Bromke, *Poland's Politics: Idealism vs. Realism* (Cambridge, MA: Harvard University Press, 1967).

Broszat 1963: Martin Broszat, *Zweihundert Jahre deutsche Polenpolitik* (Munich: Ehrenwirt, 1963).

Brubaker 1992: Rogers Brubaker, *Citizenship and Nationhood in France and Germany* (Cambridge, MA: Harvard University Press, 1992).

Brubaker 1996: Rogers Brubaker, *Nationalism Reframed: Nationhood and the National Question in the New Europe* (Cambridge: Cambridge University Press, 1996).

Bufacchi and Burgess 1998: Vittorio Bufacchi and Simon Burgess, *Italy Since 1989: Events and Interpretations* (London: Macmillan, 1998).

Bugajski 2000: Janusz Bugajski, "Nationalist Majoritarian Parties: The Anatomy of Ethnic Domination," in Jonathan P. Stern (ed.), *The Politics of National Minority Participation in Post-Communist Europe* (Armonk, NY: M. E. Sharpe, 2000).

Burdeau 1966: Georges Burdeau, *Droit constitutionnel et institutions politiques*, 12th ed. (Paris: Librairie Générale de Droit et Jurisprudence, 1966).

Burgess 1997: Adam Burgess, *Divided Europe: The New Domination of the East* (London: Pluto Press, 1997).

Cadat and Fennema 1996: Brieuc-Yves Cadat and Meindert Fennema, "Het zelfbeeld van Amsterdamse migrantenpolitici in de jaren zeventig" (*Amsterdams Sociologisch Tijdschrift* 22, 1996).

Campbell 1971: John C. Campbell, *French Influence and the Rise of Romanian Nationalism* (New York: Arno [1957] 1971).

Chateaubriand 1849–50: François Auguste-René de Chateaubriand, *Mémoires d'Outre-Tombe* (Paris: Pénaud frères, 1849–50).

Chevalier 1958: Louis Chevalier, *Classes laborieuses et classes dangereuses à Paris pendant la première moitié du XIX siècle* (Paris: Plon, 1958).

Churchill 1974: *Winston S. Churchill: His Complete Speeches 1897–1963*, edited by Robert Rhodes James, vol. 7, *1943–1949* (New York and London: Chelsea House Publishers, 1974).

Clapham 1982: Christopher Clapham (ed.), *Private Patronage and Public Power* (London: Frances Pinter/New York: St. Martin's Press, 1982).

Cohen 1998: Daniel Cohen et al., *France: les révolutions invisibles* (Paris: Calmann-Levy, 1998).

Cohen 1995: Lenard J. Cohen, *Broken Bonds: Yugoslavia's Disintegration and Balkan Politics in Transition* (Boulder, CO: Westview Press, 1995).

Crankshaw 1963: Edward Crankshaw, *The Fall of the House of Habsburg* (New York: Viking Press, 1963).

Dahl 1989: Robert A. Dahl, *Democracy and Its Critics* (New Haven: Yale University Press, 1989).

Davies 1982: Norman Davies, *God's Playground: A History of Poland*, vol 2, *1795 to the Present* (Oxford: Clarendon Press, 1982).

Dawn 1991: Ernest Dawn, "The Origins of Arab Nationalism," in Rashid Khalidi et al. (eds.), *The Origins of Arab Nationalism* (New York: Columbia University Press, 1991).

Dawning 1992: Brian M. Dawning, *The Military Revolution and Political Change: Origins of Democracy and Autocracy in Early Modern Europe* (Princeton: Princeton University Press, 1992).

De Haan 1998: Ido de Haan, "Het onderwijs in de grondwet. Van staatszorg tot vrijheidsrecht," in Niek C .F. van Sas and Henk te Velde (eds.), *De eeuw van de Grondwet. Grondwet en politiek in Nederland, 1798–1917* (The Hague: Ministerie van Binnenlandse Zaken en Koninkrijksrelaties, 1998).

De Haan 2000: Ido de Haan, "Een gevelde Goliath? Liberale onderwijspolitiek 1848–1920," in T. J. van der Ploeg et al. (eds.), *De vrijheid van onderwijs, de ontwikkeling van een bijzonder grondrecht* (Utrecht: Lemma, 2000).

De Haan 2003: Ido de Haan, *Het beginsel van leven en wasdom. De constitutie van de Nederlandse politiek in de negentiende eeuw* (Amsterdam: Wereldbibliotheek, 2003).

De Jong 1999: Ron de Jong, *Van standspolitiek naar partijloyaliteit. Verkiezingen voor de Tweede Kamer 1848–1887* (Hilversum: Verloren, 1999).

De Rijk 1980: G. de Rijk, *Joegoslavië* (Haarlem: Romen, 1980).

De Swaan 1988: Abram de Swaan, *In Care of the State: Health Care, Education and Welfare in Europe and the USA in the Modern Era* (Cambridge: Polity Press, 1988).

Den Doolaard 1954: A. Den Doolaard, *Het land van Tito. Portret van mijn tweede vaderland* (Amsterdam: Querido, 1954).

Denitch 1994: Bogdan D. Denitch, *Ethnic Nationalism: The Tragic Death of Yugoslavia* (Minneapolis: University of Minnesota Press, 1994).

Diamond, Linz, and Lipset 1995: Larry Diamond, Juan J. Linz, and Seymour Martin Lipset, "Introduction: What Makes for Democracy," in Larry Diamond, Juan J. Linz, and Seymour Martin Lipset (eds.), *Politics in Developing Countries: Comparing Experiences with Democracy* (Boulder, CO: Lynne Rienner, 1995).

Diamond and Platter 1994: Larry Diamond and Marc F. Platter, "Introduction," in Larry Diamond and Marc F. Platter (eds.), *Nationalism, Ethnic Conflict, and Democracy* (Baltimore and London: The Johns Hopkins University Press, 1994).

Dietz 1932: Frederick Dietz, *The Political History of England* (New York: Macmillan, 1932).

Dittrich 1987: Zdenek R. Dittrich, *Midden-Europa? Een anti-nostalgie* (Utrecht, printed valediction, 1987).

Dittrich 1991: Zdenek R. Dittrich, *Uitgestelde bevrijding. Volkeren van oostelijk Europa na de Tweede Wereldoorlog* (Zeist: Het Spectrum, 1991).

Dittrich 1992: Zdenek R. Dittrich, "Oost-Europa tot circa 1870–1880," in Leonard H. M. Wesssels and Antoon Bosch (eds.), *Veranderde grenzen, Nationalisme in Europa, 1815–1919* (Heerlen/Nijmegen: SUN, 1992).

Droz 1960: Jacques Droz, *L'Europe centrale. Evolution historique de 1'idée de "Mitteleuropa"* (Paris: Payot, 1960).

Duijzings 1999: Ger H.J. Duijzings, *Religion and Politics of Identity in Kosovo* (PhD diss., University of Amsterdam, 1999).

Dunn and Fraser 1996: Seamus Dunn and Thomas G. Fraser (eds.), *Europe and Ethnicity: World War I and Contemporary Ethnic Conflict* (London: Routledge, 1996).

Durkheim 1963: Emile Durkheim, *Suicide*, translated by George Simpson (Glencoe, IL: The Free Press, 1963).

Durkheim 1964: Emile Durkheim, *The Division of Labor in Society*, translated by George Simpson (Glencoe, IL: The Free Press, 1964).

Eekman 1955: Tom A. Eekman, *Joegoslavië: Opstandig stiefkind van Europa* (Meppel: Boom, 1955).

Ehrenburg 1967: Ilya Ehrenburg, *The War: 1941–45*, translated by Tatyana Shebunina (Cleveland, OH: World Pub. Co., 1967).

Eidelberg 1974: Philip G. Eidelberg, *The Great Romanian Peasant Revolt of 1907: Origins of a Modern Jacquerie* (Leiden: E. J. Brill, 1974).

Eisenstadt 1981: Shmuel N. Eisenstadt, "Cultural Orientations and Center-Periphery in Europe in a Comparative Perspective," in Per Torsvik (ed.) *Mobilisation, Center-Periphery Structures and Nation-Building: A Volume in Commemoration of Stein Rokkan* (Bergen: Universitetsforlaget, 1981).

Emmert 1990: Thomas E. Emmert, *Serbian Golgotha: Kosovo, 1389* (New York: Columbia University Press, 1990).

Europa 1992: Europa im Krieg. Die Debatte über den Krieg im ehemaligen Jugoslawien (Frankfurt: Suhrkamp, 1992).

European Bank 1996: *European Bank for Regional Development Report 1994* (Brussels, 1996).

Fennema and Cadat 2000: Meindert Fennema and Brieuc-Yves Cadat, "Raadsleden met twee antennes. Ter Inleiding," in Saron Petronilia (ed.), *Raadsleden met dubbele antenne* (Amsterdam: Instituut voor Publiek en Politiek, 2000).

Ferenczi 1984: Caspar Ferenczi, "Nationalismus und Neoslawismus in Russland vor dem ersten Weltkrieg" (*Forschungen zur osteuropäischen Geschichte* 34, 1984).

Fink 1995: Carole Fink, "The League of Nations and the Minorities Question" (*World Affairs* 157, no. 4, spring 1995).

Finney 1995: Patrick B. Finney, "'An Evil for All Concerned': Great Britain and Minority Protection after 1919" (*Journal of Contemporary History* 30, no. 3, July 1995).

Fischer-Galati 1969: Stephen Fischer-Galati, *The Socialist Republic of Rumania* (Baltimore: Johns Hopkins University Press, 1969).

Fischer-Galati 2000: Stephen Fischer-Galati, "Romania: Crisis Without Compromise," in Dirk Berg-Schlosser and Jeremy Mitchell (eds.), *Conditions of Democracy in Europe, 1919–39: Systematic Case-Studies* (Houndmills: Macmillan, 2000).

Fish 1998: M. Steven Fish, "Democratization's Requisites: The Postcommunist Experience" (*Post-Soviet Affairs* 14, July-September 1998).

Fish 2001: M. Steven Fish, "The Dynamics of Democratic Erosion," in Richard D. Anderson Jr. et al., *Postcommunism and the Theory of Democracy* (Princeton: Princeton University Press, 2001).

Fountain 1980: Alvin Marcus Fountain II, *Roman Dmowski: Party, Tactics, Ideology, 1895–1907* (Boulder, CO: East European Monographs, 1980).

Gadgil 1975: Dhananjay R. Gadgil, "The Protection of Minorities," in William F. Mackey and Albert Verdoodt (eds.), *The Multinational Society: Papers of the Ljubljana Seminar* (Rowley, MA: Newbury House Publishers, 1975).

Garrigou 1992: Alain Garrigou, *Le vote et la vertu. Comment les Français sont devenus électeurs* (Paris: Presses de la Fondation nationale des sciences politiques, 1992).

Gellner and Waterbury 1977: Ernest Gellner and James Waterbury (eds.), *Patrons and Clients in Mediterranean Societies* (London: Duckworth, 1977).

Gerrits 1992: André W. M. Gerrits, *Nationalism and Political Change in Post-Communist Europe* (The Hague: Clingendael, 1992).

Gesemann 1979: Gerhard Gesemann, *Heroische Lebensform. Zur Literatur und Wesenskunde der Balkanische Patriarchalität* (Neuried: Hieronymus Verlag, 1979).

Ginsberg 1965: Morris Ginsberg, "The Sociology of Pareto," in James H. Meisel (ed.), *Pareto and Mosca* (Englewood Cliffs, NJ: Prentice–Hall, 1965).

Glassl 1967: Horst Glassl, *Der mährische Ausgleich*, (Munich: Fides Verlagsgesellschat, 1967).

Glenny 1996: Misha Glenny, *The Fall of Yugoslavia: The Third Balkan War* (London: Penguin Books, 1996).

Goldblatt 1997: David Goldblatt, "Democracy in the 'Long Nineteenth Century', 1760–1919," in David Potter et al. (eds.), *Democratization* (Cambridge: Milton Keynes, 1997).

Goldsworthy 1998: Vesna Goldsworthy, *Inventing Ruritania: The Imperialism of the Imagination* (New Haven: Yale University Press, 1998).

Gorbatsjov 1999: Michail Gorbatsjov, *Mijn Rusland. De dramatische geschiedenis van een grootmacht* (Amsterdam: Balans, 1999).

Gover 1875: William C. Gover, *The Tammany Hall Democracy of the City of New York, and the general committee for 1875, being a brief history of the Tammany Hall democracy from 1834 to the present time* (New York: M. B. Brown Printer, 1875).

Greenfeld 1992: Liah Greenfeld, *Nationalism: Five Roads to Modernity* (Cambridge, MA: Harvard University Press, 1992).

Grmek 1993: Mirko Grmek et al. (eds.), *Le nettoyage etnique. Documents historiques sur une idéologie serbe* (Paris: Fayard, 1993).

Gross 1997: Jan Gross, "War as Revolution," in Norman Naimark and Leonid Gibianskii (eds.), *The Establishment of Communist Regimes in Eastern Europe, 1944–1949* (Boulder, CO: Westview Press, 1997).

Gutterbock 1980: Thomas Gutterbock, *Machine Politics in Transition* (Chicago: University of Chicago Press, 1980).

Haas 1997: Ernst B. Haas, *Nationalism, Liberalism, Progress* (Ithaca, NY: Cornell University Press, 1997).

Hackett 1980: John Hackett, *The Third World War. August 1985: A Future History* (London: Sphere Books, 1980).

Hagen 1980: William W. Hagen, *Germans, Poles, and Jews: The Nationality Conflict in the Prussian East, 1772–1914* (Chicago: University of Chicago Press, 1980).

Hall 1994: Brian Hall, *The Impossible Country: A Journey Through the Last Days of Yugoslavia* (London: Penguin Books, 1994).

Halpern and Kerewsky Halpern 1972: Joel M. Halpern and B. Barbara Kerewsky Halpern, *A Serbian Village in Historical Perspective* (Prospect Heights: Waveland Press, 1972).

Hanák 1988: Peter Hanák, *Magyarország Története, 1890–1918* (Budapest: Akadémiai Kiadó, 1988).

Hanioglu 1995: M. Sükrü Hanioglu, *The Young Turks in Opposition* (New York: Oxford University Press, 1995).

Hašek 1930: Jaroslav Hašek, *The Good Soldier Schweik*, translated by Paul Selver (Garden City, NY: Doubleday, 1930).

Haslam 1984: Jonathan Haslam, *The Soviet Union and the Struggle for Collective Security in Europe, 1933–39* (London: Macmillan, 1984).

Hayes 1992: Paul Hayes (ed.), *Themes in Modern European History, 1890–1945* (London: Routledge, 1992).

Hazareesingh 1998: Sudhir Hazareesingh, *From Subject to Citizen: The Second Empire and the Emergence of Modern French Democracy* (Princeton: Princeton University Press, 1998).

Held 1987: David Held, *Models of Democracy* (Cambridge: Cambridge University Press, 1987).

Henderson 1976: Thomas M. Henderson, *Tammany Hall and the New Immigrants: The Progressive Years* (New York: Arno Press, 1976).

Hilhorst 2001: Pieter Hilhorst, "Onmogelijke spagaat. Dubbele opdracht verlamt allochtone politici" (*Contrast*, December 20, 2001).

Hitchins 1994: Keith Hitchins, *Rumania, 1866–1947* (Oxford: Clarendon Press, 1994).

Hitler 1971: Adolf Hitler, *Mein Kampf*, translated by Ralph Manheim (Boston: Houghton Mifflin, 1971).

Hobsbawm 1994: Eric Hobsbawm, *Age of Extremes: A History of the World, 1914–1991* (London: Michael Joseph, 1994).

Holbrooke 1998: Richard Holbrooke, *To End a War* (New York: Random House, 1998).

Hollinger 1994: Robert Hollinger, *Postmodernism and the Social Sciences: A Thematic Approach* (Thousand Oaks, CA: Russel Sage Publications, 1994).

Horak 1961: Stephen M. Horak, *Poland and Her National Minorities, 1919–1939* (New York: Vantage, 1961).

Horowitz 1985: Donald L. Horowitz, *Ethnic Groups in Conflict* (Berkeley and Los Angeles: University of California Press, 1985).

Hosking 1997: Geoffrey Hosking, *Russia: People and Empire, 1552–1917* (Cambridge, MA: Harvard University Press, 1997).

Hourani 1962: Albert Hourani, *Arabic Thought in the Liberal Age, 1798–1939* (Oxford: Oxford University Press, 1962).

Hroch 1999: Miroslav Hroch, *Na prahu národní existence. Touha a skutecnost* (Prague: Mladá Fronta, 1999).

Huntington 1996: Samuel P. Huntington, *The Clash of Civilizations and the Remaking of World Order* (New York: Simon & Schuster, 1996).

Ilincioiu 1991: Ion Ilincioiu (ed.), *The Great Romanian Peasant Revolt of 1907* (Bucureşt: Editura Academiei Română, 1991).

Janos 1982: Andrew C. Janos, *The Politics of Backwardness in Hungary, 1825–1945* (Princeton: Princeton University Press, 1982).

Janos 1989: Andrew C. Janos, "The Politics of Backwardness in Continental Europe, 1780–1945" (*World Politics* 41, no. 3, April 1989).

Janos 2000: Andrew C. Janos, *East Central Europe in the Modern World: The Politics of the Borderlands from Pre- to Postcommunism* (Stanford, CA: Stanford University Press, 2000).

Janos 2001: Andrew C. Janos, "From Eastern Empire to Western Hegemony: East Central Europe Under Two International Regimes" (*East European Politics and Societies* 15, no. 2, 2001).

Jaszi 1929: Oscar Jaszi, *The Dissolution of the Habsburg Monarchy* (Chicago: University of Chicago Press, 1929).

Jelavich 1990: Charles Jelavich, *South Slav Nationalisms: Textbooks and Yugoslav Union Before 1914* (Columbus: Ohio State University Press, 1990).

Jelavich and Jelavich 1993: Charles Jelavich and Barbara Jelavich, *The Establishment of the Balkan National States, 1804–1920: A History of East Central Europe*, vol. 8 (Seattle and London, University of Washington Press, 1993).

Johnson 1985: Douglas Johnson, "Jules Ferry et les protestants," in François Furet (ed.), *Jules Ferry, fondateur de la République* (Paris: École des Hautes Études en Sciences Sociales, 1985).

Johnson 1996: Martin Phillip Johnson, *The Paradise of Association: Political Culture and Popular Organizations in the Paris Commune of 1871* (Ann Arbor: University of Michigan Press, 1996).

Judah 1997: Tim Judah, *The Serbs: History, Myth, and the Destruction of Yugoslavia* (New Haven: Yale University Press, 1997).

Judt 1992: Tony Judt, *Past Imperfect: French Intellectuals, 1944–1956* (Berkeley and Los Angeles: University of California Press, 1992).

Kale 1992: Steven D. Kale, *Legitimism and the Reconstruction of French Society, 1852–1883* (Baton Rouge: University of Louisiana Press, 1992).

Kalvoda 1986: Josef Kalvoda, *The Genesis of Czechoslovakia* (Boulder, CO: East European Monographs, 1986).

Kamiński 2000: Andrzej S. Kamiński, *Historia Rzeczypospolitej Wielu Narodów, 1505–1795* (Lublin: Instytut Europy Stodkowo Wschodniej, 2000).

Kann 1950: Robert A.Kann, *The Multinational Empire: Nationalism and National Reform in the Habsburg Monarchy, 1848–1918*, 2 vols. (New York: Columbia University Press, 1950).

Kann 1974: Robert A. Kann, *A History of the Habsburg Empire, 1526–1918* (Berkeley and Los Angeles: University of California Press, 1974).

Kaplan 1981: Karel Kaplan, *Der kurze Marsch. Kommunistische Machtübernahme in der Tschechoslowakei, 1945–1948* (Munich/Vienna: Oldenbourg, 1981).

Kappeler 1993: Andreas Kappeler, *Russland als Vielvölkerreich: Entstehung, Geschichte, Zerfall* (Munich: C. H. Beck, 1993).

Kaser and Radice 1975: Michael C. Kaser and Edward A. Radice, *The Economic History of Eastern Europe, 1991–1975* (Oxford: Clarendon Press, 1975).

Kaufman 2001: Stuart J. Kaufman, *Modern Hatreds: The Symbolic Politics of Ethnic War* (Ithaca, NY: Cornell University Press, 2001).

Kayali 1997: Hasan Kayali, *Arabs and Young Turks: Ottomanism, Arabism, and Islamism in the Ottoman Empire, 1908–1918* (Berkeley and Los Angeles: University of California Press, 1997).

Kenney 1997: Padraic Kenney, *Rebuilding Poland: Workers and Communists, 1945–1950* (Ithaca, NY: Cornell University Press, 1997).

Kenrick and Puxon 1972: Donald Kenrick and Grattan Puxon, *The Destiny of Europe's Gypsies* (Sussex: Sussex University Press, 1972).

Kerr 1966: Malcolm H. Kerr, *Islamic Reform: The Political and Legal Theories of Muhammad Abduh and Rashid Rida* (Berkeley and Los Angeles: University of California Press, 1966).

Kersten 1991: Krystyna Kersten, *The Establishment of Communist Rule in Poland, 1943–1948*, translated by John Micgiel and Michael H. Bernhard (Berkeley and Los Angeles: University of California Press, 1991).

Khalidi 1991: Rashid Khalidi "Ottomanism and Arabism in Syria Before 1914: A Reassessment," in Rashid Khalidi et al. (eds.), *The Origins of Arab Nationalism* (New York: Columbia University Press, 1991).

Khoury 1983: Philip Khoury, *Urban Notables and Arab Nationalism: The Politics of Damascus, 1860–1920* (Cambridge: Cambridge University Press, 1983).

King 2001: Jeremy King, "The Nationalisation of East Central Europe: Ethnicism, Ethnicity, and Beyond," in Nancy Wingfield and Maria Bucur (eds.), *Staging the Past: The Politics of Commemoration in Habsburg Central Europe, 1848 to the Present* (West Lafayette, IN: Purdue University Press, 2001).

King 1973: Robert R. King, *Minorities Under Communism: Nationalities as a Source of Tension Among Balkan Communist States* (Cambridge, MA: Harvard University Press, 1973).

Klier 1995: John Doyle Klier, *Imperial Russia's Jewish Question, 1855–1881* (Cambridge: Cambridge University Press, 1995).

Koch 1887: Adolf Koch, *Prince Alexander of Battenberg* (London: Whitaker, 1887).

Kohser-Spohn 2001: Christiane Kohser-Spohn, "Staatliche Gewalt und der Zwang zur Eindeutigkeit: Die Politik Frankreichs in Elsaß-Lothringen nach dem Ersten Weltkrieg," in Philipp Ther und Holm Sundhaussen (eds.), *National-itätenkonflikte im 20. Jahrhundert: Ursachen von inter-ethnischer Gewalt im Vergleich* (Wiesbaden: Harrassowitz, 2001).

Kossmann 1986: Ernst H. Kossmann, *De Lage Landen 1780–1980. Twee Eeuwen Nederland en België Deel I. 1798–1914* (Amsterdam: Elsevier, 1986).

Křen 1990: Jan Křen, *Konfliktní společenství češi a Nemci, 1780–1918* (Prague: Academia, 1990).

Křen 2000: Jan Křen, "Die Tradition der tschechischen Demokratie," in Manfred Hildermeier, Jürgen Kocka, and Christoph Conrad (eds.), *Europäische Zivilgesellschaft in Ost und West* (Berlin: Campus, 2000).

Kučera 1999: Jaroslav Kučera, *Minderheit im Nationalstaat, Die Sprachenfrage in den tschechisch-deutschen Beziehungen, 1918–1938* (Munich: Oldenbourg, 1999)

Kučera (2000): Jaroslav Kučera, "Von der 'nationalen' zur 'sozialen' Revolution: die Zwangsaussiedlung der Deutschen aus der Tschechoslowakei und der Februar-Sieg der Kommunisten" (*Mitteilungen des Oberösterreichischen Landesarchivs* 19, Linz 2000).

Kundera 1984: Milan Kundera, "Central European 'Tragedy'" (*The New York Review of Books*, April 26, 1984).

Kuyper 1880: Abraham Kuyper, *Souvereiniteit in eigen kring* (Amsterdam: Kruyt, 1880).

Kymlicka 1995: Will Kymlicka, *Multicultural Citizenship* (Oxford: Oxford University Press, 1995).

Kymlicka and Opalski 2001: Will Kymlicka and Magda Opalski, "Introduction," in Will Klymicka and Magda Opalski (eds.), *Can Liberal Pluralism Be Exported? Western Political Theory and Ethnic Relations in Eastern Europe* (Oxford: Oxford University Press, 2001).

Lach 1993: Stanisław Lach, *Przeksztalcenia ustrojowo-gospodarcze w rolnictwie ziem zachodnich i pólnocnych w latach 1945–1949: studium historyczne* (Slupsk: Wyzsza Szkola Pedagogiczna w Slupsku, 1993).

Landau 1995: Jacob Landau, *Pan-Turkism: From Irredentism to Cooperation* (Bloomington and Indianapolis: Indiana University Press, 1995).

Langlois 1992: Claude Langlois, "Catholiques et laïcs," in Pierre Nora, *Les lieux de mémoire III: Les France: 1: Conflits et partages* (Paris: Gallimard, 1992).

Lawrence 1974: Daniel Lawrence, *Black Migrants, White Natives: A Study of Race Relations in Nottingham* (Cambridge: Cambridge University Press, 1974).

Lederer 1969: Ivo J. Lederer, "Nationalism and the Yugoslavs," in Ivo J. Lederer and Peter Sugar (eds.), *Nationalism in Eastern Europe* (Seattle: University of Washington Press, 1969).

Leijenaar, Niemöller, and Van der Kooij 1999: Monique Leijenaar, Kees Niemöller, and Astrid van der Kooij, *Kandidaten gezocht. Politieke partijen en het streven naar grotere diversiteit onder gemeenteraadsleden* (Amsterdam: Instituut voor Publiek en Politiek, 1999).

Lévi-Strauss 1952: Claude Lévi-Strauss, *Race et Histoire* (Paris: UNESCO, 1952).

Lévi-Strauss 1983: Claude Lévi-Strauss, *Le Regard éloigné* (Paris: Plon, 1983).

Lieven 2000: Dominic Lieven, *Empire: The Russian Empire and its Rivals* (New Haven: Yale University Press, 2000).

Lijphart 1968: Arend Lijphart, *The Politics of Accommodation: Pluralism and Democracy in the Netherlands* (Berkeley and Los Angeles: University of California Press, 1968).

Lilge 1978: Hans-Georg Lilge, *Arbeiterselbstverwaltung. Das Beispiel Jugoslawien* (Bern/Stuttgart: Haupt, 1978).

Lipset 1960: Seymour Martin Lipset, *Political Man: The Social Bases of Politics* (Garden City, NY: Doubleday, 1960).

Lipset and Rokkan 1967: Seymour Martin Lipset and Stein Rokkan, *Party Systems and Voter Alignments: Cross-National Perspectives* (New York: The Free Press, 1967).

Lorenz 1997: Chris Lorenz, *Konstruktion der Vergangenheit. Eine Einführung in die Geschichtstheorie* (Cologne: Böhlau, 1997).

Luebbert 1991: Gregory M. Luebbert, *Liberalism, Fascism, or Social Democracy: Social Classes and the Political Origins of Regimes in Interwar Europe* (New York/Oxford: Oxford University Press 1991).

Luža 1964: Radomír Luža, *The Transfer of the Sudeten Germans: A Study of Czech-German Relations, 1933–1962* (New York: New York University Press, 1964).

Macartney 1934: Aylmer C. Macartney, *National States and National Minorities* (London: Oxford University Press, 1934).

Macartney 1937: Aylmer C. Macartney, *Hungary and Her Successors* (London: Oxford University Press, 1937).

Macartney 1968: Aylmer C. Macartney, *The Habsburg Empire, 1790–1918* (London: Weidenfeld and Nicholson, 1968).

Magocsi 1997: Paul Magocsi, *The History of the Ukraine* (Toronto: Toronto University Press, 1997).

Malia 1999: Martin Malia, *Russia Under Western Eyes: From the Bronze Horseman to the Lenin Mausoleum* (Cambridge, MA: Belknap, 1999).

Mamatey 1973: Victor S. Mamatey, "The Development of Czechoslovak Democracy, 1920–1938," in Victor S. Mamatey and Radomír Luža (eds.), *A History of the Czechoslovak Republic, 1918–1948* (Princeton: Princeton University Press, 1973).

Mann 1988: Michael Mann, *States, War, and Capitalism* (New York: Basil Blackwell, 1988).

Mann 1993: Michael Mann, *The Sources of Social Power II: The Rise of Classes and Nation-States, 1760–1914* (Cambridge: Cambridge University Press, 1993).

Marrus 1985: Michael Marrus, *The Unwanted: European Refugees in the Twentieth Century* (Oxford: Oxford University Press, 1985).

May 1951: Arthur J. May, *The Hapsburg Monarchy, 1867–1914* (Cambridge, MA: Harvard University Press, 1951).

Mayeur 1973: Jean-Marie Mayeur, *Les débuts de la IIIe République, 1871–1898* (Paris: Seuil, 1973).

Mazower 1998: Mark Mazower, *Dark Continent: Europe's Twentieth Century* (London: Allen Lane, 1998).

Mazower 2002: Mark Mazower, "Violence and the State in the Twentieth Century" (*The American Historical Review* 107, no. 4, 2002).

McKenzie and Silver 1967: Robert T. McKenzie and Allan Silver, "The Delicate Experiment: Industrialism, Conservatism and Working-Class Tories in England," in Seymour Martin Lipset and Stein Rokkan (eds.), *Party Systems and Voter Alignments: Cross-National Perspectives* (New York: The Free Press, 1967).

Meeus and Raaijmakers 1984: Wilhelmus H. J. Meeus and Quintin A. W. Raaijmakers, *Gewoon gehoorzaam. Een sociaal-psychologisch onderzoek naar gehoorzaamheid* (PhD diss., Utrecht University, 1984).

Meisel 1965: James H. Meisel, "Introduction," in James H. Meisel (ed.), *Pareto and Mosca* (Englewood Cliffs, NJ: Prentice-Hall, 1965).

Meister 1970: Albert Meister, *Où va l'autogestion yougoslave?* (Paris: Seuil, 1970).

Milgram 1974: Stanley Milgram, *Grenzeloze gehoorzaamheid. Een experimenteel onderzoek* (Utrecht-Antwerp: Het Spectrum, 1974).

Mill 1958: John Stuart Mill, *Considerations in Representative Government* [1861] (New York: Liberal Arts Press, 1958).

Mill 1963: John Stuart Mill, *Collected Works* (London: Routledge and Kegan Paul, 1963).

Miller 1999: Nicholas Miller, "Review of Branimir Anzulovic *Heavenly Serbia: From Myth to Genocide*" (*Habsburg H-Net Reviews*, May 1999).

Moore 1967: Barrington Moore Jr., *Social Origins of Dictatorship and Democracy: Lord and Peasant in the Making of the Modern World* (Boston: Beacon Press, 1967).

Musil 1995: Robert Musil, *The Man Without Qualities*, 2 vols., translated by Sophie Wilkins (New York: Alfred A. Knopf, 1995).

Naimark 1995: Norman M. Naimark, *The Russians in Germany* (Cambridge, MA: Harvard University Press, 1995).

Naimark 2001: Norman M. Naimark, *Fires of Hatred: Ethnic Cleansing in Twentieth-Century Europe* (Cambridge, MA: Harvard University Press, 2001).

Nairn 1977: Tom Nairn, *The Break-Up of Britain: Crisis and Neo-Nationalism* (London: Humanities Press, 1977).

Nation 1995: R. Craig Nation, "Balkan Images in the West," (*Balkan Forum* 3, no. 3, September 1995).

Newman 1954: Bernard Newman, *Rood Joego-Slavië* (Tilburg: Nederlands Boekhuis, 1954).

Noiriel 1988: Gérard Noiriel, *Le Creuset français. Histoire de l'immigration XIXe-XXe sciècles* (Paris: Seuil, 1988).

Nora 1984: Pierre Nora, "Lavisse, instituteur national," in Pierre Nora (ed.), *Les lieux de mémoire*, vol. 1, *La République* (Paris: Gallimard, 1984).

Nord 1995: Philip Nord, *The Republican Moment: Struggles for Democracy in Nineteenth Century France* (Cambridge, MA: Harvard University Press, 1995).

Nurkse 1962: Ragnar Nurkse, *Problems of Capital Formation in Underdeveloped Countries* (New York: Oxford University Press, 1962).

Office of Research 2000: United States Department of State, Office of Research, *Ten Years After the Fall of the Wall: Public Opinion in Central and Eastern European Countries in Transition* (Washington, DC, 2000).

Opalski and Bartal 1992: Magdalena Opalski and Israel Bartal, *Poles and Jews: A Failed Brotherhood* (Hanover/New Hampshire: University Press of New England, 1992).

The Other Balkan Wars 1993: *The Other Balkan Wars: A 1913 Carnegie Endowment Inquiry in Retrospect with a New Introduction and Reflections on the Present Conflict by George F. Kennan* (Washington, DC: Carnegie Endowment for International Peace, 1993).

Ozouf and Ozouf 1984: Jacques Ozouf and Mona Ozouf, "La tour de la France par deux enfants. Le petit livre rouge de la République," in Pierre Nora (ed.), *Les lieux de mémoire*, vol. 1, *La République* (Paris: Gallimard, 1984).

Paczkowski 1993: Andrzej Paczkowski, *Referendum z 30 czerwca 1946 r. Przebieg i wyniki* (Warsaw: Instytut Studiów Politycznych Polskiej Akademii Nauk, 1993).

Palmer 1972: Alan Palmer, *Metternich* (London: Weidenfeld & Nicolson, 1972).

Parsons and Shils 1951: Talcott Parsons and Edward Shils, "Personality as a System of Action," in Parsons and Shils (eds.), *Towards a General Theory of Action* (New York: Harper and Row, 1951).

Partacz 1996: Czeslaw Partacz, *Od Badeniego do Potockiego: Stosunki polsko-ukrainskie w Galicji w latach 1888–1908* (Torun: Wydawn. Adam Marszalek, 1996).

Péter 1997–98: László Péter, "The Autocratic Principle of the Law and Civil Rights in Nineteenth-Century Hungary," in *Central European University History Department Yearbook* (Budapest: Central European University Press, 1997–98).

Pipes 1964: Richard Pipes, *The Formation of the Soviet Union: Communism and Nationalism, 1917–1923*, rev. ed. (Cambridge, MA: Harvard University Press, 1964).

Pipes 1992: Richard Pipes, *Russia Under the Old Regime*, 2nd ed. (New York: Macmillan, 1992).

Podkaminer 1998: Leon Podkaminer et al., *Transition Countries* (Vienna: Wiener Institut für Internationale Wirtschaftsvergleiche Monograph, 1998).

Popović 1988: Tatyana Popović, *Prince Marko. The Hero of South Slavic Epics* (Syracuse, NY: Syracuse University Press, 1988).

Porter 2000: Brian Porter, *When Nationalism Began to Hate: Imagining Modern Politics in Nineteenth-Century Poland* (New York: Oxford University Press, 2000).

Potter 1955: Henry Potter, *History of France, 1460–1560: The Emergence of a Nation State* (New York: St. Martin's Press, 1955).

Preece 1998: Jennifer Jackson Preece, *National Minorities and the European Nation-States System* (Oxford: Clarendon Press, 1998).

Pulpán 1993: Karen Pulpán, *Nástin Českých a československých hospodařskych dějin* (Prague: Charles University Press, 1993).

Putnam 1993: Robert D. Putnam, *Making Democracy Work: Civic Traditions in Modern Italy* (Princeton: Princeton University Press, 1993).

Pynsent 1994: Robert Pynsent, *Questions of Identity: Czech and Slovak Ideas of Nationality and Personality* (Budapest: Central European University Press, 1994).

Rabushka and Shepsle 1972: Alvin Rabushka and Kenneth A. Shepsle, *Politics in Plural Societies: A Theory of Democratic Instability* (Columbus, OH: Charles E. Merrill, 1972).

Rachamimov 1996: Alon Rachamimov, "Diaspora Nationalism's Pyrrhic Victory: The Controversy Regarding the Electoral Reform of 1909 in Bukowina," in John Micgiel (ed.), *State and Nation Building in East Central Europe: Contemporary Perspectives* (New York: Institute on East Central Europe, Columbia University, 1996).

Radvanovský 2001: Zdeněk Radvanovský, "The Social and Economic Consequences of Resettling Czechs into Northwestern Bohemia, 1945–1947," in Philipp Ther and Ana Siljak (eds.), *Redrawing Nations: Ethnic Cleansing in East Central Europe, 1944–1948* (Lanham: Rowman & Littlefield, 2001).

Ramet 1996: Sabrina P. Ramet, *Balkan Babel: The Disintegration of Yugoslavia from the Death of Tito to Ethnic War* (Boulder, CO: Westview Press, 1996).

Randeraad and Wolffram 2001: Nico Randeraad and Dirk Jan Wolffram, "Dutch Administrative Culture in a Historic Perspective," in Frank Hendriks and Theo Toonen (eds.), *Polder Politics: The Re-invention of Consensus Democracy in the Netherlands* (Aldershot: Ashgate, 2001).

Renan 1947: Ernest Renan, "Qu'est-ce qu'une nation?" *Oeuvres complètes* 1 (Paris: Henriette Psichari, 1947).

Rida 1909: Rashid Rida, "Al-`Arab wa al-Turk", in *al-Manar* (Cairo), vol. 12 (1909). Reprinted in Yusuf Husayn Ibish and Yusuf Quzma Khuri (eds.), *Maqalat al-Shaykh Rashid Rida al-siyasiyyah*, vol. 2 (Beirut: Dar Ibn Arabi, 1994).

Rogger 1986: Hans Rogger, *Jewish Policies and Right-Wing Politics in Imperial Russia* (London: Macmillan, 1986).

Rokkan and Urwin 1982: Stein Rokkan and Derek Urwin, *The Politics of Territorial Identity: Studies in European Regionalism* (London: Sage, 1982).

Römhildt 1994: Kerstin Römhildt, *Nationalismus und ethnische Identität im 'spanischen' Baskenland* (Münster: Lit, 1994).

Rosanvallon 1990: Pierre Rosanvallon, *L'État en France de 1789 à nos jours* (Paris: Seuil, 1990).

Rosanvallon 1992: Pierre Rosanvallon, *Le sacre du citoyen. Histoire du suffrage universel en France* (Paris: Gallimard, 1992).

Rosanvallon 2000: Pierre Rosanvallon, *La démocratie inachevée. Histoire de la souveraineté du people en France* (Paris: Gallimard, 2000).

Rose 1997: Richard Rose, "Where Are the Post-Communist Countries Going?" (*Journal of Democracy* 8, no. 3, July 1997).

Rosenau 1991: Marie Pauline Rosenau, *Post-Modernism and the Social Sciences: Insights, Inroads, and Intrusions* (Princeton: Princeton University Press, 1991).

Roshwald 2001: Aviel Roshwald, *Ethnic Nationalism and the Fall of Empires: Central Europe, Russia and the Middle East, 1914–1923* (London: Routledge, 2001).

Roth 1995: Joseph Roth, *The Radetzky March*, translated by Joachim Neugroschel (Woodstock, NY: Overlook Press, 1995 [1932]).

Rothschild 1974: Joseph Rothschild, *A History of East Central Europe*, vol. 9, *East Central Europe Between the Two World Wars* (Seattle: University of Washington Press, 1974).

Rueschemeyer 1992: Dietrich Rueschemeyer et al., *Capitalist Development and Democracy* (Cambridge: Polity Press, 1992).

Słabek 1972: Henryk Słabek, *Dzieje polskiej reformy rolnej 1944–48* (Warsaw: Wiedza Powszechna, 1972).

Sartori 2002: Giovanni Sartori, *Pluralismo, multiculturalismo ed estranei: saggio sulle società multietniche* (Milan: Rizzoli 2002).

Schlesinger 1998: Arthur M. Schlesinger Jr., *The Disuniting of America* (New York: Norton, 1998).

Schlesinger 2000: Arthur M. Schlesinger Jr., *A Life in the Twentieth Century: Innocent Beginnings, 1917–1950* (Boston: Houghton Mifflin, 2000).

Schmidt-Hartmann 1990: Eva Schmidt-Hartmann, "The Fallacy of Realism: Some Problems of Masaryk's Approach to Czech National Aspirations," in Stanley B. Winters (ed.), *T. G. Masaryk (1850–1937)*, vol. 1 (New York: St. Martin's Press, 1990).

Schmitt 1985: Carl Schmitt, "On the Contradiction Between Parliamentarism and Democracy," in *The Crisis of Parliamentary Democracy*, translated by Ellen Kennedy (Cambridge, MA: MIT Press, 1985).

Scholten 1987: Ilja Scholten, *Political Stability and Neo-corporatism: Corporatist Integration and Societal Cleavages in Western Europe* (London: Sage, 1987).

Schöpflin 1989: George Schöpflin, "Central Europe: Definitions Old and New," in George Schöpflin and Nancy Wood, *In Search of Central Europe* (Cambridge: Polity Press, 1989).

Schrenk 1979: Martin Schrenk et al. (eds.), *Yugoslavia: Self-management, Socialism, and the Challenges of Development* (Baltimore/London: Johns Hopkins University Press, 1979).

Schroevers 1961: Marinus Schroevers, *Op zoek naar Joego-Slavië* (The Hague: Servire, 1961).

Schulze 1994: Hagen Schulze, *Staat und Nation in der europäischen Geschichte* (Munich: Verlag C. H. Beck, 1994).

Scurtu 1988: Ioan Scurtu, *Contributii privind viata politica din Romania* (Bucureşti: Editura Stiintifica si Enciclopedica, 1988).

Seton-Watson 1945: Hugh Seton-Watson, *Eastern Europe Between the Wars, 1918–1941* (Cambridge: Cambridge University Press, 1945).

Seton-Watson 1962: Hugh Seton-Watson, *Eastern Europe Between the Wars, 1918–1941*, 3rd ed. (New York: Harper, 1962).

Seton-Watson 1963: Robert W. Seton-Watson, *A History of the Romanians from Roman Times to the Completion of Union* (New York: Archon Books, 1963).

Silber and Little 1995: Laura Silber and Allan Little, *The Death of Yugoslavia* (London: Penguin–BBC Books, 1995).

Simić 1991: Andrei Simić, "Obstacles to the Development of a Yugoslav National Consciousness: Ethnic Identity and Folk Culture in the Balkans" (*Journal of Mediterranean Studies* 1, no. 1, 1991).

Sked 1989: Alan Sked, *The Decline and Fall of the Habsburg Empire, 1815–1918* (London: Longman, 1989).

Skilling 1994: H. Gordon Skilling, *T. G. Masaryk: Against the Current, 1882–1914* (University Park, PA: Pennsylvania State University Press, 1994).

Skinner 1980: Andrew Skinner, "Introduction" to Adam Smith, *The Wealth of Nations. Books I–III* (New York: Penguin Books, 1980).

Skocpol 1979: Theda Skocpol, *States and Social Revolutions: A Comparative Analysis of France, Russia and China* (Cambridge: Cambridge University Press, 1979).

Slapnicka 1975: Helmut Slapnicka, "Der neue Staat und die burokratische Kontinuitaet: die Entwicklung der Verwaltung," in Karl Bosl (ed.), *Die demokratisch-parlamentarische Struktur der Ersten Tschechoslowakischen Republik* (Muenchen: Oldenburg, 1975).

Smit 1958: Cornelis Smit (ed.), *Bescheiden betreffende de buitenlandse politiek van Nederland: Derde periode 1899–1919*, vol. 2, *Tweede Deel: 1903–1907* (The Hague: Staatsuitgeverij, 1958).

Smith 1995: Anthony D. Smith, *Nations and Nationalism in a Global Era* (Cambridge: Cambridge University Press, 1995).

Smith 1997: Denis Mack Smith, *Modern Italy: A Political History* (New Haven/London: Yale University Press, 1997).

Snyder 2000: Jack Snyder, *From Voting to Violence: Democratization and Nationalist Conflict* (New York/London: W.W. Norton, 2000).

Soergel 1979: Wolfgang Soergel, *Arbeiterselbstverwaltung oder Managersozialismus? Eine empirische Untersuchung in Joegoslawischen Industriebetrieben* (Munich: Oldenbourg, 1979).

Somakian 1995: Manoug Somakian, *Empires in Conflict: Armenia and the Great Powers, 1895–1920* (London: I. B. Tauris, 1995).

Spence 1981: Richard B. Spence, *Yugoslavs, the Austro-Hungarian Army, and the First World War* (PhD diss., University of California at Santa Barbara, 1981).

Speyer 1951: Paul Speyer, *Zuid Slavië 1950. Noch Stalin, noch Marshall. 'Volksgazet' in het land van Tito* (Antwerp: Ontwikkeling, 1951).

Statistički Godisnjak 1989: *Statistički Godisnjak. Savezni Zavod za statistiku* (Belgrade, 1989).

Stavrianos 1993: Leften S. Stavrianos, "The Influence of the West on the Balkans," in Charles Jelavich and Barbara Jelavich, *The Establishment of the Balkan National States, 1804–1920: A History of East Central Europe* (Seattle and London, University of Washington Press, 1993).

Steiner and Ertman 2002: Jürg Steiner and Thomas Ertman (eds.), *Consociationalism and Corporatism in Western Europe: Still the Politics of Accommodation?* (*Acta Politica* 37, special issue, 2002).

Sternhell 1991: Zeev Sternhell, "The Political Culture of Nationalism'," in Robert Tombs (ed.), *Nationhood and Nationalism in France: From Boulangism to the Great War, 1889–1918* (London/New York: HarperCollinsAcademic, 1991).

Stourzh 1985: Gerald Stourzh, *Die Gleichberechtigung der Nationalitäten in der Verfassung und Verwaltung Österreichs 1848–1918* (Vienna: Verlag der östereichischen Akademie der Wissenachaften, 1985).

Ströhm 1976: Carl G. Ströhm, *Ohne Tito. Kann Jugoslawien überleben?* (Cologne: Verlag Styria, 1976).

Sugar 1980: Peter F. Sugar (ed.), *Ethnic Diversity and Conflict in Eastern Europe* (Santa Barbara, CA/London: ABC-Clio, 1980).

Sugar 1999: Peter F. Sugar, *East European Nationalism, Politics and Religion* (Aldershot: Ashgate, 1999).

Suny 1993: Ronald Grigor Suny, *Looking Toward Ararat: Armenia in Modern History* (Bloomington: Indiana University Press, 1993).

Suppan 1997: Arnold Suppan, "Zur sozialen und wirtschaftlichen Lage im Protektorat Böhmen und Mähren," in Richard G. Plaschka, Horst Haselsteiner, Arnold Suppan, and Anna M. Drabek, *Nationale Frage und Vertreibung in der Tschechoslowakei und Ungarn 1938–1948: aktuelle Forschungen* (Vienna: Verlag der österreichischen Akademie der Wissenschaften, 1997).

Swift 1737: Jonathan Swift, *A Proposal for Giving Badges to the Beggars in all the Parishes of Dublin* (London and Dublin, 1737).

Szporluk 1981: Roman Szporluk, *The Political Thought of Thomas G. Masaryk* (Boulder, CO: East European Monographs, 1981).

Taylor 1964: A.J.P. Taylor, *The Habsburg Monarchy: A History of the Austrian Empire and Austria-Hungary* (London: Penguin Books, 1964).

Taylor 1989: Charles Taylor, *Sources of the Self: The Making of Modern Identity* (Cambridge, MA: Harvard University Press, 1989).

Tellegen 1968: Egbert Tellegen, *De sociologie in het werk van Max Weber* (Meppel: Boom, 1968).

Te Velde 1992: Henk te Velde, *Gemeenschapszin en plichtsbesef. Liberalisme en nationalisme in Nederland, 1870–1918* (The Hague: SDU Uitgeverij, 1992).

Te Velde 1999: Henk te Velde, "Van Grondwet tot Grondwet. Oefenen met parlement, partij en schaalvergroting, 1848–1917," in Remieg Aerts et al., *Land van kleine gebaren. Een politieke geschiedenis van Nederland 1780–1990* (Nijmegen: SUN, 1999).

Te Velde 2002: Henk te Velde, *Stijlen van leiderschap. Persoon en politiek van Thorbecke tot Den Uyl* (Amsterdam: Wereldbibliotheek, 2002).

Ther 1998: Philipp Ther, *Deutsche und Polnische Vertriebene. Gesellschaft und Vertriebenenpolitik in der SBZ/DDR und in Polen 1945–1956* (Göttingen: Vandenhoeck & Ruprecht, 1998).

Ther 2001a: Philipp Ther, "A Century of Forced Migration: The Origins and Consequences of Ethnic Cleansing," in Philipp Ther and Ana Siljak (eds.), *Redrawing Nations: Ethnic Cleansing in East Central Europe, 1944–1948* (Lanham: Rowman & Littlefield Publishers, 2001).

Ther 2001b: Philipp Ther, "Chancen und Untergang einer multinationalen Stadt: Die Beziehungen zwischen den Nationalitäten in Lemberg in der ersten Hälfte des Zwanzigsten Jahrhunderts," in Philipp Ther und Holm Sundhaussen (eds.), *Nationalitätenkonflikte im 20. Jahrhundert: Ursachen von inter-ethnischer Gewalt im Vergleich* (Wiesbaden: Harrassowitz, 2001).

Ther 2001c: Philipp Ther, "Die Grenzen des Nationalismus: Der Wandel von Identitäten in Oberschlesien von der Mitte des 19. Jahrhunderts bis 1939," in Ulrike Von Hirschhausen and Jörn Leohard (eds.), *Nationalismen in Europa: West und Osteuropa im Vergleich* (Göttingen: Wallstein Verlag, 2001).

Tibi 1997: Bassam Tibi, *Arab Nationalism: Between Islam and the Nation-State*, 3rd ed. (New York: St. Martin's Press, 1997).

Tillie and Fennema 2000: Jean Tillie and Meindert Fennema, *De etnische stem: opkomst en stemgedrag van migranten tijdens de gemeenteraadsverkiezingen, 1986–1998* (Utrecht: Forum, 2000).

Tilly 1975: Charles Tilly, *The Formation of National States in Western Europe* (Princeton: Princeton University Press, 1975).

Tocqueville 1981: Alexis de Tocqueville, *De la démocratie en Amérique*, 2 vols. (Paris: Flammarion, 1981).

Todorova 1997: Maria Todorova, *Imagining the Balkans* (Oxford/New York: Oxford University Press, 1997).

Torzecki 1993: Ryszard Torzecki, *Polacy i Ukraincy. Sprawa ukrainska w czasie II wojnie światowej na terenie II Rzeczpospolitej* (Warsaw: Wydawnictwo Naukowe, 1993).

Tóth 1997: Agnes Tóth, "Zwang oder Möglichkeit. Die Annahme der Maxime von der Kollektivschuld und die Bestrafung der deutschen Minderheit in Ungarn," in Richard G. Plaschka, Horst Haselsteiner, Arnold Suppan, and Anna M. Drabek, *Nationale Frage und Vertreibung in der Tschechoslowakei und Ungarn 1938–1948: Aktuelle Forschungen* (Vienna: Verlag der Österreichischen Akademie der Wissenschaften, 1997).

Touraine 1994: Alain Touraine, *Qu'est-ce que la démocratie?* (Paris: Artème Fayard, 1994).

Touraine 2001: Alain Touraine, *La Différence culturelle* (Paris: Artème Fayard, 2001).

Tromp 1995: Hylke Tromp, "On the Nature of War and the Nature of Militarism," in Robert A. Hinde and Helen E. Watson (eds.), *War, a Cruel Necessity? The Bases of Institutionalized Violence* (London: Tauris Academic Studies, 1995).

Truman 1970: David Truman, "Interest Groups and the Nature of the State," in Maurice Zeitlin (ed.), *American Society, Inc.: Studies in the Social Structure and Political Economy of the United States* (Chicago: Markham Publishing, 1970).

Udovićki and Ridgeway 1997: Jasminka Udovićki and James Ridgeway (eds.), *Burn This House: The Making and Unmaking of Yugoslavia* (Durham, NC: Duke University Press, 1997).

U.S. Department of State 2000: U.S. Department of State, Office of Research, *Ten Years After the Fall of the Wall: Public Opinion in Central and Eastern European Countries in Transition* (Washington, DC, 2000).

Vakar 1956: Nicholas Vakar, *Belorussia: The Making of a Nation* (Cambridge: Cambridge University Press, 1956).

Van de Port 1994: Mattijs van de Port, *Het einde van de wereld. Beschaving en redeloosheid en zigeunercafés in Servië* (Amsterdam: Babylon–De Geus, 1994).

Van de Port 1999: Mattijs van de Port, "'It Takes a Serb to Know a Serb.' Uncovering the Roots of Obstinate Otherness in Serbia," in *Imagining the Balkans* (*Press Now/Balie*, January 1999).

Verba 1965: Sidney Verba, "Comparative Political Culture," in Lucian W. Pey and Sidney Verba, *Political Culture and Political Development* (Princeton: Princeton University Press, 1965).

Visser and Hemerijck 1997: Jelle Visser and Anton Hemerijck, *A Dutch Miracle: Job Growth, Welfare Reform and Corporatism in the Netherlands* (Amsterdam: Amsterdam University Press, 1997).

Vucinich 1963: Wayne S. Vucinich, "Some Aspects of the Ottoman Legacy," in Charles and Barbara Jelavich (eds.), *The Balkans in Transition: Essays on the Devel-*

opment of Balkan Life and Politics Since the Eighteenth Century (Berkeley and Los Angeles: University of California Press, 1963).

Vucinich 1965: Wayne S. Vucinich, *The Ottoman Empire: Its Record and Legacy* (Princeton, NJ: Van Nostrand Cy, 1965).

Vucinich 1979: Wayne S. Vucinich, "Serbian Military Tradition," in Béla K. Király and Gunther E. Rothenberg (eds.), *War and Society in East Central Europe* (New York: Brooklyn College Press, 1979).

Vysny 1977: Paul Vysny, *Neo-Slavism and the Czechs: 1898–1914* (Cambridge: Cambridge University Press, 1977).

Wachtel 1998: Andrew B. Wachtel, *Making a Nation, Breaking a Nation: Literature and Cultural Politics in Yugoslavia* (Stanford, CA: Stanford University Press, 1998).

Wallerstein 1974: Immanuel M. Wallerstein, *The Modern World System* (New York: Academic Publishers, 1974).

Wallerstein 1984: Immanuel Wallerstein, *The Politics of the World-Economy: The States, the Movements, and the Civilizations: Essays* (Cambridge: Cambridge University Press, 1984).

Warren 1999: Mark E. Warren, "Democratic Theory and Trust," in Mark E. Warren (ed.), *Democracy and Trust* (Cambridge: Cambridge University Press, 1999).

Weber 1964: Max Weber, *Theory of Social and Economic Organization*, translated by Alexander M. Henderson and Talcott Parsons (Glencoe, IL: The Free Press, 1964).

Weber 1976: Eugen Weber, *Peasants into Frenchmen: The Modernization of Rural France, 1870–1914* (Stanford, CA: Stanford University Press, 1976).

Weber 1986: Eugen Weber, *France, Fin de Siècle* (Cambridge, MA: Harvard University Press, 1986).

Weeks 1996: Theodore R. Weeks, *Nation and State in Late Imperial Russia: Nationalism and Russification on the Western Frontier, 1863–1914* (DeKalb, IL: Northern Illinois University Press, 1996).

Wehler 1995: Hans-Ulrich Wehler, *Deutsche Gesellschaftsgeschichte, Dritter Band. Von der Deutschen Doppelrevolution bis zum Beginn des Ersten Weltkrieges* (Munich: C. H. Beck, 1995).

Weil 1988: Patrick Weil, "La politique française d'immigration" (*Pouvoirs. Revue française d'études constitutionelles et politiques* 47, 1988).

Werner 1928: Morris Robert Werner, *Tammany Hall* (Garden City: Doubleday, Doran & Co. Inc, 1928).

Williams 1989: Patrick Williams (ed.), *Tsiganes: identité, evolution* (Paris: Syros Alternatives, 1989).

Williamson 1991: Samuel R. Williamson Jr., *Austria-Hungary and the Origins of the First World War* (New York: St. Martin's Press, 1991).

Winock 1990: Michel Winock, "Nationalisme ouvert et nationalisme fermé," in *Nationalisme, antisémitisme et fascisme en France* (Paris: Seuil, 1990).

Wolchik 1991: Sharon Wolchik, *Czechoslovakia in Transition: Politics, Economics, Society* (New York: Pinter, 1991).

Wolff 1994: Larry Wolff, *Inventing Eastern Europe: The Map of Civilization on the Mind of the Enlightenment* (Stanford, CA: Stanford University Press, 1994).

World Bank 1996: World Bank, *World Development Report, 1996: From Plan to Market* (New York: Oxford University Press, 1996).

Zeine 1958: Zeine N. Zeine, *Arab-Turkish Relations and the Emergence of Arab Nationalism* (Beirut: Khayat's, 1958).

Zeldin 1973: Theodore Zeldin, *France, 1848–1945*, vol. 1, *Ambition, Love and Politics* (Oxford: Oxford University Press, 1973).

Zimbardo 1969: Philip G. Zimbardo, "The Human Choice: Individuation, Reason, and Order versus Deindividuation, Impulse, and Chaos," in William J. Arnold and David Levine (eds.), *Nebraska Symposium on Motivation, 1969* (Lincoln: University of Nebraska Press, 1969).

Zimbardo 1973: Philip G. Zimbardo, "On the Ethics of Intervention in Human Psychology with Special Reference to the Stanford Prison Experiment" (*Cognition: International Journal of Cognitive Psychology* 2, 1973).

Zürcher 1984: Erik Zürcher, *The Unionist Factor: The Role of the Committee of Union and Progress in the Turkish National Movement* (Leiden: Brill, 1984).

Zweig 1964: Stefan Zweig, *The World of Yesterday* (Lincoln and London: University of Nebraska Press, 1964).

Index

Absolutism, 55, 75, 77, 83, 98, 123
Accountable government, 52, 54
Acculturation, 8, 145, 150–53
Acton, Lord John Emerich Edward, 2
Africa, 121
Agricultural revolution, 98, 101
Aix, 99
Albania, 46ff, 105ff, 115ff, 127, 137
Albert, Michel, 152
Aletheia, 154
Alexander the Great, 31
Alien Act of 1905 (Great Britain), 20
Alsace, 86, 91
American Revolution, 152
Ancien regime, 148
Andrić, Ivo, 139
Ankersmit, Frank, 8
Annales, 159n1
Anticapitalism, 113
Anti-Dreyfusards, 62
Antirevolutionaire Partij (Netherlands), 59
Antirevolutionary protestants, 49
Anti-Semitism, 20, 22, 38–44 *passim*, 68f, 72
Appeasement, 87
April Movement (Netherlands), 55
Aristocracy, 54f, 97, 136
Aristocratic rule, 55
Aristotle, 31, 120
Asia, 69, 121, 124
Assimilation, 10, 48, 79–82 *passim*, 90f, 103, 110, 115
Atlantic Europe, 98
Augustus, 24
Ausgleich, Austro-Hungarian, 42, 102

Ausgleich, Galician, 84
Australia, 24f
Austria, 11, 24f, 35–38 *passim*, 46, 67–73 *passim*, 80–85 *passim*, 90f, 105
Austria-Hungary, 44, 46, 74, 105, 160n5
Austria, imperial, 83, 85, 91
Austro-Hungarian Monarchy, 103
Auvergne, 99

Bácska-Bánát, 102
Balkan man, myth of the, 132, 141, 143
Balkans, 15, 38, 40, 69, 112, 125–32 *passim*, 137, 141ff, 146; in interwar years, 48, 125; part of Ottoman Empire, 34, 83, 132; postcommunist, 118, 121, 132, 135
Banac, Ivo, 132
Banat, 38
Bataillons Scolaires, 62
Battenberg, Prince Alexander von, 38f
Bauer, Otto, 67
Bax, Mart, 138
Béchard, Ferdinand, 60
Belgium, 5, 24, 37
Belle Époque, 21
Beller, Steven, 70, 158n2
Benda, Julien, 20
Beneš, Edvard, 88
Beneš decrees, 88
Berend, Ivan, 8
Berlin, 39, 82
Berlin Treaty (1878), 38f
Berlin Wall, 7, 126
Bessarabia, 38, 47, 102
Beust, Friedrich von, 124